Sustainable Development Goals Series

The **Sustainable Development Goals Series** is Springer Nature's inaugural cross-imprint book series that addresses and supports the United Nations' seventeen Sustainable Development Goals. The series fosters comprehensive research focused on these global targets and endeavours to address some of society's greatest grand challenges. The SDGs are inherently multidisciplinary, and they bring people working across different fields together and working towards a common goal. In this spirit, the Sustainable Development Goals series is the first at Springer Nature to publish books under both the Springer and Palgrave Macmillan imprints, bringing the strengths of our imprints together.

The Sustainable Development Goals Series is organized into eighteen subseries: one subseries based around each of the seventeen respective Sustainable Development Goals, and an eighteenth subseries, "Connecting the Goals," which serves as a home for volumes addressing multiple goals or studying the SDGs as a whole. Each subseries is guided by an expert Subseries Advisor with years or decades of experience studying and addressing core components of their respective Goal.

The SDG Series has a remit as broad as the SDGs themselves, and contributions are welcome from scientists, academics, policymakers, and researchers working in fields related to any of the seventeen goals. If you are interested in contributing a monograph or curated volume to the series, please contact the Publishers: Zachary Romano [Springer; zachary.romano@springer.com] and Rachael Ballard [Palgrave Macmillan; rachael.ballard@palgrave.com].

More information about this series at https://link.springer.com/bookseries/15486

Cedric de Coning • Ako Muto
Rui Saraiva
Editors

Adaptive Mediation and Conflict Resolution

Peace-making in Colombia, Mozambique, the Philippines, and Syria

palgrave
macmillan

Editors
Cedric de Coning
Norwegian Institute of
International Affairs (NUPI)
Oslo, Norway

Ako Muto
JICA Ogata Sadako Research Institute
for Peace and Development
Tokyo, Japan

Rui Saraiva
JICA Ogata Sadako Research Institute
for Peace and Development
Tokyo, Japan

ISSN 2523-3084 ISSN 2523-3092 (electronic)
Sustainable Development Goals Series
ISBN 978-3-030-92576-5 ISBN 978-3-030-92577-2 (eBook)
https://doi.org/10.1007/978-3-030-92577-2

Cover illustration: Sue Mcdonald / EyeEm / Getty Images

This Palgrave Macmillan imprint is published by the registered company Springer Nature Switzerland AG.
The registered company address is: Gewerbestrasse 11, 6330 Cham, Switzerland

Foreword

At this very moment, armed conflicts are occurring in many places in the world. We need to address this crisis as immediately and practically as we can. Mediation is a commonly used method to resolve conflict, understood as some type of dialogic support provided to the armed conflict parties through a neutral third actor. Among various approaches to mediation is adaptive mediation, a new mechanism which means that such an actor facilitates the will of the parties themselves to the conflict to resolve it through negotiation, rather than external actors leading toward a predesigned solution. This book, *Adaptive Mediation and Conflict Resolution—Peace-making in Colombia, Mozambique, the Philippines, and Syria*, explores the significance and challenges of adaptive mediation in armed conflicts based on the findings from the field.

As the Cold War came to an end, the United Nations and other international organizations became actively involved in mediation operations to resolve conflicts that had previously been significantly affected by major powers. Mechanisms to implement mediation in the process of peacemaking and peacekeeping were put in place, and institutional mediation capabilities were developed with international cooperation. However, since the 2010s, there has been a noticeable increase in the number of protracted and recurrent conflicts. These conflicts not only are internationalized and subject to interventions by other countries but also tend to become more complex and uncertain with the emergence of nonstate actors such as nonstate armed groups. Ceasefires are either not reached and conflicts are prolonged, or the agreed ceasefires are dissolved again and again in a short period, resulting in relapsing conflicts. In conflicts that result in ineffective and incomplete ceasefires, United Nations peacekeeping operations, whose mission is to sustain the truce, have also stagnated. Additionally, some of those conflicts do not move toward democratic state-building, reflecting the recent global regression of democracy; in such conflicts, application of the nonimpunity principle has been impractical and even harmful. In other words, internationally initiated and standardized mediations do not always work in complex armed conflicts in modern times.

In such cases of protracted and recurrent conflicts, where it is difficult to establish a sustainable ceasefire, it is extremely important to take a pragmatic approach according to the local context of the conflicts. One possible reason why externally initiated mediation does not work is that the parties to the conflict may not want to resolve the conflict through mediation, or they are not satisfied with the results of the mediation even if they accepted the process. The context of the conflicts is affected by such local actors, and thus their proactive involvement in the mediation becomes important. In other words, local ownership in peace negotiations is absolutely crucial. What the external actors can do is to support and facilitate the peace negotiations between the parties with neutral standpoints. I would say that adaptive mediation consists of local ownership and external facilitation, which sheds light on the new structure of the possible peace process. This book discusses the cases of mediation in protracted, recurrent, and thus complex conflicts in Colombia, Mozambique, the Philippines, and Syria from an adaptive perspective. Each case study is a mixture of successful and unsuccessful mediation activities. In terms of achieving a sustainable peace agreement, the cases of Colombia, Mozambique, and the Philippines present thought-provoking elements of adaptive mediation through which various challenges arising from complex situations were overcome. Together with the case study of Syria, which argues that some useful insights can be extracted even from failed mediation, all cases definitely provide valuable lessons for mediators around the world.

This book is a timely and significant contribution to understanding the complex dynamics of the mediation landscape by presenting both a theoretical framework of adaptive mediation and practical means of conflict resolution that address the complexity and uncertainty faced by mediators in contemporary armed conflicts. What this book consistently argues is that conflict resolution requires both the stable willingness of the parties to resolve the conflict and the proactive participation of a broad range of citizens in the country. Adaptive mediation is an approach in which a neutral third actor deeply understands the local context and supports the contested parties in reaching a peace agreement. I hope that this book will provide new perspectives in mediation to open a new conversation on the effective transition from violent conflict to sustaining peace.

President, Japan International Cooperation Agency, Tokyo, Japan

Shinichi Kitaoka

Acknowledgments

This book is one of the outputs of the research project, *Contextualizing International Cooperation for Sustaining Peace: Adaptive Peacebuilding Pathways*, organized by the Japan International Cooperation Agency (JICA) Ogata Sadako Research Institute for Peace and Development. Several people have given valuable guidance and great inspiration to this book project. We would like to express our gratitude to Prof. Izumi Ohno, former director of JICA Ogata Research institute, and to former deputy director, Dr. Megumi Muto, for their continued support and encouragement for a book project idea that emerged during the beginning of the COVID-19 pandemic, a particularly challenging time to proceed with research activities worldwide. We also thank Prof. Akio Takahara, Director of JICA Ogata Research Institute, and the Deputy Director, Mr. Koji Makino, for their insightful feedback provided during the implementation of our research project.

In December 2020, in the context of presentations made at the 31st Japan Association for International Development (JASID) annual conference, we received insightful comments from Prof. Daisaku Higashi (Sophia University), Prof. Yuichi Kubota (Nihon University), and Prof. Yukako Tanaka-Sakabe (Aoyama Gakuin University).

We are most grateful to all the book contributors for their patience and skillful revisions to the manuscripts. Furthermore, we are thankful to all the research project advisors and experts for the discussion and feedback on a wide range of topics related to peacemaking, peacebuilding, and conflict resolution. We are also grateful to all local interviewees and local researchers, as well as the staff of JICA offices in each country where the chapter authors conducted fieldwork. Finally, we would like to acknowledge the professional support given by the staff of JICA Ogata Research Institute: editorial advice by Mr. Yasuhiko Sato, editorial work and project coordination by the project research officer, Mr. Kaito Takeuchi, and the valuable contribution of the project research assistants, Dr. Udeni Appuhamilage, Ms. Asti Metami Asak, Dr. César Rodrigues, and Ms. Marcela Perić.

Praise for *Sustainable Development Goals Series*

"In an increasingly unpredictable and uncertain world, conflicts are becoming more complex and difficult to resolve and sustain peace agreements. Local ownership of peace processes, as a way to build sustainable peace, has been a mantra preached for decades but until now, this has been, at best, a cliché. This book on adaptive mediation, focusing on local ownership of peace processes, is therefore timely, refreshing and original, and should be compulsory reading for students and practitioners alike."

—Vasu Gounden, Founder and Executive Director, *African Centre for the Constructive Resolution of Disputes (ACCORD), South Africa*

"This is an important book. The international community has been struggling for decades to pivot from its standard top-down, linear, one-size-fits-all approach to mediation, conflict resolution and peacebuilding, and this insightful book lays out a practical, albeit challenging, alternative path forward. Combining concepts from complexity science with grounded experiences and empirical case studies of some of the more challenging protracted conflicts of our time, the authors offer a hopeful but realistic sense of what effective adaptive mediation and peacebuilding can look like—in fact, must look like—as the degree and pace of complexity in our world continues to rise. Peace scholars, peacebuilders, policy makers and donors would do well to take heed."

—Peter T. Coleman, *Professor of Psychology at Columbia University, and Director of The Morton Deutsch International Center for Cooperation and Conflict Resolution, USA*

"The reforms liberal peacebuilding badly needs have been rehearsed in thousands of books, articles, program evaluations and UN resolutions. But the findings and recommendations rarely go beyond platitudes of inclusion, local ownership, and flexibility. This volume presents an alternative that grapples seriously with what it would mean to put these principles into concrete concepts and grounded practice in the real world of peace mediation and conflict resolution. It turns out that adaptive mediation mostly means that the role of internationals is to accompany self-organized home-grown peace processes and even protect them from overly international interference. It is a must-read for policy makers, practitioners and students alike!"

—Thania Paffenholz, Executive Director, *Inclusive Peace, Switzerland*

"This book is a theoretically groundbreaking and empirically rich study on adaptive mediation. It is a must-read for scholars and students of peace and conflict research, as well as for peace practitioners and policymakers interested in how peace mediation practices can better recognise the complexity of societies and conflict realities, redefine the role of the mediator, and address the demands of locally owned inclusive peace processes."

—Marko Lehti, *Senior Research Fellow and Deputy Director of Tampere Peace Research Institute (TAPRI), Tampere University, Finland*

"Adaptive mediation is exactly what is needed for today's international conflict resolution. Based on a deep understanding of complexity theory, this book offers an accessible and practical set of tools to analyze and resolve the most intractable wars of today and tomorrow. Adaptive mediation will change the way you understand how conflict evolves and will revolutionize the field of mediation. It will be required reading in all my courses, and should guide how we deal with future conflicts."

—Adam Day, *Director of Programmes at United Nations University Centre for Policy Research, New York, USA*

"This is a laudable and timely effort to debate the merits of fundamental concepts of mediation today. The authors correctly identify and criticize cookie cutter approaches to mediation. In several country cases, the concept of adaptive mediation is demonstrated to be workable and convincing. Whether it is applicable in a wider number of varying contexts, especially the more complex conflicts involving foreign armies, is however yet to be proven."

Asif R. Khan, *Chief of Mediation Support and Gender, Peace & Security, UN Department of Political and Peacebuilding Affairs*

"This book, through both theoretical analysis and concrete examples, leads us to understand the importance of the ownership by the parties to the conflict of the peace and reconciliation process. Mediators' delicate and yet key roles are discussed. Respect for the local realities is paramount for a sustainable peace; but without sometimes facilitation to break the deadlock, the process would not advance. Adaptive mediation proposed here serves as an answer to help conflict resolution in the current complex context. When I look back on the Afghan conflict, the importance of what the book argues as key elements becomes apparent. The lack of one party's will to seek settlement through talks led to stalling of the peace talks between the Taliban and the Republic; and the lack of proactive participation of diversified citizens was one of the reasons which threw the country into deep confusion after the Taliban's return to power."

—Tadamichi Yamamoto, Visiting Professor, *Doshisha University, Japan, and Former Special Representative of the United Nations Secretary-General for Afghanistan and Head of the United Nations Assistance Mission in Afghanistan*

Contents

1 **Adaptive Mediation and Conflict Resolution in Contemporary and Future Armed Conflicts** 1
Cedric de Coning, Ako Muto, and Rui Saraiva

2 **Adaptive Mediation** 19
Cedric de Coning

3 **Adaptive Mediation in Colombia: Toward Institutional Capacity Building Amid Complexity and Uncertainty** 57
Lina Penagos

4 **Peacemaking from Within: Adaptive Mediation of Direct Dialogue in Mozambique's New Peace Process (2013–2019)** 81
Rui Saraiva

5 **Adapting from Outsider to Insider Mediation in the Bangsamoro Peace Process, Southern Philippines** 111
Miyoko Taniguchi

6 **Exploring Mediation Efforts Amid Systemic and Domestic Constraints: The Case of the Syrian Conflict** 137
Ako Muto

7 **Adapting to Uncertainty: What Have We Learned from Mediation and Conflict Resolution in Colombia, Mozambique, the Philippines, and Syria** 165
Cedric de Coning, Ako Muto, and Rui Saraiva

Index 185

Notes on Contributors

Cedric de Coning is a research professor with the Norwegian Institute of International Affairs (NUPI) Center for UN and Global Governance, where he coordinates the Effectiveness of Peace Operations Network (EPON) and leads the Climate-related Peace and Security Risk (CPSR) project. He is also a senior advisor for the African Centre for the Constructive Resolution of Disputes (ACCORD) and Chief Editor of ACCORD's *COVID-19 Conflict and Resilience Monitor*. He holds a PhD from the Department of Philosophy at the University of Stellenbosch South Africa. His research focuses on strengthening the resilience and sustainability of social-ecological systems under pressure from climate change, conflict, and other stressors. He has served in several advisory capacities for the African Union and United Nations, including the UN Secretary-General's Advisory Board for the Peacebuilding Fund, and as an advisor to the Special Representative of the Chairperson of the African Union Commission for the Peace Fund.

Ako Muto currently serves as executive senior research fellow at the Japan International Cooperation Agency (JICA) Ogata Sadako Research Institute for Peace and Development, and is involved in research on peacebuilding, human security, and humanitarian crises. Based on her experiences as an aid practitioner, she works on bridging aid practices with academic work. Her publications include "Assessing Context-Specific Peacebuilding Approaches in Contemporary Armed Conflicts: From High-Level Mediation to Middle-Out Linkage in Syria and from Adaptive Mediation to Nationally-Owned Peacebuilding in Mozambique" (with

R. Saraiva, *Asian Journal of Peacebuilding*, 2020), and "Variations to Humanitarian and Development Assistance during Conflict: A Case Study Analysis of Assistance provided to Syria" (in Japanese, *The United Nations Studies*, 2019). She is also a coeditor of the book *Human Security Norms in East Asia* (with Y. Mine and O.A. Gómez, Palgrave Macmillan, 2019).

Lina Penagos is involved in scientific research on underground economies, SDGs, migrations, and peace studies. She is currently a PhD candidate in Political Science at Université Gustave Eiffel (Laboratoire Interdisciplinaire d'étude du Politique Hannah Arendt - Paris-Est (LIPHA-PE)), France. Her thesis analyses gray zones from an underground economy perspective. The research focuses on power shifts, security outlooks, and peacebuilding challenges in the Colombian and Venezuelan borderlands. She graduated in International Relations from the School of International Relations and Security Strategy at Nueva Granada Military University, Colombia, and holds a master's degree in economics from Saint Thomas University, Miami, USA. She has lectured in Colombia and France at Saint Thomas University, La Salle University, Université Paris-Est Créteil, and Université Catholique de Lille.

Rui Saraiva is a research fellow in the Peacebuilding and Humanitarian Support Team at the Japan International Cooperation Agency (JICA) Ogata Sadako Research Institute for Peace and Development. His current research focuses on conflict resolution, peacebuilding, and preventing violent extremism in Africa. He holds a PhD in International Public Policy from Osaka University, Japan, as a recipient of the Japanese Government Monbukagakusho (MEXT) Scholarship, and a master's degree in Political Science and International Relations from NOVA University of Lisbon, Portugal. His recent publications include "Assessing Context-Specific Peacebuilding Approaches in Contemporary Armed Conflicts: From High-Level Mediation to Middle-Out Linkage in Syria and from Adaptive Mediation to Nationally-Owned Peacebuilding in Mozambique" (with A. Muto, *Asian Journal of Peacebuilding*, 2020) and "Contextualizing the Sustaining Peace Approach in Contemporary Armed Conflicts: From High-Level International Mediation to Pragmatic Peacebuilding Initiatives in Syria" (with A. Muto, *Journal of Human Security Studies*, 2020).

Miyoko Taniguchi is currently senior advisor on peacebuilding at the Japan International Cooperation Agency (JICA). She holds a PhD in Human Security from the University of Tokyo, Japan. Over the last 20 years, she has been working at various development agencies as an expert on conflict resolution, mediation/reconciliation, peacebuilding, and reconstruction, especially in the area of governance in conflict-affected areas and countries, including the Southern Philippines (Mindanao), Sri Lanka, India, Cambodia, the Balkans, Guatemala, Colombia, Liberia, Democratic Republic of Congo, Uganda, Sierra Leone, Turkey, Jordan, and Lebanon. She has also published numerous academic articles and policy papers based on her extensive fieldwork, including *Assisting Peacebuilding: Mindanao Conflict and Road to Peace* (in Japanese, University of Nagoya Press, 2020). She recently received several academic awards, including the Asia Pacific Academic Award by the Asian Affairs Research Council in 2020, and was nominated for the International Book Award by the International Convention of Asia Scholars in 2021.

Abbreviations

ACCORD	African Centre for the Constructive Resolution of Disputes
ADO	Workers Self-Defense
AFP	Armed Forces of the Philippines
AGI	African Governance Initiative
ANAPO	National Popular Alliance
ANSA	Armed nonstate actor
ARCSS	Agreement on the Resolution of Conflict in the Republic of South Sudan
ARMM	Autonomous Region in Muslim Mindanao
ARN	National Agency for Reincorporation
ASEAN	Association of Southeast Asian Nations
AU	African Union
AUC	Autodefensas Unidas de Colombia (United Self-Defense Forces of Colombia)
BARMM	Bangsamoro Autonomous Region in Muslim Mindanao
BATNA	Best Alternative to a Negotiated Settlement
BBL	Bangsamoro Basic Law
BDA	Bangsamoro Development Agency
BIFF	Bangsamoro Islamic Freedom Fighters
BLMI	Bangsamoro Leadership and Management Institute
BOL	Bangsamoro Organic Law
BTA	Bangsamoro Transition Authority
BTC	Bangsamoro Transition Commission
CAB	Comprehensive Agreement on the Bangsamoro
CHD	Center for Humanitarian Dialogue
CMHA	Cessation of Military Hostilities Agreement

CMI	Crisis Management Initiative
CODESA	Convention for a Democratic South Africa
CRNR	Center for Reconciliation, Normalization, and Rehabilitation
CSI	Common Space Initiative
CSO	Civil society organization
CSSR	Civil Society Support Room
CSV	Commission on the Study of Violence
DDR	Demobilization, disarmament, and reincorporation
ECOWAS	Economic Community of West African States
ELN	Ejército de Liberación Nacional (National Liberation Army)
EMOCHM	Equipa de Observação da Cessação das Hostilidades Militares (Team of Military International Observers on the Cessation of Military Hostilities)
EPL	Ejército Popular de Liberación (Popular LiberationArmy)
ETCR	Espacios Territoriales de Capacitación y Reincorporación (Territorial Spaces of Capacitation and Reincorporation)
EU	European Union
FAB	Framework Agreement on the Bangsamoro
FADM	Forças Armadas de Defesa de Moçambique (Mozambican armed forces)
FARC-EP	Fuerzas Armadas Revolucionarias de Colombia—Ejército del Pueblo (Revolutionary Armed Forces of Colombia)
FELM	Finnish Evangelic-Lutheran Mission
FIP	Fundación Ideas Para La Paz
FPA	Final Peace Agreement
FRELIMO	Frente de Libertação de Moçambique (Mozambique Liberation Front)
GAO	Grupos Armados Oganizados (Organized Armed Groups)
GLF	Global Leadership Foundation
GMV	Grupo de Monitoria e Verificação (Monitoring and Verification Group)
GOE	Grupo de Operações Especiais (Special Operations Group)
GPA	General Peace Agreement
GPH	Government of the Philippines
GTCDDR	Grupo Técnico Conjunto de Desarmamento, Desmobilização e Reintegração (Joint Technical Group for Disarmament Demobilization and Reintegration)
GTCE	Grupo Técnico Conjunto de Enquadramento (Joint Technical Framework Group)
HCP	High Commission for Peace
HD	Centre for Humanitarian Dialogue

HNC	High Negotiations Committee
ICB	Institutional Capacity Building
ICG	International Contact Group
IDP	Internally displaced persons
IMF	International Monetary Fund
IMG	Insider Mediation Group
IMT	International Monitoring Team
INGO	International NGO
IO	International organizations
ISIL/ISIS	The Islamic State of Iraq and the Levant
ISSG	International Syria Support Group
JCCCH	Joint Coordinating Committee on the Cessation of Hostilities
JEP	Jurisdicción Especial para la Paz (Special Jurisdiction of Peace)
JICA	Japan International Cooperation Agency
LAS	League of Arab States
LMT	Local Monitoring Teams
M-19	April 19 Movement
MAPR	Maputo Accord for Peace and Reconciliation
MAQL	Quintin Lame Armed Movement
MDM	Movimento Democrático de Moçambique
MEO	Mozambican Electoral Observatory
MILF	Moro Islamic Liberation Front
MNLF	Moro National Liberation Front
MOA-AD	Memorandum of Agreement on Ancestral Domain
MoU	Memorandum of Understanding
MP	Members of Parliament
NAFS	National Agenda for the Future of Syria
NDP	National Development Plan
NGO	Nongovernmental organization
NIAC	Non-international armed conflicts
NOREF	Norwegian Peacebuilding Resource Centre
NPR	National Plan of Rehabilitation
NRA	National Reincorporation Agency
NSAGs	Non-State Armed Groups
OIC	Organisation of Islamic Cooperation
P5	Five permanent members of the UNSC—China, France, Russia, the UK, and the US
PAM	Peace Agreement Matrix
PARES	Fundación Paz y Reconciliación
PLA	Pedro León Arboleda Comando
PRM	Mozambique Republic Police

RENAMO	Resistência Nacional Moçambicana (Mozambican National Resistance)
SADC	Southern African Development Community
SARS-CoV-2	Severe acute respiratory syndrome coronavirus 2
SCR	Special Commission for Rehabilitation
SI	Syria Initiative
SISE	Serviços de Informação e Segurança do Estado (State Security and Intelligence Services)
SOC	Syrian Opposition Coalition
TAF	The Asian Foundation
TOR	Terms of reference
TPMT	Third-Party Monitoring Team
UIR	Unidade de Intervenção Rápida (Rapid Intervention Unit)
UK	United Kingdom
UN	United Nations
UNDP	United Nations Development Programme
UNESCWA	United Nations Economic and Social Commission for Western Asia
UNGA	United Nations General Assembly
UNHCR	United Nations High Commissioner for Refugees
UNSC	United Nations Security Council
UNSG	United Nations Secretary General
UNSMIS	UN Supervision Mission in Syria
US	United States

List of Figures

Fig. 3.1 Main drivers of mediation processes with irregular groups in Colombia (Source: García-Durán 2004) 70
Fig. 5.1 Overall peacebuilding architecture between the GPH and the MILF. (Source: Author) 122

List of Tables

Table 1.1	Research questions	11
Table 1.2	The case studies and respective distinguishing features	12
Table 3.1	Irregular groups participating in mediation processes 1991–2016	68

CHAPTER 1

Adaptive Mediation and Conflict Resolution in Contemporary and Future Armed Conflicts

Cedric de Coning, Ako Muto, and Rui Saraiva

Since the 1990s, mediation and conflict resolution processes have often been intimately related to liberal peacebuilding interventions, helping first to bring the fighting to an end with cease-fire agreements and then shaping the post-conflict phase through more comprehensive peace agreements. A characteristic feature of this period is that the content of the peace agreements typically reveals more about the liberal peace values of the mediators than they do about the values or context-specific interests of the parties to the conflict. Most of these peace agreements share at their core a similar logic and structure, deriving from a determined-designed model based on a liberal peace ideology and the so-called international

C. de Coning
Norwegian Institute of International Affairs (NUPI), Oslo, Norway
e-mail: cdc@nupi.no

A. Muto • R. Saraiva (✉)
JICA Ogata Sadako Research Institute for Peace and Development, Tokyo, Japan
e-mail: Muto.Ako@jica.go.jp; Farosaraiva.Rui@jica.go.jp

C. de Coning et al. (eds.), *Adaptive Mediation and Conflict Resolution*, Sustainable Development Goals Series,
https://doi.org/10.1007/978-3-030-92577-2_1

best practices, which tend to be linear, staged, normative, and individualistic in orientation (Bagshaw and Porter 2013). The reality is that, for the most part, domestic actors did not have control over these mediation processes, and third-party mediation became associated with imposed conflict transformation and power mediation (Eriksson and Kostić 2013). It is thus not surprising that Collier and colleagues found that 50 percent of peace agreements reached relapsed into conflict within ten years (Collier et al. 2003).

Since 2010, trends in violent armed conflicts have also been shifting significantly, which has had an impact on the ability of international, national, and local mediators to respond to related crises effectively. David Harland (2018) argues that geopolitical rivalry, the atomization of conflict, and the internationalization of internal conflicts have reduced the space for mediation, pointing to a number of failures in Sri Lanka, Libya, Darfur, South Sudan, Yemen, and Syria as examples to support his argument (see also Lehti 2020; Paffenholz 2021).

One feature of the changing nature of armed conflict is that the drivers of violence tend not to be resolved by peace agreements, because these agreements often result in elite power-sharing arrangements aimed at ending the fighting rather than addressing the causes of the conflict. As a result of this focus on short-term conflict management rather than long-term conflict resolution, tensions frequently reemerge not long after mediation processes are completed. As a consequence, once a country or society is on a violent path, changing its trajectory toward peace becomes more difficult over time.

Today, in many places, from Colombia to the Philippines and from Syria to Mozambique, armed conflicts often coexist with the rise of violent extremism, and this scenario is often coupled with additional human security threats, such as climate change, natural disasters, infectious diseases, and organized crime (OECD 2016; United Nations and World Bank 2018). Therefore, despite the collective desire to achieve sustainable peace in fora such as the United Nations (UN), the effectiveness of mediation to bring an end to violent conflicts is challenged by many conflicts across the world.

One exacerbating factor is that conflicts are more interconnected and complex than ever before. Local conflict dynamics such as marginalization and exclusion can be closely entangled with global jihadist ideologies, and local conflict resolution efforts may be disrupted by major power interventions that have little to do with addressing local conflict drivers. There is thus a growing sense that the mainstream approach to mediation and peacemaking is unable to address the changing conflict landscape effectively, and there is an interest in exploring alternative approaches to peacemaking that can enrich the peacemaking toolbox available to mediators around the world.

With the recent transition to a more complex and multipolar international order, mediation has become less sought after and more challenging to implement in volatile and uncertain conflict-affected situations (Milián et al. 2019). The peace and security environment after 9/11 dramatically reduced the space for dialogue with especially extremist armed groups that show little interest in recognition of their cause or negotiating for control over existing governing structures. In addition, the rise and fragmentation of Non-State Armed Groups (NSAGs) resulted in more complex and unpredictable scenarios. On the one hand, traditional rebel groups are subject to several challenges deriving from increasingly complex environments, making it difficult for them to decide whether they should engage in dialogue or continue fighting (Zartman and Alfredson 2019). On the other hand, the behavior of decentralized insurgencies, often labeled as violent extremism or terrorism, has limited the effectiveness of regional and international mediation. However, the challenges resulting from NSAGs behavior have also triggered the development of innovative mediation strategies, such as more adaptive and pragmatic negotiations and city-based dialogues involving civil society actors (Mcquinn and Courche 2020).

Against this background, a fundamental research problem has been identifying the most effective strategy for mediators amid increasing complexity and uncertainty. In this context, this book introduces adaptive mediation as an alternative approach that enables mediators to go beyond liberal peace mediation or other determined-design models of mediation. Adaptive mediation is an approach to mediation that has its foundations in Complexity Theory, and that is specifically designed to cope with highly dynamic conflict situations characterized by uncertainty and a lack of predictability. Adaptive mediation is also a facilitated mediation process whereby the content of agreements emerges from the parties to the conflict themselves, informed by the context within which the conflict is situated. The core principles and practices of adaptive mediation are presented in this book in conjunction with empirical evidence from four diverse case studies—Colombia, Mozambique, the Philippines, and Syria—in an attempt to generate recommendations for how mediators can apply adaptive mediation approaches to resolve and transform contemporary and future armed conflicts.

Mediation, conflict management, and conflict resolution are relatively new but expanding research areas of central importance in peace and conflict studies. In the academic literature, mediation has been described as some form of interactive assistance to the conflict parties with the aim of solving a conflict. This assistance is, in general, offered by a third party who lacks the authority to impose an outcome (Kressel and Pruitt 1989). Mediation has also been central to peacebuilding. It can occur at any phase of conflict and intends to eliminate the causes and impact of armed violence to prepare the ground for a more sustained dialogue. Although many have considered mediation as an isolated process that brings about a cease-fire or a political agreement, it may be considered instead as part of a more holistic peacebuilding approach and seen as a comprehensive and ongoing process that supplements other conflict management dimensions (Bercovitch and Kadayifci 2002). The qualities, skills, and methods of mediators are crucial to the effectiveness of mediation, as external mediators need to respond to and consider the context of the conflict to be successful. Today, more complex models of third-party engagement—regional organizations, ad hoc coalitions of actors, and nongovernmental bodies—are increasingly involved in bringing legitimacy to international mediation processes (Crocker et al. 2018).

Since 1945, the UN has been one of the key international organizations advancing the practice and support of mediation processes. According to its charter, peacemaking is an "action to bring hostile parties to agreement, essentially through such peaceful means as those foreseen in Chapter VI of the Charter of the United Nations; Pacific Settlement of Disputes" (United Nations 1945). In the UN system, peacemaking emerges as a conflict resolution tool that intends to move a violent conflict into a nonviolent dialogue. The objective of peacemaking in this context is to end violence between the contending parties through a variety of tools: negotiation, mediation, conciliation, arbitration, and international law mechanisms (Otunnu and Doyle 1998). In addition, the UN views peacekeeping as a technique designed to preserve peace where fighting has been halted and assist in implementing agreements achieved by peacemakers. In the UN system, peacemaking and peacekeeping are also clearly interlinked with peacebuilding, which aims at reducing the risk of conflict by strengthening capacities and addressing the core issues that affect the functioning of the society and the state. Considering the complexity of current armed conflict trends, the current UN secretary-general, António Guterres, encouraged a new focus on mediation support and facilitation, which entails fostering inclusivity and local engagement, strengthening national capacities, increasing women's participation in peace processes, promoting capacity-building, and professionalizing the field of mediation. The UN is now perceived as more effective in its role as an enabler, emphasizing the importance of greater investment in partnerships with regional and subregional organizations, such as the African Union, the Economic Community of West African States (ECOWAS), the Southern African Development Community (SADC), and the League of Arab States (United Nations Secretary General (UNSG) 2017).

The providers of international mediation include not only international, regional, and subregional organizations but also states, nongovernmental organizations (NGOs), and individuals. Since the Treaty of Westphalia (1648), states have been the dominant actor in the international system and the most frequent provider of conflict mediation. More recently, the five permanent members of the UN Security Council account for most of the state-conducted mediation since 1945, but a number of other countries, such as Finland, Norway, Switzerland, and, more recently, Qatar, have also been recognized as countries that have a special focus on mediation. On the other hand, within the realm of mediation efforts led by faith-based actors, the International Red Cross, the Catholic Church, and smaller religious groups such as the Quakers and the Sant'Egidio Foundation for Peace and Dialogue, have been some of the most active providers. In addition, private individuals, such as the former South African president Nelson Mandela, former Finnish president Martti Ahtisaari, and the former UN secretary-general Kofi Annan, have also served as key mediators to armed conflicts around the world (Greig and Diehl 2012). However, the cross-border and highly fragmented nature of current armed conflicts propelled the need to go beyond dominant track-one mediation activities.

As state actors felt reluctant to engage with nonofficial or nonrecognized actors, informal mediation activities conducted by private peacemakers became more common. NGOs such as the African Centre for the Constructive Resolution of Disputes (ACCORD), the Crisis Management Initiative (CMI)—Martti Ahtisaari Peace Foundation, and the Centre for Humanitarian Dialogue (HD) became some of the most prominent private peacemakers preparing and engaging in both formal and direct but informal mediation activities (Lehti 2019). Therefore, the last 20 years have also observed relevant innovations in the field of mediation with the rise of informal peace diplomacy often implemented by these nongovernmental organizations (NGOs). Private peacemakers coordinate their mediation activities with official actors and are now increasingly perceived as fundamental mediation actors in contemporary peace processes. The current transformation in peacemaking practices and actors reveals the emergence of alternative methods in the peace mediation field, which Marko Lehti (2020) highlights as a dialogic turn in peacemaking, contrasting it with standard mediation methods and approaches.

A new mediation environment with fragmented and cross-border NSAGs also raises concerns about the impact of a liberal-illiberal divide on the mediators' agency. Mandate-givers are increasingly expecting mediators to be more "inclusive" in their overall strategy. However, mediators are also under pressure to develop mediation processes that purposefully exclude some NSAGs designated as "terrorists," thus adopting a form of illiberal "exclusivity" that prevents these proscribed groups from participating in peace processes (Federer 2019).

On the issue of inclusivity, women and youth remain disproportionately underrepresented. With increasing pressure from women's groups and international actors, women have been gradually more included in mediation initiatives. The United Nations Security Council resolution 1325 in the year 2000 brought women, peace, and security onto the UN agenda. It called for recognizing women as peacemakers, peacekeepers, and peacebuilders rather than only as victims of armed conflicts. Since the 2000s, there have been concerted efforts to increase the participation of women in peace negotiations in a variety of ways, including via direct representation at the negotiating table, observer status, informal discussions, and public decision-making. However, research demonstrates that it is women's actual influence on the peace negotiations, not only their formal involvement, that is positively connected with a higher possibility of achieving long-term peace (Paffenholz 2018).

Youth involvement also became a vital component of local peacemaking activities. Many conflict-afflicted contexts have comparably young populations, giving youth a significant role in either sustaining the peace or fueling conflict in their respective sociopolitical environments. Youth can play a crucial role in the mitigation of ongoing armed conflicts and contribute significantly to the dissemination of mediation outcomes, particularly through social media (Pospisil et al. 2020).

On the other hand, digital transformation is also increasingly influencing the mediation context. Digital technologies are being used in a variety of ways. For example, some stakeholders may use social media to put pressure on the parties to the conflict. The mediator and the parties often use social media alongside low-tech forms of media like national and local radio stations to keep the public informed about the progress being made in the mediation process. Once an agreement has been reached, these different forms of media can also be used to share information on the agreement and to encourage support for the cease-fire or peace agreements. Digitalization has increased the volume, scope, and speed with which information can be shared directly between, for example, parties and their supporters. This can be positive when it is encouraging and reenforcing a message of peace, but it can also be used to promote hatred, stir up emotions, and even encourage violence (Hirblinger 2020). Digital platforms have also been utilized for monitoring elections, documenting human rights abuses, and facilitating contact among people of various parties in conflict-affected societies. Information and communication technologies, both digital and web based, can be utilized to prevent and manage armed violence, helping both peacemakers and peacebuilders to foster more positive outcomes (Duursma and Karlsrud 2021).

Despite recent innovations in the field of mediation, conflict management, and conflict resolution, newly signed peace agreements remain under increasing strain and are marked by high rates of relapse into conflict. Measuring the effectiveness of mediation is also becoming more difficult. The ability to achieve an agreement to end violence has been a standard method; however, this metric alone fails to properly assess the impact of the agreement in relation to the context and complexity of the conflict. Because peace processes are nonlinear and expand into multiple dimensions, it is impossible to assess their impact as a single process (Baumann and Clayton 2017).

Despite the changing nature of war and warring parties, the increasing internationalization and regionalization of conflicts, and the unprecedented acceleration in the speed and spread of information and knowledge, standard methods used in mediation are still predominantly trapped in linear and determined-designed thinking (Paffenholz 2021). From directed-mediation to facilitation, the mediators and the parties to the conflict might use a variety of techniques. Using directed-mediation techniques, the mediator strives to influence the parties' behavior both during and after the mediation. On the other hand, the mediator who acts as a facilitator throughout the peace process is primarily concerned with acting as a moderator and developing trust between the parties. Facilitation can also provide facilities and resources, as well as safeguard against unwanted external disruption and interference.

Adaptive Mediation and Conflict Resolution Amid Increasing Uncertainty

In the last decade, intrastate conflicts have become longer (protracted), more complex, and more frequent, not only in low-income but also in middle-income countries. As conflicts are by their nature complex and uncertain, contemporary conflict resolution is rendered even more complex by significant disruptions to and changes in the global order. Most recently, the COVID-19 pandemic further exacerbated the unpredictability and uncertainty within the international peace mediation environment and significantly disrupted the way regional and international mediation teams operate. The pandemic had a reduced impact on the underlying causes or dynamics of violent conflicts. Instead, it was able to ramp up current armed conflict trends and provided armed groups with more strategic options. The weakening of state structures and lack of media attention resulting from the health crisis allowed for more military actions with less opposition (Ide 2021).

It is increasingly recognized that the standard methods used in mediation are inadequate for coping with the levels of uncertainty and complexity that most mediators face today. In this book, we will introduce an alternative method—Adaptive Mediation—that is specifically designed to cope with uncertainty and complexity. This method will be analyzed within the context of four contemporary case studies—Colombia, Mozambique, the Philippines, and Syria—to test its assumptions and learn from and refine the approach to adaptive mediation based on the empirical experiences of mediation in these cases.

Here, mediation is broadly understood as a third-party-facilitated peacemaking process that includes formal and informal talks, dialogues, and other confidence-building initiatives that lead up to formal negotiations, such as negotiations over humanitarian access, cease-fires, and comprehensive peace agreements. The standard mediation method can be described as determined-designed thinking. It is based on the assumption that mediation experts have the agency to analyze a conflict, identify its root causes, and design solutions for the conflict based on international best practices. These options can then be presented to the conflicting parties in a mediation setting. Mediation is then understood as a process through which the parties, based on the information and analysis presented, will be led through a facilitated negotiation during which they should agree on one or more of the options presented to them.

In practice, most of the limited solutions offered follow a standard range of options, informed by the so-called best practices from other peace mediation experiences. The determined-design theory of change is flawed because social systems are empirically complex, highly dynamic, nonlinear, and emergent. This uncertainty is an intrinsic quality of complex adaptive systems, not a result of imperfect knowledge or inadequate analysis, planning, or implementation. This recognition has specific implications for the planning and implementation of mediation.

The adaptive mediation approach provides us with a methodology for coping with this complexity and uncertainty. Firstly, it recognizes that an analysis of the conflict system has to be emergent from a collaborative engagement with the parties to the conflict. A conflict analysis should not be developed by experts and presented to the parties to the conflict. It is something that has to be developed as a collaborative process with the parties to the conflict. Arriving at a shared understanding of the conflict is the first building block of the adaptive mediation process and a prerequisite for a self-sustainable mediated settlement. Secondly, based on such a shared understanding, the parties to the conflict should generate their own potential range of settlement options.

Generating a range of options together builds confidence and broadens the scope of potential solutions beyond the narrow range that parties typically enter a negotiation with. Generating future options can also be complemented with associated collaborative and inclusive processes such as national dialogues or other forms of popular consultation. Thirdly, adaptive mediation approaches recognize that a mediation process is not limited to one series of talks or agreements but is, in reality, a cumulative transition process that typically spans decades and includes negotiations and agreements on many aspects of the social contract that take place at different times and in different fora. It is thus important to think of mediation as a process, not an event, and to think about any agreement reached as one building block in this larger process. It thus takes a whole-of-system, relational, and spatial approach that is open-ended, fluid, and flexible. Adaptive mediation is an approach that shifts the focus of mediation away from its fixation on the mediator, the mediation table, and the settlement agreement, instead approaching mediation as a participatory, adaptive, and iterative facilitation process that accompanies a society in its journey from conflict to sustainable peace.

Adaptive mediation differs from the mainstream determined-design and directed-mediation model in that it is an approach that is specifically designed to cope with the uncertainty, unpredictability, and irreproducibility inherent in the complex social change process. Adaptive mediation is a process that is aimed at empowering the parties participating in the mediation to generate solutions themselves. For a peace agreement to be self-sustainable, it has to emerge from both a collaborative process owned by the parties to the conflict and an inductive iterative adaptive engagement with the context. The role of the mediator is limited to facilitating the process. Adaptive mediation is especially concerned with enhancing the self-sustainability of peace agreements and, in this context, understands the role of the mediator as facilitating a process of emergent self-organization.

When this approach is applied to conflict analyses, planning, monitoring, and evaluation, the ability of mediation processes to navigate uncertainty and adapt to changing dynamics will be enhanced. In order for more resilient and more self-sustainable agreements to emerge, adaptive mediation requires mediators to apply a light touch that encourages greater interdependence among the parties and discourages dependence upon the mediator. As a result, utilizing an adaptive mediation approach should result in generating peace agreements that are more locally grounded, self-sustainable, and resilient to withstand setbacks and shocks.

The Structure of the Book

This book explores mediation practices in four conflict-affected countries: Colombia, Mozambique, the Philippines, and Syria. Each case study will examine several mediation episodes and the complexities of sustaining peace in situations of protracted and recurring conflicts. In these four cases, the authors will question and identify some of the limitations of determined-designed mediation efforts, explore the extent to which adaptive approaches to mediation have been implemented, and examine the effects of these initiatives. For that purpose, the authors have followed a common analytical framework and attempted to answer the research questions mentioned in Table 1.1.

Table 1.1 Research questions

Main research question	• How do mediators adapt to uncertainty and complexity in contemporary armed conflicts?
Case study research questions	• What are the key characteristics of standard or alternative, and formal or informal, mediation practices in your case study? • How did mediators or parties to the conflict adapt or fail to adapt to uncertainty and complexity in your case study? • Which mediation good practices or lessons learned can you extract from your case study?

By extracting empirical evidence from the structure and practice of mediation in various conflict-affected contexts, this study attempts to reveal the conditions under which different types of formal and informal mediation events occurred in four case studies with distinct features (see Table 1.2).

Given the diversity of geopolitical and socioeconomic contexts, the evidence and lessons learned from each case study should help mediators dealing with similar contexts of uncertainty and complexity. The authors of each chapter analyzed each conflict-affected situation and respective mediation initiatives using process tracing, archival and database research, and field or remote semi-structured interviews. While the theoretical chapter presents an alternative pathway for effective mediation in the context of a more complex and newly emerging international order, four case studies have explored the contemporary challenges, opportunities, and limitations of mediation activities on the ground.

In Chap. 2, Cedric de Coning introduces the adaptive mediation approach, explains its roots in the study of complex adaptive systems, and addresses the key principles and characteristics of adaptive mediation, informing contemporary peacemakers on how to plan, analyze, assess, and undertake adaptive mediation processes. The chapter examines the attributes of complex systems, namely systems dynamics, nonlinearity, and self-organization. In the process, it explores the relationship between complexity and adaptive mediation, introducing emergence, adaptation, and feedback in this context. The adaptive mediation approach highlights the role of the mediator as the facilitator of the mediation process and is especially concerned with enhancing the self-sustainability of peace agreements.

The authors of the country case studies applied the insights of adaptive mediation to the variety of practices observed in four contexts, reflecting

Table 1.2 The case studies and respective distinguishing features

Case studies	*Distinguishing features*
Colombia Latest peace agreement in 2016	• High level of complexity and variety of nonstate actors in a long period of mediation with 12 processes occurring in parallel between 1991 and 2016. • Standard and adaptive meditation practices have coexisted and mediators focused on promoting institutional capacity building and communitarian bottom-up peacebuilding.
Mozambique Latest peace agreement in 2019	• In the context of a small-scale conflict recurrence, initial ineffective domestic and international mediation attempts led to a more effective process-facilitation of direct dialogue and adaptive mediation. • In the last mediation stage, the small mediation team's discretion and adaptiveness enabled positive outcomes in a nationally owned peace process.
The Philippines Latest peace agreement in 2014	• Adaptive peace process featuring a multilayered mediation framework with insider mediators and development agencies playing a crucial role. • Peace gains were sustained by building trust among stakeholders through vertical and horizontal relations.
Syria At the time of writing, no peace agreement has been reached	• High-level international mediation was conditioned by structural factors but enabled various negotiation platforms. • A combination of standard and adaptive approaches enabled positive outcomes. Mediation efforts enabled humanitarian actions to save lives and paved the ground for the creation of a constitutional committee. The process became increasingly inclusive of civil society and women's groups.

on whether and how adaptive approaches have helped mediators cope with uncertainty and complexity, and the extent to which mediators and the parties to the conflicts in these case studies adapted (or not) to changing dynamics on the ground. It is important to note that the case study authors retroactively applied the adaptive mediation lens to these cases. Adaptive mediation is a new concept, and none of the mediators in these cases have consciously applied the approach. They have instead analyzed these four cases to see if there were elements of an adaptive mediation approach in the mediation styles applied in them, and what it is we can learn from those approaches and the results they have achieved.

In Chap. 3, Lina Penagos reflects on Colombia's mediation experiences during the last three decades, encompassing 12 peace processes between the Colombian government and various Non-State Armed Groups. From the negotiation with the Popular Liberation Army in 1991 to the peace agreement with the Revolutionary Armed Forces of Colombia (FARC-EP) in 2016, mediation initiatives in Colombia combined standard and adaptive approaches. Despite the variety of violent nonstate actors involved in lengthy and overlapping peace negotiations, in retrospect, Colombian mediation experiences show evidence of the flexibility and adaptiveness of domestic mediators often supported by the national government and external partners. The author focused on mediation initiatives that enabled institutional capacity building and effective disarmament, demobilization, and reintegration outcomes.

In Chap. 4, Rui Saraiva examines the adaptive nature of the new mediation process in Mozambique's recent small-scale armed conflict recurrence (2013–2019). This chapter extracts the key factors and strategies that enabled the signature of the Maputo Accord for Peace and Reconciliation on August 6, 2019. It argues that adaptive mediation and a nationally owned direct dialogue were essential to address the complexity of the conflict situation and the impact of unexpected events such as the sudden death of the Mozambican National Resistance (RENAMO) leader Afonso Dhlakama in 2018. The effectiveness of the later stage of the mediation process resulted from the discreet and adaptive strategies used by a small mediation team led by the Swiss Ambassador, Mirko Manzoni. Adaptive mediation in Mozambique accentuated the agency, interdependence, and direct dialogue between both parties, making it possible for peacemaking to emerge from within.

In Chap. 5, Miyoko Taniguchi explores the adaptation from outsider to insider mediation as a nonlinear process in response to the complexity of the protracted conflict and armed violence in Mindanao, the Philippines. For more than 50 years, continuous efforts by international and national mediators have been able to sustain peace in the region. This chapter identifies four factors that have led to the creation of a new autonomous region through a multilayered mediation framework that has broadened the definition of mediation from transitional (international-external-predetermined) to innovative (local-insider-adaptive). The author concludes that the adaptation from outsider to insider mediation, especially under the Duterte administration, fostered trust-building among the involved parties and increased the domestic ownership of the peace process.

In Chap. 6, Ako Muto examines standard and adaptive mediation approaches, efforts, and initiatives in the context of the Syrian armed conflict. The author assesses the impact of domestic and external constraints in the mediation process and reveals how the mediators attempted, to varying degrees, to "adapt" to contextual complexities in unique ways. The Syrian mediation context struggled with the extensive fragmentation of NSAGs, and progress in the negotiations has been dependent on the consent of major conflict parties and respective external allies. This chapter demonstrates how standard and adaptive mediation approaches have coexisted and mitigated the impact of the conflict despite the fact that a peace agreement has not yet been reached. It underlines that adaptive approaches contributed to saving lives and finding inclusive ways for more Syrian civil society actors to participate in the ongoing peace process.

Conclusion

Many peace agreements today are signed or pursued amid volatile political instability and uncertainty. War and other forms of armed violence reoccur more often, as renewed tensions at the ground level frequently erupt not long after the signature of new peace accords, and while the underlying root causes of conflict remain to be adequately addressed by peacebuilding actions. The rise of violent extremism coexisting with traditional armed conflicts, the fragmentation and changing behavior of armed groups, the cross-border nature, and the increasing internationalization and regionalization of armed conflicts have all contributed to the ineffectiveness of dominant mediation strategies. Mediators often struggle with increasing uncertainty and unpredictability and more complex peace architectures than ever before. Previous determined-designed methods applied to interstate wars have been subsequently adjusted to increasingly complex intrastate conflicts and are now insufficient to respond to contemporary challenges.

Determined-designed mediation approaches are based on static and linear conflict analysis and planning. They lead mediators to seek cause-and-effect interactions, prompting surprise when unwanted results emerge. In addition, mediators following determined-designed approaches will undervalue the uniqueness of local contexts, while applying models that were used elsewhere but that might not work in a different context. Peace mediation has largely remained state-centric and continued to rely on determined-designed approaches. However, in the last decade, there has also been an increase in the number of peace mediation actors, including official actors such as small states and international organizations, and private actors such as nongovernmental organizations, both attempting to implement alternative and innovative approaches.

In line with the current transformation of peacemaking practices and with the dialogic turn, adaptive mediation rests on the basis of two main pillars: self-organization and resilience. Mediators are encouraged to promote the national and local ownership of the mediation process (self-organization) and help conflict-affected societies to gain the capacity to deal with future shocks and uncertainty (resilience). An adaptive approach sees external mediators as facilitators of a process that emerges from within, with monitoring and evaluation activities focused on the ability of mediators to adapt to uncertainty and complexity rather than to achieve predetermined objectives. In this context, this book reflects on the limitations of standard determined-designed mediation approaches and introduces adaptive mediation as an alternative. This approach questions the top-down determined-design nature of mainstream mediation and calls for an approach where the role of mediator is to be limited to process facilitation and where the sustainability of peace agreements is to be grounded in the agency and participation of the parties to the conflict reaching their own context-specific agreements.

References

Bagshaw, Dale, and Elisabeth J. Porter. 2013. *Mediation in the Asia-Pacific Region: Transforming Conflicts and Building Peace*. London: Routledge.

Baumann, Jonas, and Govinda Clayton. 2017. Mediation in Violent Conflict. *CSS Analyses in Security Policy* 211 (June).

Bercovitch, Jacob, and Ayse Kadayifci. 2002. Exploring the Relevance and Contribution of Mediation to Peace-Building. *Peace and Conflict Studies* 9 (2): 21–40.

Collier, Paul, V. L. Elliott, Håvard Hegre, Anke Hoeffler, Marta Reynal-Querol, and Nicholas Sambanis. 2003. *Breaking the Conflict Trap: Civil War and Development Policy*. A World Bank Policy Research Report, World Bank and Oxford University Press, Washington, DC. https://openknowledge.worldbank.org/handle/10986/13938.

Crocker, Chester A., Fen Osler Hampson, and Pamela Aall. 2018. *International Negotiation and Mediation in Violent Conflict: The Changing Context of Peacemaking*. London: Taylor and Francis.

Duursma, Allard, and John Karlsrud. 2021. Technologies of Peace. In *The Oxford Handbook of Peacebuilding, Statebuilding, and Peace Formation*, ed. Oliver

P. Richmond and Gëzim Visoka. Oxford University Press. https://doi.org/10.1093/oxfordhb/9780190904418.013.28.

Eriksson, Mikael, and Roland Kostić. 2013. *Mediation and Liberal Peacebuilding: Peace from the Ashes of War?* London: Routledge.

Federer, Julia Palmiano. 2019. We Do Negotiate with Terrorists: Navigating Liberal and Illiberal Norms in Peace Mediation. *Critical Studies on Terrorism* 12 (1): 19–39.

Harland, David. 2018. *The Lost Art of Peacemaking*. Geneva: HD Centre for Humanitarian Dialogue.

Greig, J. Michael, and Paul F. Diehl. 2012. *International Mediation. War and Conflict in the Modern World*. Cambridge: Polity Press.

Hirblinger, Andreas T. 2020. *Digital Inclusion in Peacemaking: A Strategic Perspective*. CCDP Working Paper, Centre on Conflict, Development and Peacebuilding (CCDP) Graduate Institute of International and Development Studies, Switzerland. https://repository.graduateinstitute.ch/record/298396.

Ide, Tobias. 2021. COVID-19 and Armed Conflict. *World Development* 140 (April): 105355.

Kressel, Kenneth, and Dean G. Pruitt. 1989. *Mediation Research: The Process and Effectiveness of Third-Party Intervention*. San Francisco: Jossey-Bass.

Lehti, Marko. 2019. *The Era of Private Peacemakers: A New Dialogic Approach to Mediation*, Rethinking Peace and Conflict Studies. London: Palgrave Macmillan. https://doi.org/10.1007/978-3-319-91201-1.

———. 2020. Private Peacemaking and Dialogic Approach to Mediation. In *The Palgrave Encyclopedia of Peace and Conflict Studies*, 1–13. Cham: Springer International Publishing. https://doi.org/10.1007/978-3-030-11795-5_53-1.

Mcquinn, Brian, and Laura Courche. 2020. Armed-Group Proliferation: Origins and Consequences. *Armed Conflict Survey* 6 (1): 14–18.

Milián, Ivan Navarro, Josep Maria Royo Aspa, Jordi Urgell García, Pamela Urrutia Arestizábal, Ana Villellas Ariño, and María Villellas Ariño. 2019. *Peace Talks in Focus 2019*. Report on Trends and Scenarios, Escola de Cultura de Pau. https://reliefweb.int/report/world/peace-talks-focus-2019-report-trends-and-scenarios-enes.

OECD. 2016. *States of Fragility 2016: Understanding Violence*. Paris: OECD Publishing. https://doi.org/10.1787/9789264267213-en.

Otunnu, Olara A., and Michael W. Doyle. 1998. *Peacemaking and Peacekeeping for the New Century*. Lanham: Rowman & Littlefield.

Paffenholz, Thania. 2018. Women in Peace Negotiations. In *Gendering Diplomacy and International Negotiation*, Studies in Diplomacy and International Relations, ed. Karin Aggestam and Ann E. Towns, 169–191. Cham: Springer International Publishing.

———. 2021. Perpetual Peacebuilding: A New Paradigm to Move Beyond the Linearity of Liberal Peacebuilding. *Journal of Intervention and Statebuilding* 15 (3): 367–385.

Pospisil, Jan, Laura Wise, and Christine Bell. 2020. *Untangling Conflict: Local Peace Agreements in Contemporary Armed Violence*. ASPR Report No. 5, Austrian Study Centre for Peace and Conflict Resolution, Stadtschlaining, Austria. https://www.politicalsettlements.org/publications-database/untangling-conflict-local-peace-agreements-in-contemporary-armed-violence/.

United Nations. 1945. *Charter of the United Nations and Statute of the International Court of Justice*. San Francisco: United Nations. https://treaties.un.org/doc/publication/ctc/uncharter.pdf.

United Nations and World Bank. 2018. *Pathways for Peace: Inclusive Approaches to Preventing Violent Conflict*. Washington, DC: World Bank. https://openknowledge.worldbank.org/handle/10986/28337.

United Nations Secretary General (UNSG). 2017. *United Nations Activities in Support of Mediation*. Report of the Secretary General A/72/115, United Nations. https://peacemaker.un.org/sites/peacemaker.un.org/files/DPA%20Report%20REV9%20ENG%20WEB_0.PDF.

Zartman, I. William, and Tanya Alfredson. 2019. Negotiating with Terrorists and the Tactical Question. In *I William Zartman: A Pioneer in Conflict Management and Area Studies: Essays on Contention and Governance*, Pioneers in Arts, Humanities, Science, Engineering, Practice, ed. I. William Zartman, 195–223. Cham: Springer International Publishing.

CHAPTER 2

Adaptive Mediation

Cedric de Coning

In this chapter, I will introduce the Adaptive Mediation approach, explain its roots in the study of complex adaptive systems, and address some of the key principles and characteristics of Adaptive Mediation that will inform how one plans for, analyzes, assesses, and undertakes Adaptive Mediation processes.

Mediation can be defined as a "complex process of conflict management that purports to facilitate a voluntary agreement between conflict parties at different levels" (Bercovitch and Houston 1993, 297). In the context of this definition, peace mediation is typically understood as a process in which two or more parties to a conflict are assisted by a neutral third-party mediator to pursue a cease-fire or peace agreement (Bercovitch 1991). It can also be used more broadly to describe neutral third-party support of national dialogue or other types of peace initiatives (Lehti 2019).

C. de Coning (✉)
Norwegian Institute of International Affairs (NUPI), Oslo, Norway

African Center for the Constructive Resolution of Disputes (ACCORD), Durban, South Africa
e-mail: cdc@nupi.no

C. de Coning et al. (eds.), *Adaptive Mediation and Conflict Resolution*, Sustainable Development Goals Series,
https://doi.org/10.1007/978-3-030-92577-2_2

There are a few widely agreed-upon prerequisites for effective mediation. The first is that the parties to the conflict must have arrived at a point where they have recognized the need to seek a negotiated solution and where they themselves choose to enter into a mediation process. This implies that they have reached what Zartman (2001) has termed a "mutually hurting stalemate." This is a point in the conflict where neither party can achieve victory over the other(s) through violence or other coercive means, and the positions they are in are untenable.

It is thus a point in the conflict where each of the parties themselves come to the realization that their best option is to pursue a negotiated end to the conflict. In other words, when weighing all their options, they must come to the conclusion themselves that they are more likely to secure their interests through a negotiated outcome than through violent conflict or other means. In negotiation theory, this is also known as considering the Best Alternative to a Negotiated Settlement (BATNA), that is, if a party believes there is a better alternative than a negotiated settlement, they will pursue that option (Fisher et al. 2011). BATNA is also used to analyze the specific options and choices a party may have during a negotiation or a mediation process when faced with certain decision points, but the first decision is of course whether to negotiate or not.

Zartman uses the mutually hurting stalemate analysis to assess the degree to which a conflict is ripe for resolution. If the parties have not reached this point, they are unlikely to opt for mediation. If they do engage in mediation, for instance under international pressure, then the process is unlikely to succeed. If they reach an agreement, it is unlikely to hold for long, if one or more of the parties believe they can achieve a better outcome for themselves through other means. This is not an idle concern. Collier and colleagues have found that approximately 50 percent of all peace agreements fail within ten years (Collier et al. 2003). Adaptive Mediation is an approach to mediation that is particularly concerned with enhancing the self-sustainability of the agreements reached, and laying the foundation for this self-sustainability through the mediation process itself.

The second prerequisite is that the parties to the conflict must choose mediation—as opposed to, for example, direct negotiation or arbitration if that is an option—and agree on the choice of the mediator. This could be a choice for an institution, for example the African Union or the United Nations, but often it also includes the choice of a specific person, or at the very least the option to veto anyone the parties object too. This is because the parties must have confidence in the neutrality, impartiality, and integrity of the mediator (Bercovitch and Houston 1993). In Adaptive Mediation, the mediator plays an important but limited facilitation role in the mediation process, and the approach has very specific guidance for how mediators should manage their role in the mediation process to avoid disrupting the emergent self-organization process necessary to generate self-sustainable peace agreements.

Many conflicts don't reach this point and are not ripe for mediation. In some cases, one party achieves victory over the others, or at least sufficient dominance to take over or remain in control of the state. Many others end up in a kind of no-peace-no-war situation where the conflict has reached an impasse, but where it is not formally acknowledged or settled. In these situations, the choice not to formally settle the conflict is a kind of temporary settlement in itself (Pospisil 2019). Some degree of typically low-level violent conflict may continue, but for the time being the conflict is paused. At the same time, trying to resolve the conflict may be too risky for the parties as attempting resolution may reignite violence. Thus, leaving it unresolved may be their best option for the time being. Often this is because important elements of the particular conflict are linked to a rivalry between major or regional powers (Lehti 2020). This is why dozens of conflicts suddenly became ripe for resolution at the end of the Cold War. Sometimes peace agreements may also contain elements of preferred unsettlement, where parties agree to address at a later stage in the process those aspects that are too sensitive to address at the outset. It is thus important to assess each conflict to determine if it is ripe for mediation. If not, other techniques, including Adaptive Peace Operations (de Coning 2020b) or Adaptive Peacebuilding (de Coning 2018) may be more suitable.

In increasingly complex armed conflicts, mediators have been challenged on several fronts and obliged to reassess the effectiveness of their methods (Paffenholz 2021). The 2016 Oslo Forum also addressed the question of whether mediation is still the most effective tool to solve the pressing conflicts of our time. The forum participants recognized that in recent years mediation has been ineffective; despite many attempts to initiate peace processes, violence continues to flare in Syria, Afghanistan, Yemen, and other locations (Dziatkowiec et al. 2016). Peace mediation has been criticized for remaining state-centric and for relying on rationalistic, interest-based, and materially driven approaches. However, in the last decade, there was also an increase in peace mediation actors among official actors, such as small states and international organizations, and an increasing number of nongovernmental actors (Lehti 2019, 2–3).

Mediation is thus widely understood as a delicate and complex undertaking that is more likely to fail then succeed. Although, as Andrew Mack (2012) pointed out, statistically even failed peace agreements save lives.[1] The potential for success depends on many factors, most of which are outside the control of the mediator and, in some cases, even the parties to the conflict. There are many stakeholders involved. In addition to the parties directly involved, there are the people affected by the conflict, including specific groups that may be associated with some of the parties. Some of these are likely to be in the diaspora, from where they may exert influence on the process. Many other actors inside and outside the country will have a stake in the outcome, and as a result may try to influence the process. This may include important private sector interests inside and outside the country, countries in the region, or rival regional or global powers. Some will try to disrupt the process or even derail the mediation itself.

In an ideal model, the mediator understands the history and context of the conflict and takes into account the interests and perspectives of the various parties to the conflict as well as others who may have an interest in the outcome and may be trying to influence the process (Lehti 2019). The mediator also has to understand the complex psychological, group, and intergroup relational dynamics of the mediation process itself in order to assess the pace of the process and determine when to introduce new elements, when to take a break, and so on (Deutsch and Coleman 2012). At the same time, the mediator is expected to facilitate a process of growing trust, first in the process and eventually in the emerging agreement and in each other (Paffenholz 2014).

In reality, no mediator, no matter how extensive and professional their support team, can meaningfully comprehend and factor in all these complex dynamics. The Adaptive Mediation approach recognizes that this complexity, unpredictability, and uncertainty is an intrinsic quality of complex systems, not a result of imperfect knowledge, poor analysis, or inadequate planning (Popolo 2011, 209). Adaptive Mediation is an approach that anticipates and accepts this complexity and employs a set of principles and practices that help mediators cope with uncertainty, setbacks, and shocks when attempting to facilitate such complex social change processes (de Coning and Gray 2018). Peter Coleman and colleagues defined

[1] See also *Human Security Report* 2012.

adaptive mediation as "the capacity to read important changes in the fundamental dimensions of mediation situations and to respond to them with strategies and tactics that are more 'fitting' and thus more effective in those situations" (Coleman et al. 2017).

Those who interpret adaptation to imply conflict management may feel that it does not go far enough, and that what is needed to truly bring an end to a conflict is a transformation of the system that generated the conflict. In the field of conflict resolution, the dichotomy between "problem-solving" and "transformation" approaches has been a key debate (Kriesberg 2007). Kriesberg (2007) underlined that one of the matters of dissensus among scholars and practitioners resides in the differentiation between "conflict" and "dispute" and their settlement, resolution, or transformation. While a dispute is an easily negotiable matter and contains more elements of compromise, a conflict is about deep-rooted problems. While "conflict resolution" implies solving these problems, "transformation" changes the relationships between the conflict parties, and "settlement" suppresses the conflict but does not address its deeper causes or relations. Bush and Folger (1994) characterized both evaluative and facilitative mediation as problem-solving approaches and introduced *transformative* mediation as an alternative. A transformative mediation approach focuses on the opportunity to transform the interaction between conflict parties, while mediators would only intervene when necessary to support empowerment and recognition shifts. Transformative mediators will be more focused on the process of transformation rather than reaching an agreement (Bush and Folger 1994).

In contrast to *problem-solving styles*, Kenneth Kressel underlined that *relational styles* "focus less on agreement making and more on open lines of communication and clarifying underlying feelings and perceptions" (Kressel 2014, 651). The *relational style* focuses on the self-organization and self-management of both parties, combined with improving their long-term relationship through humanistic values. Some examples of this new emerging paradigm are the transformational (Bush and Folger 1994), narrative (Winslade and Monk 2001), and victim-offender mediation approaches (Umbreit 2010). In addition to this debate, Kressel (2014) highlights that the mediator style is interdependent with the context where the conflict is occurring. Therefore, mediators are encouraged to be flexible and adaptive to the context.

The last 20 years in particular have seen the rise of informal peace diplomacy executed by nongovernmental organizations. They are frequently viewed as supporting actors in peace processes, and their participation is widely acknowledged to be fundamental. In most cases, peace processes are carried out by independent nongovernmental institutions, for example the African Centre for the Construction Resolution of Disputes (ACCORD), the Finnish Crisis Management Initiative (CMI) and the Centre for Humanitarian Dialogue (HD) (Lehti 2019, 40). The current transformation in peacemaking practices and actors reveals the emergence of bottom-up methods in the peace mediation field, which has been highlighted by Marko Lehti (2019, 6) as a dialogic turn in peacemaking, contrasting it with the methods and approaches of classical mediation.

Adaptive Mediation is transformative, relational, and dialogic, but it is important to understand that the term "adaptive" in this case does not refer to the degree or extent of the change in the conflict system, that is, conflict management, resolution, or transformation, but to the theory of change, that is, the way in which the change in the system is brought about.

Two concepts that are important to understand when it comes to the theory of change of Adaptive Mediation are resilience and self-organization. Resilience refers to the capacity of social institutions "to absorb and adapt in order to sustain an acceptable level of function, structure and identity under stress" (Dahlberg 2015, 541). Self-organization refers to the ability of a complex system to organize, regulate, and maintain itself without a controlling agent. In complex social systems, the resilience to withstand shocks and challenges grows as social institutions develop increasingly complex forms of self-organization, which distributes and dilutes vulnerability across a network of interdependent parts.

In a mediation context, self-organization begins to emerge when the parties involved in the mediation cross the interdependence tipping point, that is, when they recognize that they can't achieve their interests on their own and that they need each other's cooperation. It is at this point that they start to collaboratively work toward mutually acceptable agreements. This is the most delicate part of the mediation process because the mediator can use this moment to influence the agreement. Agreements reached through a self-organizing mediation process are, however, more resilient because the ownership and commitment are distributed among all the participants who co-created it. Adaptive Mediation challenges mediators to accentuate rather than constrain the agency and interdependence of the parties. Adaptive Mediation encourages a process whereby the content of agreements emerge from the interaction among the participants—as opposed to from inputs by the mediation team or from so-called international best practice—and where the emergent dynamics of the mediation process creates the basis for the self-sustainability and resilience of the agreements reached (de Coning 2018).

The negotiations that brought an end to the Apartheid era in South Africa are an example of self-organized mediation. The Convention for a Democratic South Africa's (CODESA) multiparty talks (1992–1994) were managed by the parties themselves. The talks broke down on several occasions due to various setbacks, such as the Boipatong massacre in June 1992 and the inability of the parties to find common ground on particularly challenging issues. However, the relationships and self-organizing networks that had developed among and around the parties were resilient enough to enable them to find creative ways to resume talks and ultimately reach an agreement (Sparks 1996).

Adaptive Mediation is thus a specific approach to mediation designed to cope with complexity and uncertainty, which is especially concerned with enhancing the self-sustainability and resilience of peace agreements and sees the role of the mediator as limited to facilitating a process of emergent self-organization. Before we unpack these aspects in more detail, let's first explore the theoretical foundation of Adaptive Mediation to understand how it is grounded in what we know about the behavior of complex social systems.

Complexity

We often hear it said that a particular conflict is complex, or that conflict resolution and mediation is a complex undertaking. What does it mean when we say a particular conflict, or the international response to it, is complex? What can we learn from applying the knowledge generated by the study of complexity to the peacemaking context? Could insights from the study of complex adaptive systems assist us in improving our understanding of how to influence complex social systems, and can we use this knowledge to improve how we help societies resolve conflict? Beyond the common use of the term, there is a science of complexity or complex adaptive systems that studies the behavior and characteristics of complex systems. This science is also increasingly applied to the social world, and is gaining ground in economics, political science, international relations, and peace and conflict studies (de Coning 2020a), with insights about social behavior and relations that are highly relevant for conflict resolution and mediation (Hendrick 2009).

Mediation is about facilitating a process whereby parties that are in an adversarial relationship are seeking to find an agreement according to which they can peacefully coexist in a shared social system. Insights from complexity science that help us understand how to influence the behavior of complex social systems and how such systems evolve and respond to pressure should thus be valuable for those involved in trying to understand and manage mediation processes.

Studying complexity can, for instance, help us understand where mediators can have the most impact when trying to influence complex social relationships. Donella Meadows (1999) found that when we try to influence complex systems, we often devote most of our efforts to aspects that, counterintuitively, have only weak leverage. In the context of mediation, this could be time spent reaching agreements on things such as the composition of committees, position assignments, deadlines for certain processes, and so on. These may be important and sensitive areas in a negotiation process, but they are weak leverage points for social change because on their own they do not change the system within which they function. In conflict resolution terminology, we can say they do not address the root causes or key drivers of the conflict. Meadows points out that high leverage points in complex systems—where relatively small shifts can have the most impact—are rules, structures, goals, and paradigms. These are also the aspects of any mediation process that will be the most sensitive but most important in terms of bringing about real change in the way a society is organized and future conflict is resolved.

Studying complex systems has also taught us that change does not always occur gradually. Pressure for change accumulates, but often without much evidence during the build-up phase. And then suddenly, when a tipping point is reached, a system can change significantly in a short period of time (Coleman et al. 2006). This is a dynamic we often experience in mediation, where breakthroughs are typically not reached as a result of steady progress, but rather under pressures of deadlock or even potential breakdown. This is partly due to the importance of path dependency in system dynamics (Mitchell 2009). The choices available to individuals, even powerful leaders and political elites, are constrained by initial conditions and by the choices they and others have made earlier in the process. This helps explain why most important systemic changes occur during periods of turbulence when path dependency is disrupted. From a mediation perspective, such transitions create opportunities to exert influence on higher-order leverage points.

As these examples show, social systems and social interactions—like mediation processes—are empirically complex (Byrne 1998). This means that they demonstrate the ability to adapt, and that they have emergent properties, including self-organizing behavior (Kaufmann 2013). As social systems are highly dynamic, nonlinear, and emergent, it is not possible to find general laws or rules that will help us predict with certainty how a particular society or community will behave or how a specific mediation process will develop (Cilliers 2002).

Complexity explains that a complex system, for example a society, is a particular type of holistic system that has the ability to adapt, and that demonstrates emergent properties, including self-organizing behavior. Such systems emerge and are maintained as a result of the dynamic and nonlinear interactions of their elements, based on the information available to them locally, as a result of their interaction with their environment, as well as from the modulated feedback they receive from the other elements in the system (Cilliers 1998, 3).

One way to highlight the unique characteristics of complex adaptive systems is to contrast them with complicated systems. A complicated system can potentially be fully understood and predicted, provided sufficient information is available. Designing, building, and launching a rocket into space is highly complicated, but once it is mastered, the same process can be repeated with a reasonable chance of success. In fact, the most frequently used rocket to send people and goods into space is the Russian Soyuz rocket, which has a core design that has been in use since 1967 (European Space Agency 2019). In contrast, nonlinearity plays a critical role in the emergence and self-regulation of complex adaptive systems (Cilliers 1998, 3). Even if a particular process helped to generate a peaceful outcome in one society, for example the CODESA process in South Africa mentioned earlier, it cannot be repeated in another context with any reasonable expectation that it will have the same outcome. In fact, it can't even be repeated in South Africa with any expectation that it will have the same outcome.

I will explain three of the core characteristics of complexity that have been mentioned several times by now, namely systems, nonlinearity, and self-organization, in more detail. In the process, I will also introduce a number of related concepts that form the basis of our understanding of complexity and its relationship with Adaptive Mediation, including emergence, adaptation, and feedback.

Systems

A system can be defined in a very general sense as a collection of interacting elements that together produce, by virtue of their interactions, some form of system-wide behavior (Mitchell 2009). In other words, a system is a community of elements that, as a result of their interconnections, form a whole. In complex systems, the interaction is dynamic; that is to say, a complex system changes over time (Cilliers 1998). Complexity is interested in how the elements interact and how this interaction fosters the development of new system capacities that did not exist within the individual elements.

From a mediation perspective, we can say that the parties to the conflict can be viewed as elements in a system and that the mediation process is aimed at facilitating the emergence of a new system. At the start of the process, they represent separate systems that are in competition with each other; if successful, by the end they represent elements (subsystems) of a new system, where the parts have recognized their interdependence and found a formula for coexisting peacefully. This does not imply that they no longer compete with each other, or that they no longer have their own interests, but that they have arrived at an agreement on how to manage that competition, and the disputes that may arise as a result, peacefully in the future while coexisting within the same system.

In complex systems, the whole has properties that cannot be found in the constituent elements or in the sum of their properties. In social systems, for instance, the society as a whole develops and maintains norms and identities that serve the common needs of the community. In some ways, this results in suppressing some of the interests and needs of the individual and of special interest groups in the interest of the general well-being and survival of the society as a whole. Morin (2005, 11) points out that in social systems, not only is the whole more than its elements because new qualities or properties emerge due to the organization of the elements in the whole, but the whole can also be less than the sum of its parts because "a certain number of qualities and properties present in the parts can be inhibited by the organization as a whole." This fits well with the mediation context where parties are expected to give up some of their demands in order to enter into a new relationship that will enable them to secure their most important interests.

The concepts "social" and "society" conjure up images of systems made up of people who share a common sociocultural, national, or civic bond.

When studying people in the context of them being part of a society, as opposed to studying them as individuals, a different side of their being—including aspects related to their role in society as well as to the restrictions that conforming to society places on them—is revealed. These are aspects of their being that could not be revealed by studying them in isolation from their place in a social system. By studying the society as a whole made up by the patterns of activity of the individuals and the various networks and subsystems—such as family, clan, and tribe that develop out of these patterns—we reveal insights into the way individuals derive meaning from their roles in a community and how the interactions between these individual roles shape, sustain, and transform both the society as a whole and the individuals who make up that society. These are insights that could never be identified by studying only the individual.

In moving from the individual to the community and society, we come across organization. Complex systems cannot do without hierarchy and structure, but in complex systems hierarchy is not hardwired or externally determined and controlled; the hierarchy of a complex system is emergent and self-organized and thus changes with the system as it adapts and evolves in response to its environment (Cilliers 2001). The vitality of the system depends on its ability to transform itself, including its structure and hierarchy. Hierarchy is a typical characteristic of complex adaptive systems, but it is important to note that the hierarchies themselves exhibit complex adaptive characteristics (Chapman 2002). A peace agreement is literally an agreement to change the political, economic, security, and other hierarchies and structures of a society from the current and immediate past state that contributed to the conflict to a future state that the parties to the conflict believe will enable them to coexist more fairly and equally.

The last aspect of a whole-of-systems approach that should be discussed is the role of boundaries and borders in complex systems. Complex systems are open systems, which implies that interactions take place across their boundaries (Cilliers 2002). These interactions take place with other systems and the environment: for instance, there is a flow of information between the system and its environment through its boundaries. Systems consist of interrelated subsystems, and some boundaries can thus fall within larger systems or share borders with them (Chapman 2002). Not all subsystems are neighbors physically; some are virtually linked—in social systems, agents far away from each other may be interlinked, for example via social media, and collaborate, coordinate, or otherwise influence each other's systems and in this way interpenetrate such systems. In the mediation context, we can think of the system as the society experiencing conflict, and of the environment as the wider national, regional, and international context within which that conflict plays out. Conflicts are typically influenced and interlinked to various interests and developments in their wider environment, but the underlying causes of the conflict are typically to be found in the structure and operation of the primary social system in which the parties are located and identify with. Conflicts generate displacement and refugees, and there are usually people living outside the territory with a great interest in—and sometimes influence over—what happens in the system. They are part of the system, although they are not at present physically located in the territorial space associated with the system, and they thus have to be factored in, both in the analysis of the conflict dynamics and in its potential resolution. We will return to the issue of boundaries and borders when we consider aspects related to delineating between internal or local and international actors in the broader mediation context.

Complexity thus builds on and is grounded in systems thinking. However, it is concerned with a specific type of system, namely complex adaptive systems, and to gain more understanding of that differentiation we turn to another set of important properties of complexity, namely nonlinearity and self-organization.

Nonlinearity

The previous section introduced a systems perspective, explaining that complexity is interested in the patterns of interconnections among the elements and how this dynamic interaction generates properties beyond those that exist in its constituent parts. This section introduces the second characteristic of complexity, namely that in complex systems the causal patterns of these interactions are nonlinear, that is, the outputs are not proportional to the inputs (Hendrick 2009). Nonlinearity refers to behaviors in which the relationships between variables in a system are dynamic and disproportionate (Kiel 1995).

Jervis (1997) points out that we tend to intuitively expect linear relationships. For example, if a little foreign aid slightly increases economic growth, it is expected that more aid should produce greater growth. However, complex systems often display behavior that cannot be understood by extrapolating from its units or their relations, and many of the results of actions are unintended. Thus, an important characteristic of complex systems is that nonlinear variables may have a disproportionate impact at one end of its range (Byrne 1998). Nonlinearity thus refers to behaviors in which the relationships between variables in a system are dynamic and disproportionate (Kiel 1995).

This leads us to the first characteristic of nonlinearity in complex systems, that the outputs they generate are not proportionate to their input; that is, they are asymmetrical. In complex social systems, we often talk of indirect or unintended consequences. For instance, in preparation for a mediation one of the parties may organize a training course with the aim of improving their negotiation skills, but then it turns out that the most important benefit that the participants gained from the training was not necessarily the new skills, but the team-building, social networking, or opportunity to develop a common understanding of their interests and expected gains from the mediation process.

The second aspect of nonlinearity is that nonlinear systems do not follow a predetermined, and thus predictable, cause-and-effect path. Nor can such a path, once traced in hindsight, be replicated to generate the same effect. This irreproducibility is one of the core characteristics of complex systems, implying that what has worked in one peace process cannot be replicated in another with any predetermined or predictable likelihood of success.

A third aspect of nonlinearity is that it cannot be reduced to something simpler, like a set of laws or rules that can help us to predict and thus control the behavior of the system. Cilliers (1998, 4) explains that "a large system of linear elements can usually be collapsed into an equivalent system that is much smaller." Nonlinear data sequences and nonlinear system processes cannot be reduced to formulae or rules that can compress the amount of information necessary to manage them, or to make them otherwise predictable and controllable. This is why we are not going to find an algorithm for peace, the one formula that will help us predetermine the outcome of a mediation or that can predict what a perfect peace agreement should contain in a given context.

As these three characteristics have demonstrated, our commonsense understanding of nonlinearity is often closely associated with the concepts of disorder, chaos, and randomness because we typically explain nonlinearity as the opposite of the linear, the logical, and the orderly. It is thus important to emphasize that, in the context of complexity, nonlinearity is not associated with disorder. In fact, nonlinearity is an essential ingredient in the processes of emergence and self-organization that generate order in complex systems.

Nonlinearity has been presented as the element that distinguishes a complex system from a linear, deterministic, or mechanical system. The latter is fully knowable, predictable and, therefore, controllable in principle. It, therefore, is also unable to do anything that is not preprogrammed or designed. In contrast, nonlinearity in complex systems makes it possible for these systems to adapt and evolve, in other words to create something new that goes beyond what is preprogrammed within the parts that make up the system. Without nonlinearity, parties will not be able to change their positions, make compromises, or create new solutions. Nonlinearity is thus an essential part, in fact a precondition, for emergence, self-regulation, and adaption in complex systems (Cilliers 1998).

One of the ways in which complex systems use constraints to maintain themselves within certain parameters is through the use of feedback mechanisms. When certain thresholds are crossed, positive or negative feedback is used to correct the system back to within its parameters. While complex systems may thus theoretically be capable of a huge variety or range of actions, their behavior is typically constrained within a fairly limited range of options. Individuals may be theoretically free to choose any action, but in reality our behavior is constrained to within a fairly limited range of options by influences such as what would be regarded as legal, moral, and appropriate by an individual's society, family, and friends. This is why our lives are relatively stable and broadly predictable, and why we have such an interest in peace and stability. However, while this may be true for most people most of the time, it is not true for all individuals all the time—some choose to act in their own interest despite social constraints—hence the inherent uncertainty of complex social systems. The difference between a system that is able to sustain peace and one that is vulnerable to lapses of violent conflict lies in the degree to which the society has a resilient network of social institutions that can prevent, manage, and resolve disputes and tensions peacefully, and can generate and maintain social norms against using violence to pursue political, social, and other interests. When an individual acts outside of these social norms or parameters, negative feedback is applied through a range of social sanctions that, in most cases, serve to direct the individual back to within the social norm. Similarly, a society will also use positive feedback to encourage and reward the kind of behavior it desires. In the mediation context, we also see positive and negative feedback being used by stakeholders to exert influence on the parties to the conflict. Feedback is also used by the parties themselves during the mediation, for example positive feedback to signal to each other where agreement may be reached and negative feedback to indicate where their respective redlines lie.

At this point, the first two complex-systems characteristics have been introduced, namely systems dynamics and nonlinearity. Let us turn now to the third characteristic: self-organization.

Self-Organization

Self-organization refers to the ability of a complex system to organize, regulate, and maintain itself without the need for an external or internal managing or controlling agent. A typical system that is designed to maintain a certain state, for example the temperature in a refrigerator, has a controlling mechanism, for example a thermostat in the case of a refrigerator, that increases or decreases the intensity of the cooling mechanism. Many people think that a government performs the same function in a society, but actually any social system is a self-organizing system in that it continuously and spontaneously adapts in response to the cumulative effect of all the decisions made by the individuals and social institutions that make up the system.

Individuals consider and act on the information available to them, and it is the cumulative and collective effect of their actions that determines the overall behavior of the system. Each individual and institution acts on their own, but these individual actions aggregate into swarm behavior—where the actions of some trigger behavior by others that result in large, swarm-like fluctuations in the system. This happens when a large number of individual agents respond similarly in what appears to be coordinated behavior. For instance, a few individuals or families may start fleeing when a rumor spreads that an attacking force may be approaching and then others join them and soon there is a large outflux that may appear coordinated or organized, but in fact it the cumulative effect of hundreds or thousands of individual and family decisions.

This is why governments can't control society; they can only influence our social system. They are part of the system, subject to the same influences and constraints posed by internal dynamics and resources and the external environment. They are, nonetheless, an influential part of the system. Governments do have a powerful set of instruments at their disposal, but not enough to control society. They may use taxes or tax rebates, certain types of spending and investments, interest rates, and regulation to influence and stimulate the economy, but this is not the same as controlling it. Very often these incentives or sanctions don't work, or don't have the intended effects. Similarly, the government may use social policies to nudge the society toward, for example, a more healthy lifestyle. Ultimately, a government can use force, for example, to quell a riot or to put down a rebellion, but if they use too much force, or if the use of force and other measures are perceived to be unfair and unjust, people tend to overthrow the government.

Democracy is a form of political self-organization. In democracies, we elect representatives that are given special roles—higher levels of influence in our social systems. However, their actions also only constitute another level of input into the self-organizing system. They are given the responsibility to make decision about the feedback that governments can employ to try to regulate the behavior of our social system, but they do not have control over how the system will respond to their inputs. If we look back at the last 50 or 100 years, we can see examples of governments that have been fairly successful at steering their societies into peaceful and prosperous times, but also examples of decisions that led to war and socioeconomic decline. We can also see examples of when governments tried to exercise absolute control, and in most cases this had disastrous consequences. From these experiments with different forms of government, one can conclude that societies that understand their governments are not, and should not be, in control of the political, social, and economic spheres of their society have been the most successful. They seem to grasp that if the optimal role of government is to help society develop and maintain a resilient network of social institutions, within and outside government, it needs to self-organize.

Some regimes have been able to exert more control on their society than others, but none can absolutely or totally control their society. The most successful regimes—democratic or authoritarian—have achieved high levels of public or social trust where most people believe that supporting the state is in their best interest (Kleinfeld 2018). These regimes are not resilient only because of their ability to control some parts of the system via negative feedback, but because large parts of the system are choosing to support the state due to positive feedback dynamics, such as the value they see in stability, safety, economic growth, and so on. These regimes, of course, encourage those dynamics and will try to manipulate the overall behavior of the system, but social systems are self-organizing, and no regime will ever be able to totally control the society they are part of.

The organization of the social system as a whole thus comes about as a result of the interaction between the various agents that constitute the system and its environment (Cilliers 1998). There is no single agent or group of agents controlling the system, but there are many agents trying to influence the behavior of the system, and there are many more who simply respond to what they perceive to be the current state or future direction of the system based on the information available to them locally. As a result, the society spontaneously self-organizes through an emergent process that comes about as a result of the cumulative and collective interaction of all the agents in the system.

As discussed in the previous section, this process is nonlinear and dynamic and thus cannot be predicted or controlled. So many causal reactions happen simultaneously, and influence each other in nonlinear and thus asymmetrical relationships, that no one agent or group of agents working together—not even the most powerful regime—can gain sufficient understanding of these social dynamics to control the social system.

Another important property of complexity in general, and self-organization in particular, that has been referred to several times before is known as emergence. Emergence is important because it explains how the elements in the system do not merely interact with each other in order to maintain themselves. In complex systems, the interactions of the elements generate new collective effects that would not have occurred if the different agents acted on their own. Nonlinearity plays a critical role in creating and sustaining order in complex systems, that is, in enabling order to emerge (Cilliers 1998). This change over time—the way in which a system adapts on the basis of its own internal processes as well as its interaction with its environment and the way in which it generates new structures, forms, and functions—is what is meant by emergence. All systems experience entropy, the loss of energy in a system that, if unchecked, will result in the gradual collapse of the system. Mechanical systems need to be maintained, but eventually their parts age to a point where they stop functioning. Most biological systems are able to heal and renew themselves to some extent, but they also have an age limit. Social systems seem to be some of the most enduring systems because of their capacity to continuously adapt to, and co-evolve with, their environment as a result of the process of emergence. The French Revolution is a dramatic example of how a society reordered itself in response to its own increasing dysfunction, and how out of seeming chaos and disorder, a totally new way of social organizing—the republic—emerged. A key characteristic of complex systems is thus that they emerge and maintain themselves spontaneously (Cilliers 1998).

Three of the core characteristics of complexity, namely a whole-of-systems approach, nonlinearity, and self-organization, have now been introduced, and key concepts such as feedback and emergence have also been discussed. The next sections focus on the implications of nonlinearity, self-organization, and emergence for mediation.

Implications of Complexity for Mediation and Conflict Resolution

The standard or mainstream mediation and conflict resolution method that emerged after the Cold War can be described as determined-designed thinking. It is based on the assumption that experts have the agency to analyze a conflict, identify its root causes, and design solutions for the conflict based on international norms (liberal peace ideology) and best practices (lessons based on past successes and failures). Mediation and conflict resolution in this context is understood as a process through which the parties, based on the information, analysis, best practices, and options presented by experts, are led through a directed-mediation process that ends with the parties agreeing on a version of the solutions presented to them, modestly adapted to reflect local realities and the most important interests of the parties (Bercovitch et al. 1991).

In practice, most of the limited solutions offered fall within a standard range of options, and, as a result, most peace agreements reached over this period share, at their core, a similar logic: a transitional power-sharing period during which state institutions are developed or restored according to liberal peace norms, including in some cases a constitutional review process, followed by democratic elections. The underlying theory of change is that democracy leads to good governance. Good governance leads to stability. And stability leads to peace and prosperity for all.

Unfortunately, electoral politics can—without sufficiently developed formal and informal institutions to manage the resulting tensions, power rivalries, and greed—generate new waves of violent conflict. It also often creates political systems in which one set of elites, often linked to whichever ethnic group happened to form the majority of the population, capture and corrupt the state to serve their own interests. These determined-design and directed-mediation and conflict resolution processes, measured against the extent to which they led to a self-sustainable peace process, seem to have been successful in fewer than 50 percent of the cases, when measured over a ten-year period following the adoption of the peace agreement (Collier et al. 2003).

In contrast, Adaptive Mediation recognizes that our ability to understand complex systems is inherently limited and time-bound. Complexity implies that the nonlinear and highly dynamic nature of complex systems places inherent limitations on our ability to know, predict, and control complex systems, including social systems. It also limits our ability to generate knowledge that is transferable from one context to another (Ramalingam 2013). Complexity thus reminds us to be skeptical, in principle, of results and findings that claim to be universally applicable or transferable, regardless of the method used to obtain them, because all methods are limited when considering highly dynamic and nonlinear phenomena. Complex social systems are dynamic, nonlinear, and emergent. This means that both the causes and consequences of conflict are continuously evolving. An adaptive approach recognizes this dynamism and copes with this uncertainty by employing an iterative inductive process, or theory of change, that continuously generates new analyses, as well as regular reflection points where teams or organizations reflect and make judgments regarding the changes they have identified and their implications (Brusset et al. 2016).

Conflict Analysis

Recognizing that the mediator's ability to understand and predict complex social systems is inherently limited has a number of implications for how we should approach and conduct conflict analysis. Firstly, a complex systems approach reminds the mediator to be mindful not just of the specific aspect we may be focused on, but to consider it in the context of the wider system of which it is a part, including the context and environment within which that system operates. In other words, how we think of reconciliation in a specific peace process should not in the first instance be determined by how we usually do reconciliation, or how we have done it somewhere else with relative success, but by what the context and needs of the specific situation at hand are. These contextual and specific needs can't be identified and analyzed by independent experts, but instead must emerge from the parties themselves as part of the relational(Kressel 2014) and dialogic (Lehti 2019) process during the mediation itself.

Secondly, it reminds the mediator of the importance of the dynamic and nonlinear interconnections among the agents in the system, and the way in which these interactions generate context specific meaning in the system (Bercovitch 1991, 4). It reminds us that any given manifestation of a problem is unique to that context. What may work in one context may not necessarily work in the next. Thirdly, it tells the mediator that there is no one single "state of affairs" or set of "root causes" that can be identified and solved. We cannot intervene in one system in isolation, and even if we were able to do so, that system will not be static. We will always have to deal with multiple systems constantly interacting with each other and the larger international and regional environments of which they (and us) are part. The conflict is not something static that happened in the past, nor are its causes static, as if buried in the past waiting to be uncovered. They are dynamic and emergent and further developing and changing as we speak. The parties have different, often competing, interpretations of the causes and drivers of the conflict, and these understandings are continuously evolving; how they are understood and viewed today has as much, if not more, bearing on future conflict (relapse) than on how they were perceived and understood when violent conflict erupted. To understand the (conflict) system, we need to see it in motion and in relation to the larger environment or system (which is also dynamically evolving) in which it is embedded, not in freeze-frame or in isolation. Fourthly, complex systems do not follow any predetermined causal design where certain root causes determine certain outcomes that can be discovered through a reductionist analytic method.

On the basis of these insights from complexity, Adaptive Mediation suggests that conflict analysis has to be an ongoing process of exploration and self-critical analysis. It should not be a one-off process that takes place prior to the start of the mediation. Conflict analysis also needs to be informed by an awareness of our inability to fully understand the complex systems we are dealing with, and of the fluidity and change in the system. This means that our analysis should be limited in scope and spanning a relatively short period of time. Our information gathering will need to take a multipronged and highly adaptive approach, so that it can be open and sensitive to feedback and changes in the system and environment. We need to be self-critical and open to new information that requires us to adapt earlier analysis. If a period of time passes without such an adjustment to our analysis, an understanding of a complex systems approach will caution us that we have likely missed some new developments, given the one thing we can predict is that the system will be constantly changing.

There is a lot of pressure, especially in large institutions like the UN system, for different parts of the system to cohere around a single "joint" conflict analysis. Involving different parts of the system that bring various perspectives to the table should be encouraged because it should lead to a more robust and rich analysis. However, the subsequent pressure for these parts of the system to then agree on one joint analysis is problematic, because it may lead to a simplified or generalized analysis. A shared conflict analysis that retains different perspectives and insights may result in a more textured and rich analysis. From a complexity perspective it is a good thing if different agencies have different understandings of a situation, because that results in the overall understanding being informed by many different perspectives. Others may not agree, but at least they have to take those perspectives into account, and that contributes to all participants in the process being more open to a complex and multifaceted understanding of the situation at hand.

Complexity informs us that in complex systems, including social systems, change processes emerge from the local system and are evolutionary in nature; in other words, the local system adapts to its environment and its own emergent behavior through a continuous process of inductive adaptation, regulated by its own self-organizing processes. Local in this context thus refers to processes that emerge from the local experience, while the external experience refers to the larger system or environment within which the local system is embedded and with which the elements in the local system interact. The local social system adapts and evolves in response to the stimulation of both the external environment and its own internal feedback in an ongoing iterative process. In order to apply a complex adaptive system's approach to mediation, we thus need to think in terms of local systems and the external influences in their environment, while being aware that the boundaries we utilize in the process have emerged as a result of the framing choices we have made in our analysis. This does not mean that our choices are completely arbitrary, as our analysis is based on features and factors that can be verified empirically, but we need to be aware of the degree to which our own framing choices influence our analysis (Cilliers 1998).

A complex-systems approach suggests that mediators need to understand peace processes as essentially local. The local system needs to develop its own resilient social institutions that can manage internal tensions and disputes peacefully, and in so doing sustain its own peace. The role of external actors may be helpful, for instance, to restore stability after an outbreak of violent conflict and to act as a catalyst by stimulating and facilitating the processes necessary for social regeneration. However, mediators need to recognize that external intervention is not sufficient to achieve self-sustainable peace. The essential ingredient for self-sustainable peace is local emergent self-organized complexity. It is possible for a society to become peaceful on its own, but it is not possible to make or build peace on behalf of a society from the outside. International mediators thus have to come to terms with what it really means when they say that something is context-specific.

This is why Adaptive Mediation encourages the maximum possible participation of the local parties themselves, whether independently or together, in the analysis of the conflict, so as to encourage self-organization and resilience. The more the parties (or insider neutrals associated with them if it is too sensitive for the parties themselves) participate in conflict analysis, the more likely it is that the analysis will reflect indigenous narratives and perspectives relevant to the context, rather than the assumptions, interests, and biases of the mediation team and other external experts.

An adaptive conflict analysis methodology enables mediation support teams and the parties to continuously adapt their strategies and approaches to the changing context. Context refers here to both the larger social dynamics that shape the mediation process and the internal dynamics within the mediation process itself.

Participatory conflict analysis across conflict divides can be a source of tension (or even impossible in the early stages of a mediation process), but, when skillfully facilitated, can be a source of common understanding and emerging ownership of mediated outcomes (Gray and Burns 2021). One way to think of mediation is to see it as a process through which a new shared knowledge system is developed (Lehti 2019, 2020). The parties enter the process each with its own knowledge of the problem. Each has its own interpretation of the history and often emphasizes different aspects of key events. So even where there is an acknowledged shared history, the parties' knowledge of the causes, triggers, major events, and possible futures differ in significant ways. Part of the mediation process is thus to educate each other and share knowledge, allowing a new shared knowledge system to emerge. This is also why national dialogues and other such processes that allow public participation are so important, because for such a new shared knowledge system to emerge, it needs broad participation and ownership (Paffenholz 2021).

Planning

The insights we have gained from the application of complexity to mediation thus far suggest that it is not possible to definitively identify a problem and design a solution for it at the outset, that is, during the premediation or initial planning phase, using an analytical problem solving methodology. Instead, we have to use an alternative adaptive planning methodology. Harry Jones (2008, 3) argues that "recognizing uncertainty heightens the importance of building flexibility into projects, and adapting to the available signals about performance and progress as you go along."

Ricardo Wilson-Grau (2008, 2) argues that in situations with high levels of uncertainty, intentional design tends to limit the capacity to respond and innovate, above all when the social change process is bound to achieving those predefined results in order to demonstrate success to its stakeholders, notably partners and donors. He argues that the alternative to full-fledged intentional design, as well as to the more conventional modes of strategic planning, is for the social change processes to keep the planning process light and imaginative (Wilson-Grau 2008, 2). On the basis of these insights from complexity, we argue that design and planning cannot be limited to the start of a mediation process, but need to be part of an ongoing process of adaptation, throughout the lifetime of the mediation process. The planning process should involve the broadest possible representative group of experts, including relevant and appropriate local actors and representatives or proxies of the parties to the conflict, so that it can be informed by the widest possible cross-section of information. The design process should generate multiple options, and the planning process should experiment with those most likely to have the desired effect. This is essentially an evolutionary process of iterative cycles of variation and selection.

Applying an adaptive approach to mediation in the face of uncertainty does not imply that we cannot plan, but it does suggest that we have to depart from linear causal planning approaches. Murray and Marmorek argue that an adaptive approach allows "activities to proceed despite uncertainty regarding how best to achieve desired outcomes (…) in fact, it specifically targets such uncertainty (…) and provides a science-based learning process characterized by using outcomes for evaluation and adjustment" (Murray and Marmorek 2003, 2).

Adaptive Mediation approaches planning as an iterative exploration and adaption process that continuously co-evolves with the system it is attempting to influence. Adaptive Mediation employs variation and selection to generate a variety of hypotheses or options for achieving objectives, and institutes a selection process that identifies options to explore further and those to discontinue. In contrast to traditional approaches, the adaptive approach does not privilege one potential solution or end-state, but purposefully pursues a variety of options simultaneously. For instance, Adaptive Mediation may simultaneously employ multiple-track approaches to engage with potential parties, or probe different topics for negotiation concurrently.

When multiple options are explored, special attention must be paid to the feedback generated by these different initiatives. Feedback enables purposeful selection-based adaptation of the mediation process, whereby underperforming options are modified or abandoned while promising options are expanded.

Management and Coordination

As complex systems are dynamic, our methodology for generating knowledge about the particular system we are engaging with and its environment must keep up with the rate of change in the system and its environment. A management approach that is sensitive to the need to continuously adapt our decisions based on new information is thus more likely to cope with complex systems. The reality on the ground is that approaches that worked in one specific context can rarely be guaranteed to yield results in another (Coleman 2003; Brusset et al. 2016).

Management in this context refers to directing the experimentation, assessment, and adaptation processes of the Adaptive Mediation approach. By contrast, a management style that is based on the belief that the manager or the organization has the knowledge and agency necessary to identify "the problem" and to develop the "right" solution for the problem is likely to be less effective when dealing with highly dynamic and nonlinear complex systems. According to Cilliers (1998, 112), following such a management strategy constitutes "an avoidance of complexity." Rihani (2002, 9) agrees, arguing that "command-and-control methods are useless. Complex adaptive systems respond better to light-touch styles of management based on constant monitoring of overall patterns of performance coupled with judicious small-scale incremental adjustments."

Real-time decisions will always necessitate compromise between the urgency of the action, the information currently available, and the time and opportunities available for pursuing coherence. In this highly dynamic and nonlinear environment, most decisions are made without crucial information and in the presence of major uncertainties about the potential cost, benefits, and risks involved in certain courses of action, both of which prevent informed decisions (Cloete 2004). Being aware of the limits of our knowledge in this context is very useful, reminding us not to overestimate our ability to analyze a conflict, identify root causes, and prescribe medium- to long-term solutions.

Our study of complex systems has found that distributed, decentralized control makes a system more flexible, and therefore increases its ability to cope with highly dynamic and nonlinear changes in its environment and within the system itself. Applied to the management of mediation processes, this notion argues against an overemphasis on centralized, top-down control of the process by the mediator. The critique against centralized management or rigid leadership is based on the knowledge that centralized control mechanisms will, in complex systems, lead to the degeneration of the system (Cilliers 1998). "Command-and-control methods and detailed forecasts and plans, effective for linear systems, are inappropriate as it is not possible to select sensible actions…where results cannot be traced back to specific causes" (Rihani 2002, 9).

When facilitating a peace process, a mediator typically does not have control over the inputs or resources, and can only indirectly influence the outputs that are meant to generate momentum toward the desired outcomes and impacts, as these depend on the agreements reached by the parties to the conflict. A mediator typically has the authority and credibility to convene, and can use that opportunity to facilitate and coordinate a process. The overall effect of this process can result in a much more comprehensive and all-encompassing effort than what any one of the parties could otherwise have achieved on their own if they chose to negotiate with each other without the help of a mediator. The role of the mediator is to facilitate the process that generates the strategic direction and operational coherence of the mediation process, not to control it (de Coning 2010).

Management and coordination in a complex mediation process thus require skills and approaches that are perhaps counterintuitive to most mainstream expectations of managers, namely that they should be visionary and decisive. Instead, what the Adaptive Mediation approach needs are process facilitators who are able to persuade independent agents to cooperate around shared goals and objectives and manage an adaptive process in a highly dynamic and uncertain environment, without interfering in or controlling the process so much that they end up disrupting the emergence of self-organization among the parties.

Facilitating a Self-Organizing Mediation Process

Adaptive Mediation suggests that when the aim is a self-sustainable peace agreement, mediators should, as a rule of thumb, apply a light touch. Mediators should protect parties from external interests and agendas, foster inductive processes that maximize the capability of parties to self-organize, and help to generate agreements that are rooted in the local context and narrative.

The quality of a peace agreement should be assessed on its sustainability, that is, the degree to which the parties are committed to implementing the agreement on their own after the mediation has ended. Many peace agreements fail to be implemented because the parties don't sufficiently own the mediation process or subsequent agreements. Important indicators of the sustainability of an agreement include the resilience of the agreed upon mechanisms for implementation, such as the extent to which the agreement puts in place processes that can manage future disputes or emergent issues.

Peace agreements that are not strongly owned by the parties lack resilience and sustainability. Implementation breakdowns are common, for example, when international mediation processes coerce parties to go along with processes, agreements, or externally conceived end states (for example, an accelerated election timetable) that do not necessarily reflect their interests or are not viable for implementation in the local context. One example is the August 2015 Agreement on the Resolution of Conflict in the Republic of South Sudan (ARCSS), which has been criticized for being imposed on the conflict parties by South Sudan's neighbors. This contributed to a lack of political willingness to implement the agreement, or in some cases selective implementation of parts of the agreement by some of the parties (Buchhold et al. 2017, 10).

With Adaptive Mediation, the aim of the mediator is to provide the benefits of external intervention without undermining self-organization.

Every time a mediator intervenes to solve a perceived problem among the parties, they interrupt internal feedback, and deny the parties the potential to respond to a challenge together, thereby deepening their interdependence. The result is a lost opportunity to develop self-organization and resilience.

Too little facilitation, however, may result in a lack of purpose, deadlocks, or breakdown. External influence has many advantages, including bringing leverage, opening political space, and encouraging accountability and more inclusive processes. The key to successful Adaptive Mediation lies in finding the appropriate balance between external facilitation and self-organized mediation.

Adaptive Mediation also recognizes the inherently political nature of mediation. Choices regarding who gets to participate and what criteria will be used to determine the topics included on the agenda, or the order in which they will be discussed all have political dimensions and political effects. A decision to pursue a particular initiative may face pushback from those who view it as harmful to their interests, or who were excluded from the process. All these choices are influenced by political judgments about who may lose or gain, and, as a result, it is rare that the "technical" aspects of a mediation will override what is seen as politically feasible in a given context. Even with the best expert advice, no mediator can replace the role of the political marketplace to effectively discount all political interests and considerations. Thus, as the South African example cited earlier demonstrated, the less the mediator directs the outcome, the more the parties themselves will self-organize, and in the process develop the ability to absorb and adapt to stress together, making the process more resilient to internal political trade-offs and external shocks.

Evaluation

Our linear determined-design assumptions influence how we assess success and failure, and are poorly suited to complex, dynamic peace-making environments. Ian Wadley observes that "Traditional monitoring and evaluation methods are not well suited to this task, typically imposing artificially linear project models on a dynamic conflict situation, as well as compliance reporting that moves attention away from real value" (Wadley 2017, 6).

In a linear complicated system, it is possible to explain an outcome in terms of a sequence of cascading causes, for example A caused B and B caused C. Complex systems are nonlinear. "Small changes can cause, through feedback and effects multiplying rather than just adding, very large changes elsewhere in the system. When effects are multiplicative rather than additive, it is not convincing to attribute one change to a single other change. The richness of interconnections means that any one change has several prior causes and itself may contribute to further changes in these causes" (Chapman 2002, 43).

As pointed out earlier, Morin (2005) stressed that emergence is "indeductible" from the qualities of the parts, and thus irreducible. This is why we are unable to attribute causation when studying interventions and effects, and why considering contribution—how certain activities contributed to a certain effect—is a more humble and realistic alternative in complex systems. Morin also considers the role of feedback in what he describes as a circular system wherein the effect itself intervenes in the cause, or in other words, "feedback is a process which complexifies causality" (Morin 2005, 15). In complex systems, the behavior of the system is influenced by its own internal processes and external causes, and its internal system has evolved as a result of its particular history.

Traditional results-based ideas of accountability and responsibility are associated with a simple linear theory of causation (Chapman 2002). In order to monitor whether progress is being made, it is essential to provide measures of performance and targets. In complex systems, the pursuit of any single target is likely to distort the operation of the system and thereby reduce its overall effectiveness. The feedback generated by the process of monitoring and reporting on the indicators will in turn influence the system, and have its own knock-on effects on the system. One of the significant dangers of specifying targets and simple measures of performance is that the result will be suboptimization. Emphasizing a single measure of performance leads to a decrease in overall performance. A specific target can encapsulate only one element of a complex system, and its dominance is likely to undermine other aspects of the system that are crucial to its general and long-term effects.

Feedback is critical for adaptation, and monitoring for feedback and effects should thus be a very important part of driving adaptation during mediation and conflict resolution processes. Current mediation practice neglects monitoring and evaluation, and where it does take place, its function is often limited to accountability, that is, reporting back to donors. There have been very few attempts to evaluate mediation with the aim of informing the adaptation of the mediation process itself.

An adaptive monitoring and evaluation model proposed by researchers at the Centre for Humanitarian Dialogue seeks to better assess real value in uncertain mediation contexts by ensuring that assessments measure the quality of the process, not just observable results. This is achieved by assuring the quality of professional judgments through peer review, assessing a project's strategic logic and implementation, and measuring observable results wherever possible (Wadley 2017).

An additional imperative for monitoring and evaluation in Adaptive Mediation is to shift the focus from accountability toward more real-time learning and adaptation. Mediation teams have to reflect regularly—weekly, monthly, or quarterly—on the continued validity of their hypotheses and on which aspects of their strategy, approach, or plans to disregard or pursue based on feedback from the context. As far as is possible, this process should be conducted together with representatives of the parties (or insider neutrals associated with them), to further stimulate self-organization and resilience. To encourage timely adaptation, feedback available to the mediation team must be systematic (that is, drawn from a diverse spread of actors and issues that could affect the mediation), timely (that is, preferably before rather than after context changes have affected the mediation), and accurate (that is, ideally verifiable, or not adversely affected by stakeholder bias) (de Coning and Gray 2018).

In Adaptive Mediation, conflict analysis, planning, and the assessment of results should not be understood as sequential steps in a linear project cycle with a defined beginning and end. Instead, they should be approached as interdependent dimensions of an iterative adaptive process that are undertaken simultaneously.

An Adaptive Mediation process can, for example, include iterative cycles of meetings within or between parties (or their proxies or constituencies) that simultaneously (a) reflect on the conflict context, dynamics, and drivers, and the implications for planning and implementation; (b) reflect on current activities under implementation, considering the viability of existing or alternative options; and (c) derive lessons and generate data to serve both internal decision making (planning) and external accountability functions.

Implications for the Ethics of Mediation and Conflict Resolution

The insights from complexity presented in this chapter have important ethical implications for mediation and conflict resolution. While complexity holds that we cannot predict the future and don't have the agency to control future behavior, this does not mean that we are without agency altogether. Woermann argues that a complexity approach implies a shift from trying to discover "the Truth" about given situations, to a process of making choices and developing strategies for living and acting, and for dealing with the often unexpected outcomes of these strategies (Woermann 2010, 121). An uncertain future can be anticipated, influenced, adapted to, and engaged with, but such engagement needs to be informed by an awareness of the limits of anyone's ability to ultimately fully know complex systems. That awareness has important implications for the ethical status of interventions into such systems. No party can claim moral superiority on the basis of predetermined models or lessons learned elsewhere, or on their good intent, nor can anyone hide behind unintended consequences, because we know that complex systems are nonlinear and dynamic and that any intervention in complex systems will generate side effects, some of which are likely to be harmful.

From an ethical perspective, this implies that it is necessary to acknowledge that, as mediators, we are acting on the basis of our own provisional knowledge and interest, not on superior knowledge that enables us to know how to achieve peace in complex social systems. Mediators thus have an ethical duty to proceed with caution and to monitor carefully the effects (intended and unintended) of their actions on the mediation process, with an understanding that these actions will eventually have an impact on the everyday lives and livelihoods of real people (Autesserre 2014). An explicit, reflexive awareness of the incompleteness of our knowledge and the limits of our agency are therefore vital to ensure decisions are made with a large degree of caution (and humility) while at the same time demanding that we think through the possible ramifications, especially possible harm (Hughes 2012, 116).

The ethical responsibility thus shifts from the perceived predetermined virtue of a proven model, theory of choice, or assumed good intent of the mediator, to those who have the agency to choose which model or theory of change will be applied in a given context. The outcomes and consequences that result are thus not attributable to the assumptions of the model or a misapplication of an otherwise good theory, but to the choices that have been made with the full awareness of the limitations of our pre-knowledge and the understanding that our attempts to influence mediation processes and social systems will have unintended consequences.

An awareness of complexity informs us that it is not possible to interfere in a complex system and have only one effect. Whenever we attempt to change something in a complex system, the system responds to our intervention in a number of ways. We can anticipate some of these responses, and some may have been responses we intended to elicit. The system, however, is also likely to respond in other ways that we do not anticipate. This does not mean that we are powerless in the face of unpredictable and unstable system effects. On the contrary, an improved understanding of the dynamics of complex systems should improve our ability to anticipate that there will be unpredictable and unintended consequences, and this should enable us to be more sensitive to such consequences when they occur and take steps to mitigate their effects or adjust our actions.

Aoi et al. (2007) argue that those responsible for the planning, management, and evaluation of interventions thus need to recognize that unintended consequences are a normal outcome of the dynamic nature of complex systems. They therefore recommend that the UN and other institutions undertaking such interventions develop institutional mechanisms for addressing unintended consequences, and institutionalize planning and assessment mechanisms that will enable them to anticipate and respond to emerging unintended consequences.

Complexity thus implies that mediators have to take ethical responsibility for their choices and actions. Taking responsibility means that mediators need to think through the ethical implications of both their macro theories and their specific choices and actions in any given context. They cannot base their decisions on the claimed superiority of a model or theory of change. They have to be conscious of the knowledge claims and assumptions that inform the choices they make, and the potential consequences of their actions for each specific context, and take responsibility for their decisions.

Conclusion

A fundamental implication of complexity for how we understand and approach mediation and conflict resolution is the realization that the ability of external agents to gain knowledge of the complex social systems we are dealing with in the mediation context is inherently limited. In other words, we need to recognize that international actors do not have the agency to analyze a conflict, design a solution, and apply that solution with a reasonable likelihood that such a solution can result in sustainable peace. First, in complex systems, there is no one definitive problem that can be solved. Second, for a peace process to be sustainable, any complex social system will need to develop its own institutions to manage its own conflicts peacefully; for that to happen, the process needs enough space and time to allow its own self-organizing processes to emerge. International or external mediators can assist and facilitate this process, but if they interfere too much, they will undermine and delay the self-organizing process. The key to successful mediation thus lies in finding the appropriate balance between external facilitation and local self-organization, which will differ from context to context.

Adaptive Mediation differs from the mainstream determined-design and directed-mediation model in that it is an approach specifically designed to cope with the uncertainty, unpredictability, and irreproducibility inherent in complex social change processes. Adaptive Mediation aims to empower the parties participating in the mediation to generate solutions themselves. For a peace agreement to be self-sustainable, it has to emerge from a collaborative process owned by the parties to the conflict that includes inductive iterative adaptive engagement with the context. The role of the mediator is limited to facilitating the process. Adaptive Mediation is especially concerned with enhancing the self-sustainability of peace agreements and, in this context, understanding the role of the mediator as facilitating a process of emergent self-organization.

When this approach is applied to conflict analyses, planning, monitoring, and evaluation, the ability of mediation processes to navigate uncertainty and adapt to changing dynamics will be enhanced. In order for more resilient and self-sustainable agreements to emerge, Adaptive Mediation requires mediators to apply a light touch that encourages greater interdependence among the parties and discourages dependence upon the mediator. As a result, utilizing an Adaptive Mediation approach should result in peace agreements that are more locally grounded, self-sustainable, and resilient to withstand setbacks and shocks.

The core principles of the Adaptive Mediation approach are thus:

1. A recognition that social systems are complex and thus highly dynamic and nonlinear. This means that their behavior is inherently uncertain and unpredictable.
2. In order to make sense of such complex conflict systems and to influence them—while recognizing that our agency to understand and influence such complex systems are limited—one needs to employ an inductive adaptive theory of change that is based on discovery and learning through iterative cycles of experimentation and feedback.
3. As the ultimate aim is to achieve self-sustainable peace, and the aim of peace mediation is to generate self-sustainable peace agreements, the mediation process needs to enable the maximum participation of the parties themselves in the emergence of an agreement. This means the mediators need to limit their role to process facilitation and allow the content of the agreements to emerge from the self-organizing processes of the negotiations among the parties themselves.

The chapter also touched on the ethical implications of applying a complexity lens to mediation and conflict resolution. When we attempt to influence complex systems, they will respond in several ways. Some of these we may anticipate, but a complex system, because it is nonlinear and dynamic, will also respond in ways that we cannot predict. Our interventions thus generate unintended consequences, including some that are likely to be negative or harmful to people. We know that this will be the case, so, although the specific effects are unintended, the general effect is not unknown. The United Nations and all other institutions that undertake mediation thus need to develop institutional mechanisms for addressing the inevitable unintended consequences of their mediation efforts on the peace process, and should institutionalize planning and assessment mechanisms that will enable them to anticipate and respond to such emerging unintended consequences, with the aim of preventing and mitigating any harm that may be caused by the mediation process.

References

Aoi, Chiyuki, Cedric de Coning, and Ramesh Chandra Thakur, eds. 2007. *Unintended Consequences of Peacekeeping Operations*. Tokyo: United Nations University Press.

Autesserre, Séverine. 2014. *Peaceland: Conflict Resolution and the Everyday Politics of International Intervention*. Cambridge: Cambridge University Press.

Bercovitch, Jacob. 1991. International Mediation. *Journal of Peace Research* 28 (1): 3–6. https://doi.org/10.1177/0022343391028001002.

Bercovitch, Jacob, and Allison Houston. 1993. Influence of Mediator Characteristics and Behavior on the Success of Mediation in International Relations. *International Journal of Conflict Management* 4 (4): 297–321. https://doi.org/10.1108/eb022730.

Bercovitch, Jacob, J. Theodore Anagnoson, and Donnette L. Wille. 1991. Some Conceptual Issues and Empirical Trends in the Study of Successful Mediation in International Relations. *Journal of Peace Research* 28 (1): 7–17.

Brusset, Emery, Cedric de Coning, and Hughes Bryn, eds. 2016. *Complexity Thinking for Peacebuilding Practice and Evaluation.* London: Palgrave Macmillan.

Buchhold, Christina, Jonathan Harlander, Sabrina Quamber, and Giles Pitts. 2017. *Peacemaking in a New Era of Geopolitics.* Meeting Report Oslo Forum 13–14 June 2017, Oslo, Norway. Geneva: The Centre for Humanitarian Dialogue. https://css.ethz.ch/en/services/digital-library/publications/publication.html/5651a001-78ab-47f9-8858-5e712101629d.

Bush, Robert A. Baruch, and Joseph P. Folger. 1994. *The Promise of Mediation: Responding to Conflict through Empowerment and Recognition.* San Francisco, CA: Jossey-Bass.

Byrne, David. 1998. *Complexity Theory and the Social Sciences: An Introduction.* London: Routledge.

Chapman, Jake. 2002. *System Failure: Why Governments Must Learn to Think Differently.* London: Demos.

Cilliers, Paul. 1998. *Complexity and Postmodernism: Understanding Complex Systems.* London: Routledge.

———. 2001. Boundaries, Hierarchies and Networks in Complex Systems. *International Journal of Innovation Management* 5 (2): 135–147.

———. 2002. Why We Cannot Know Complex Things Completely. *Emergence* 4 (1–2): 77–84.

Cloete, Fanie. 2004. *Chaos and Quantum Complexity Approaches to Public Management: Insights from the New Sciences.* Conference of the Association of South African Schools and Departments of Public Administration and Management, Pretoria, May 13–14.

Coleman, Peter T. 2003. Characteristics of Protracted, Intractable Conflict: Toward the Development of a Metaframework-I. *Peace and Conflict: Journal of Peace Psychology* 9 (1): 1–37. https://doi.org/10.1207/S15327949PAC0901_01.

Coleman, Peter T., Lan Bui-Wrzosinska, Robin R. Vallacher, and Andrzej Nowak. 2006. Protracted Conflicts and Dynamical Systems. In *The Negotiator's Fieldbook*, ed. Andrea Kupfer Schneider and Christopher Honeyman. Washington, DC: American Bar Association.

Coleman, Peter T., Katharina G. Kugler, and Ljubica Chatman. 2017. Adaptive Mediation: An Evidence-Based Contingency Approach to Mediating Conflict. *International Journal of Conflict Management* 28 (3): 383–406.

Collier, Paul, V. L. Elliott, Håvard Hegre, Anke Hoeffler, Marta Reynal-Querol, and Nicholas Sambanis. 2003. *Breaking the Conflict Trap: Civil War and Development Policy*. A World Bank Policy Research Report. Washington, DC: World Bank and Oxford University Press. https://openknowledge.worldbank.org/handle/10986/13938License.

de Coning, Cedric. 2010. Mediation and Peacebuilding: The Role of SRSGs in UN Integrated Missions. *Global Governance: Special Edition on Mediation in Post-Conflict Peace Operations* 16 (2): 266–281.

———. 2018. Adaptive Peacebuilding. *International Affairs* 94 (2): 301–317.

———. 2020a. Insights from Complexity Theory for Peace and Conflict Studies. In *The Palgrave Encyclopedia of Peace and Conflict Studies*, ed. Oliver Richmond and Gëzim Visoka. Cham: Palgrave Macmillan.

———. 2020b. Adaptive Peace Operations: Navigating the Complexity of Influencing Societal Change without Causing Harm. *International Peacekeeping* 27 (5): 836–858.

de Coning, Cedric, and Stephen Gray. 2018. Adaptive Mediation. ACCORD. *Conflict Trends*. https://www.accord.org.za/conflict-trends/adaptive-mediation/.

Dahlberg, Rasmus. 2015. Resilience and Complexity: Conjoining the Discourses of Two Contested Concepts. *Culture Unbound: Journal of Current Cultural Research* 7 (3): 541–557.

Deutsch, Morton, and Peter Coleman, eds. 2012. *Psychological Components of Sustainable Peace*, Peace Psychology Book Series. New York: Springer-Verlag. https://doi.org/10.1007/978-1-4614-3555-6.

Dziatkowiec, Authored Paul, Christina Buchhold, Elodie Convergne, Jonathan Harlander, and Tinahy Andriamasomanana. 2016. Oslo Forum 2016: Adapting to a New Conflict Landscape. https://www.hdcentre.org/wp-content/uploads/2016/11/OF-2016-REPORT-WEB.pdf.

European Space Agency. 2019. Soyuz Launch Vehicle: The Most Reliable Means of Space Travel. Accessed October 10. http://bit.ly/2vYRRGh.

Fisher, Roger, William Ury, and Bruce Patton. 2011. *Getting to Yes: Negotiating Agreement without Giving In*. New York: Penguin Books.

Gray, Stephen, and Danny Burns. 2021. Local Agency, Adaptation, and Vertical Integration of Bottom-Up Peacebuilding: Reflecting on Systemic Action Research in Myanmar. *Peacebuilding* 9 (1): 15–39.

Hendrick, Diane. 2009. *Complexity Theory and Conflict Transformation: An Exploration of Potential and Implications*. Working Paper 17. Centre for Conflict Resolution Department of Peace Studies, University of Bradford.

Hughes, Bryn. 2012. Peace Operations and the Political: A Pacific Reminder of What Really Matters. *Journal of International Peacekeeping* 16 (1–2): 99–118.

Jervis, Robert. 1997. *System Effects: Complexity in Political and Social Life*. Princeton University Press.

Jones, Harry. 2008. Outcome Mapping and Complexity. *Newsletter 2*. Outcome Mapping Learning Community.

Kaufmann, Mareile. 2013. Emergent Self-Organisation in Emergencies: Resilience Rationales in Interconnected Societies. *Resilience* 1 (1): 53–68.

Kiel, L. Douglas. 1995. Chaos Theory and Disaster Response Management: Lessons for Managing Periods of Extreme Instability. In *What Disaster Response Management Can Learn from Chaos Theory: Conference Proceedings May 18–19, 1995*, ed. Gus A. Koehler. Sacramento: California Research Bureau.

Kleinfeld, Rachel. 2018. *A Savage Order: How the World's Deadliest Countries Can Forge a Path to Security*. New York: Pantheon.

Kressel, Kenneth. 2014. The Mediation of Conflict: Context, Recognition, and Practice. In *The Handbook of Conflict Resolution Theory and Practice*, 640–662. San Francisco, CA: Jossey-Bass. https://learning.oreilly.com/library/view/-/9781118810323/?ar.

Kriesberg, Louis. 2007. The Conflict Resolution Field: Origins, Growth, and Differentiation. In *Peacemaking in International Conflict: Methods and Techniques*. Washington, DC: United States Institute of Peace.

Lehti, Marko. 2019. *The Era of Private Peacemakers: A New Dialogic Approach to Mediation*, Rethinking Peace and Conflict Studies. Palgrave Macmillan. https://doi.org/10.1007/978-3-319-91201-1.

———. 2020. Private Peacemaking and Dialogic Approach to Mediation. In *The Palgrave Encyclopedia of Peace and Conflict Studies*, 1–13. Cham: Springer International Publishing. https://doi.org/10.1007/978-3-030-11795-5_53-1.

Mack, Andrew. 2012. Even Failed Peace Agreements Save Lives. *Political Violence at a Glance*. August 10. https://politicalviolenceataglance.org/2012/08/10/even-failed-peace-agreements-save-lives/.

Meadows, Donella. 1999. *Leverage Points: Places to Intervene in a System*. Hartland: The Sustainability Institute.

Mitchell, Melanie. 2009. *Complexity: A Guided Tour*. New York: Oxford University Press.

Morin, Edgar. 2005. Restricted Complexity, General Complexity. Translated from French by Carlos Gershenson presented at the Colloquium "Intelligence de la complexité: épistémologie et pragma-tique," Cerisy-La-Salle, France, June 26.

Murray, Carol, and David R Marmorek. 2003. Adaptive Management: A Science-Based Approach to Managing Ecosystems in the Face of Uncertainty. Prepared for presentation at the Fifth International Conference on Science and Management of Protected Areas: Making Ecosystem Based Management Work, Victoria, British Columbia, May 11–16.

Paffenholz, Thania. 2014. Civil Society and Peace Negotiations: Beyond the Inclusion–Exclusion Dichotomy. *Negotiation Journal* 30 (1): 69–91. https://doi.org/10.1111/nejo.12046.

———. 2021. Perpetual Peacebuilding: A New Paradigm to Move Beyond the Linearity of Liberal Peacebuilding. *Journal of Intervention and Statebuilding* 15 (3): 367–385.

Popolo, Damian. 2011. *A New Science of International Relations: Modernity, Complexity and the Kosovo Conflict*. Farnham: Ashgate.

Pospisil, Jan. 2019. *Peace in Political Unsettlement: Beyond Solving Conflict*, Rethinking Peace and Conflict Studies. London: Palgrave Macmillan.

Ramalingam, Ben. 2013. *Aid on the Edge of Chaos: Rethinking International Cooperation in a Complex World*. Oxford: Oxford University Press.

Rihani, Samir. 2002. *Complex Systems Theory and Development Practice: Understanding Non-Linear Realities*. London: Zed Books.

Sparks, Allister. 1996. *Tomorrow Is Another Country: The inside Story of South Africa's Road to Change*. Chicago: University of Chicago Press.

Umbreit, Mark S. 2010. *The Handbook of Victim Offender Mediation an Essential Guide to Practice and Research*. San Francisco, CA: Jossey-Bass.

Wadley, Ian. 2017. *Valuing Peace: Delivering and Demonstrating Mediation Results*, Mediation Practice Series. Geneva: Centre for Humanitarian Dialogue.

Wilson-Grau, Ricardo. 2008. "When Is Intentionally Designing Your Work Not Useful?" *Newsletter 2*. Outcome Mapping Learning Community.

Winslade, John, and Gerald Monk. 2001. *Narrative Mediation: A New Approach to Conflict Resolution*. San Francisco, CA: Jossey-Bass.

Woermann, Minka. 2010. *A Complex Ethics: Critical Complexity, Deconstruction, and Implications for Business Ethics*. PhD Dissertation, Stellenbosch: University of Stellenbosch.

Zartman, I. William. 2001. The Timing of Peace Initiatives: Hurting Stalemates and Ripe Moments. *Global Review of Ethnopolitics* 1 (1): 8–18.

CHAPTER 3

Adaptive Mediation in Colombia: Toward Institutional Capacity Building Amid Complexity and Uncertainty

Lina Penagos

Introduction

Mediation is a method that frequently pursues a cease-fire or a peace agreement to prevent, manage, or resolve an armed conflict. When conducted under an effective and structured process, mediation becomes a fundamental tool for negotiations between two opponents that cannot be defeated through violence. The Colombian case has been known for its multiscale and regionalized conflicts and encompassed structured mediation processes since the 1980s. It has been shaped by elements of complexity and uncertainty that compromised the peacebuilding path. Simultaneously, amid this same complexity and uncertainty, this case presents one of the most effective mediation processes with the Revolutionary Armed Forces of Colombia-People's Army (FARC-EP), the oldest Marxist-Leninist guerrilla in Latin America.

L. Penagos (✉)
Laboratoire Interdisciplinaire d'étude du Politique Hannah Arendt - Paris-Est (LIPHA-PE), Université Gustave Eiffel, Champs-sur-Marne, France

C. de Coning et al. (eds.), *Adaptive Mediation and Conflict Resolution*, Sustainable Development Goals Series,
https://doi.org/10.1007/978-3-030-92577-2_3

The Norwegian Peacebuilding Resource Centre (NOREF) report "Innovations in the Colombian Peace Process" highlighted this process as a significant milestone to settling one of the most protracted and violent conflicts in the world. In that respect, Colombia is now recognized as a global reference for diagnosing political solutions to intractable conflicts (Herbolzheimer 2016). After five decades of peacemaking initiatives and three major attempts to reach a negotiated solution to the conflict, the parties assessed their past failures and took into account the lessons learned from various peace processes occurring in Colombia. They developed innovative frameworks and approaches, for example developing procedural distinctions between peace negotiations and the peace process; positioning the rights of the victims at the center of the talks; addressing issues related to rural development; and preparing for peacebuilding before the agreement was signed (Herbolzheimer 2016). These innovative trends demonstrate that the Colombian case serves as an example of adaptive mediation, which can present key lessons from a process whereby the content of agreements emerges from the interaction among the participants.

Colombia's peacebuilding path is often challenged by complexity and uncertainty resulting from the active presence of armed nonstate actors (ANSAs).[1] However, simultaneously, efforts toward Institutional Capacity Building (ICB) were revealed to be effective under such challenging conditions. The achievement of the peace agreement with the FARC-EP shows how institutional capacity building results from resilient social institutions that emerged after more than 20 years of negotiated processes and related attempts to achieve peace with various armed groups.

This chapter takes the Colombian case's example and its collective mediation initiatives leading to several demobilization processes. It highlights how the complex context of irregular groups operating as controlling agents, with illegal economies and the remains of ideology, coexists with significant mediation efforts at the heart of political and social negotiations. Self-regulation to maintain peace in regions where the conflict has profoundly affected the social structure (de Coning 2021, Chap. 2 in this volume) remains one of the main drivers of self-organization in the implementation of the peace process. In this regard, the chapter provides

[1] In the twenty-first century, non-international armed conflicts (NIACs) are dominant. Yet, their nature and scope are broad and complex. Today's armed conflicts often include well-organized armed non-state actors opposing the state.

examples of lessons learned in Colombia on promoting resilience and self-organization in an adaptive mediation process that has evolved over time.

Three main hypotheses are raised in this chapter: (1) Adaptive mediation approaches contribute to peacebuilding focused on ICB and communitarian participation within a bottom-up demobilization, disarmament, and reincorporation (DDR) process. (2) Flexibility and institutionalism are key to the effectiveness of Colombia's mediation processes. (3) Colombia's successful mediation experiences demonstrate the need for more comprehensive and participatory conflict analysis and management of adaptive practices to address the complexity and uncertainty of ANSAs' behavior.

This chapter will show, in particular, how flexibility and adaptiveness in Colombia's mediation experience offer evidence of a matured mediation strategy that has resulted in remarkable achievements. This case intends to encourage mediators to promote the resilience of social institutions in countries that face ongoing failures of peace initiatives. The need for a more comprehensive focus on the importance of resilience and self-organization becomes even more relevant when taking into account the Colombian context and the respective level of engagement and trust in the mediators operating in such a protracted and complex conflict.

This study is based on a comparative analysis of reports and academic literature produced by scholars and think tanks specializing in the Colombian case. A particular focus on the mediation process with the FARC-EP is presented based on the analyses and experience of Enrique Santos Calderón (journalist), Frank Pearl (Colombia's minister of environment), Sergio Jaramillo (presidency's security advisor), Alejandro Eder (reintegration advisor), and Jaime Avendaño and Lucía Jaramillo (presidency's public officials). These mediators led to the successful 2012 negotiations between the FARC-EP under the government of former Colombian president Juan Manuel Santos. The author conducted fieldwork in Colombia between February and March 2020, conducting 41 semi-structured interviews and 7 videoconferences, and spending eight days with Colombian peacebuilders. Although these interviews were meant to inform the peacebuilding process in Colombia, the author conducted additional remote interviews during the SARS-CoV-2 pandemic focused on the topic of mediation.

Colombia's Complexity Within an Adapting System

Complexity is a relevant variable that cannot be neglected in the design of a mediation structure. This is valid both for academia and policy research, that is, in theory and practice. One of the elements to be examined in the Colombian case is the coexistence of multiple and simultaneous conflicts at various levels. Although the FARC-EP war was one of the primary references in this context, many other conflicts have taken place with either critical negotiation processes leading to cease-fires and disintegration of armed groups, or a reformulation of conflict drivers.

Not all mediation processes have led to sustainable peacebuilding actions. The literature related to mediation presents various approaches and examples of successful practices on the ground. The Colombian case sheds light on how adaptive approaches provide a better understanding of each context's specificity and the complex network of conflict actors. In this regard, many successful mediation processes have failed with demobilization, when conflicts mutate to complex forms of violence. However, an adaptive and institutionalist pathway serving as an umbrella for negotiations contributed significantly to institutional capacity building in Colombia (ICB).

From the first negotiation process with the Popular Liberation Army (EPL[2]) in 1991, until the latest 2012–2016 peace process with the Revolutionary Armed Forces of Colombia (FARC-EP[3]), standard and adaptive meditation practices have coexisted to facilitate peace talks during long and overlapping processes. In Colombia, history shows how a multiscale phenomenon of rebel groups influenced by the communist ideology emerged during the 1960s. Poverty and inequality seemed to justify a war against the state. As a result, in the Cold War framework, relevant groups emerged in strategic geographical regions.

The EPL, the April 19 Movement (M-19), the Revolutionary Workers Party, and the Quintin Lame Armed Movement (MAQL[4]) were some of the most representative rebel groups that emerged in the second half of the twentieth century. In the heart of the Colombian countryside, high levels of complexity and uncertainty resulted in the rise of various ANSAs,

[2] Spanish acronym for *Ejército Popular de Liberación*.

[3] Spanish acronym for *Fuerzas Armadas Revolucionarias de Colombia—Ejército del Pueblo*.

[4] Spanish acronym for *Movimiento Armado Quintin Lame*.

many of them highly influenced by the communist movement in Latin America and its so-called liberation doctrine.

Disparities between regions were attributed mainly to violence that divided the country after the important *El Bogotazo* episode in 1948, which marked the beginning of a political project known as the National Front (1958–1974), a power-sharing arrangement for pacification where liberal and conservative parties alternated in the presidency every four years.

Since Alberto Lleras Camargo's presidency (1959–1962), the first step toward pacification involved incorporating the state presence into war zones to defeat rebel forces. Understanding group dynamics—particularly their connections to regions and their respective societies—required a long-standing decentralization strategy of the negotiations and permanent interactions with local mediators. This allowed the government to go beyond a deterrence strategy and improve the effectiveness of the mediation process.

By prioritizing the regions most affected by conflict, the state brought military forces to the countryside without successfully defeating rebel groups or setting a mediation process that could end the hostilities. While intensive battles between the state and rebel groups occurred, conflict regions witnessed a considerable gap in growth and development, whereas major Colombian cities showed substantial growth rates. The country was running into a perpetuation of a development model with different speeds, at least in three identifiable layers: the major cities, the countryside near cities, and the distant countryside. The level of violence and the presence or absence of structured institutionalization were all benchmarks for further peace talk agendas (Arias et al. 2010).

With the creation of the Special Commission for Rehabilitation (SCR), President Lleras Camargo consolidated the first institutional benchmark that contributed to structured conflict management. This unique body consisted of five individual commissions in the regions under a state of emergency.[5] It worked toward two distinguishing goals: (1) addressing the multiple causes of violence—varying in a large spectrum, from party ideologies to economic reasons mainly associated with the concentration of land ownership combined with common delinquency, and (2) attending to the victims and their families after years of violence. Both features determined the impossibility of managing violence with traditional

[5] As a unitary republic, Colombia is divided into 32 departments. The special commissions were settled in the departments of Cauca, Tolima, Huila, Caldas, and Valle del Cauca.

mechanisms (i.e., determined-designed deterrence, amnesty, and conciliation) to mediate conflicts (Sánchez Gómez 1988).

The SCR acted as a ministerial committee with various departments, each one of them including Colombian Army members. As the first structured institution with a limited budget, it handled some situations beyond its original goal in a country where the end of violence was important but not determinant to the private sector's economic performance. Despite the dispersion in the SCR's field of action,[6] Lleras Camargo's mediation strategy aimed at reconciliation through pacification[7] and rehabilitation of the economic order in regions severely hit by violence.

The achievement of pacification in these regions was expected to persuade irregular groups to reincorporate into civil life and to regain economic growth. However, the pacification strategy's rural focus did not succeed through the action of the National Front's governments. Initiatives such as the "Integral Rural Reform Program"[8] were difficult to implement and did not effectively contribute to the mediation objective of pacification in violent regions (Arias et al. 2010).

Official initiatives to resolve conflicts at this stage combined strategies focused on rural areas and the renewal of institutions at a national level. As proposed by the SCR, decentralized mediation processes were abandoned, and strong, centralized management of a perceived "single conflict" (instead of multiple conflicts) became the new strategy, with a particular focus on security issues. In the aftermath, the strategy to "bring the state into the war zones" was measured by the two main political parties' presence in regions with representation at the national government's

[6] The SCR acts from 1958 to 1960, restored by Gonzalo Gomez Sanchez, registered a large variety of subjects that were encompassed by the Commission: requests from widows, orphans, homeless, and abandoned children; land dispossession actions; internally displaced people by violence; and even the donation of used furniture and equipment that could be used to relieve the poor's needs (Sánchez Gómez 1988).

[7] It is worth noting that in Colombia stakeholders and policymakers did not mention the concept of peacebuilding at this stage. Also, the idea of pacification was not related to the anarchist or postcolonial thought where "structures of domination ensure that resistance in the form of direct violence against this order is less frequent" (Baron et al. 2019). In Colombia, the concept of pacification was related to the reclamation of power by the state to allow economic growth in regions with ongoing conflicts. A significant reference in the field was the pacification process led by a Spanish military campaign that occurred between 1816 and 1820, carried out to reclaim the power of its overseas territories (Universidad del Rosario 2016).

[8] Created under the presidency of Alfonso López Michelsen (1974–1978).

legislative and executive branches (López Hernández 2016, 331). However, in regions with no active party representation, organized links with political parties were based more on rebel or illegal leadership than on the society's democratic will. During the National Front period, the idea of the "state" was built around electoral opportunism, nepotism, and favoring patronages. This undermined the people's trust in the institutions. Party representation in regions where public budget priorities were determined by electoral interests led to a considerable dispersion in public investment and increased the development gap with other regions (López Hernández 2016, 331). Therefore, the impact that derives from the correlation between public investment, political representation, and violence explains how mediation processes benefit from adopting adaptive approaches to deal with such context-specific variables. This is why the Colombian peace process has failed in some mediation stages that lacked adaptiveness, for example the ELN[9] process.

Theoretical and empirical studies on the evolution of violence and power in Colombia have shown that in some regions like Norte de Santander, Chocó, and Cauca, irregular groups have imposed their own rules, playing the triple role of governors, judges, and tax collectors. These three attributes also overlap with the role of a structured state. In some municipalities of these departments, both the state and irregular groups shared the monopoly of violence within a complex social control structure. This situation has not changed since the signing of the peace agreement with the FARC-EP. During fieldwork conducted by the author in 2020, evidence of the monopoly of violence sharing was worryingly explicit in Norte de Santander, where the ELN was fighting against criminal groups such as "Los Rastrojos" and "Los Pelusos" to regain control over the territory. At the time of writing, the ELN's action has been expanded to Venezuela, where they are involved in several kinds of trafficking (Fundación Paz y Reconciliación (Pares) 2019).

The arguments of this first section suggest that violence might have exacerbated conflicts and increased inequalities, when used as an instrument to control political participation. In Colombia, the instrumentalization of violence has been exclusive to some privileged segments of the society which directly benefit from the state's institutional structure against minorities' participation in a democratic process. In this regard, the thesis developed by Claudia López Hernandez (former senator and

[9] Spanish acronym for *Ejército de Liberación Nacional.*

current mayor of Bogotá) of a Colombian political system that misrepresents the needs of the population, particularly in regions critically impacted by violence, contributes to understanding why the most significant mediation processes—that is, with the United Self-Defense Forces of Colombia (AUC[10]) until 2006 and the FARC-EP until 2016—were continuously challenged by complexity and uncertainty (Kline et al. 2021), as suggested in the third hypothesis presented in this chapter and the overall arguments of the book.

Adaptiveness Within Colombia's Domestic Mediation Experiences

This section presents relevant facts related to the contribution of adaptive mediation approaches to DDR processes in Colombia by creating an effective institutional structure, as suggested by the first and second hypotheses presented in this chapter. Since 1990, Colombia has observed at least 12 collective mediation experiences leading to various disarmament, demobilization, and reintegration processes, with the objective of ending multiscale and regionalized conflicts. From 1990 to 1998, eight guerrilla groups and three urban militias signed a peace agreement with the Colombian government. In 2006, new mediation initiatives led the AUC to participate in the DDR process, and, following the 2016 peace agreement, the FARC-EP also began its demobilization process.

These mediation experiences involved numerous negotiations with the national government, welcomed the ANSA groups' deliberations, and sealed in the peace agreements the formalization of DDR programs. However, each process was held in different political, regional, and national contexts or within specific institutional frameworks. Various mediation initiatives were flexible enough to adapt to each context and relied on the mediators' and local partners' knowledge.

Despite the National Front's intentions and pacification strategy, the SCR failed to lead the parties to the negotiation table. During the 1980s, new political parties emerged, and irregular organizations multiplied, fueling hostilities in rural areas and the country's major cities. The M-19 case is a clear example of irregular organizations, that is, organized groups operating as militias in capital cities. In the countryside, the ELN and FARC-EP guerrillas operated in very different ways. The FARC-EP had a

[10] Spanish acronym for *Autodefensas Unidas de Colombia*.

secretariat (highest level of the leadership) responsible for giving directions to the appointed bloc commanders; the ELN (the largest Colombian leftist guerrilla) had a central command that worked in a very decentralized way. The differences in leaderships caused conflict between the groups around the control of territories and assuring income from kidnapping, protection payments,[11] and ransoms (CISAC 2021).

By 1982, the FARC-EP guerilla intended to gain political power by attacking the capital, Bogota. In the same year, Belisario Betancur won the presidential elections and created a national peace commission to be in charge of mediation processes with the two prominent guerrillas. This peace commission constituted another institutional benchmark within a very complex mediation process. Betancur's initiative included 12 members from the liberal party, another 12 from the conservative party, 6 members from left movements, 1 representative from the New Liberalism party, 1 from the National Popular Alliance (ANAPO), 1 journalist, 2 bishops, and 3 retired members of the Army (Villaveces 2003).

The commission's primary purpose was to achieve the country's pacification. With this objective, it gathered the most representative sectors of the Colombian political, religious, and military sectors, and was in charge of many negotiations. However, the commission had exiguous decision-making power, as the results of negotiations had to be approved by the national government. This fact represented a delay in the negotiations, undermining the trust between the conflict parties. The peace commission failed in its peacebuilding attempt; however, the national government's efforts resulted in promoting an essential mechanism under Betancur's strategy: the Law 35th, known as the *amnesty law*.

The Colombian Congress approved the amnesty law in 1985 against critical opposition. At this stage, the mediation process was determined to reach an agreement with actual advantages for rebels, particularly those that could be achieved in the short term, that is, financial support to ensure livelihood. The revolutionary group M-19 found the amnesty law unsatisfactory, as their social demands, such as political and economic reforms, and the end of counterinsurgency groups, were not taken into account. Hence, the group rejected the amnesty. However, around 2000 former combatants from the M-19 group, the ELN, and the EPL, together

[11] A model of a security structure was created because of these practices. The evolution of the ELN has allowed consolidating security services that are still present in Colombia today, and it was very useful in Venezuela to bring security to trafficking operations.

with Pedro León Arboleda Comando (PLA) group and the Workers Self-Defense (ADO), signed the agreement (López Hernández 2016, 340).

A third institutional benchmark in the mediation process emerged in this fragile and complex context. The "High Commission for Peace," which included several commissioners mandated by the presidency, had the mission of finding ways to reintegrate former combatants into civil life. Later, the actions led by the High Commission for Peace developed significantly from its first role; with its own institutional *corpus*, it was headed by a single high commissioner assigned by the presidency, and it became a critical actor in mediation in the AUC and the FARC-EP peace processes.

The amnesty law did not include a process of disarmament and reintegration of former insurgents. This was an important lesson that was taken into account in the following peace negotiations with the United Self-Defense Forces of Colombia and the FARC-EP. The High Commission for Peace activities remained important in peace efforts with the insurgency (García-Durán 2004).

As an institutional mechanism of Betancur's national peace strategy, the National Plan of Rehabilitation (NPR) was incorporated in the National Development Plan (NDP) in 1985. The NDP was one of Colombia's main public policy tools and the roadmap for every national government. This mechanism's primary purpose was to increase social investments in rural areas, so the local population was less allied and supportive of the insurgency (García Durán 2004).

The NPR was common to the political project conceived in Colombia, which included political participation, decentralization, and poverty reduction as the three main pillars to address peace-related issues in 160 municipalities with high rates of violence. Based on reports by the National Ministry of Defense and the National Cattle Breeding Association, the public budget was allocated to these municipalities. However, extortions, kidnappings, and ransoms profoundly affected its implementation.

As President Betancur claimed in his speeches, to reestablish trust with local communities, it was essential to create the conditions for peace and secure employment sources that could become new engines of progress (Señal Memoria 2017). Correspondingly, during Virgilio Barco's presidency (1986–1990), the peace strategy was also focused on regaining the state's legitimacy in the society, that is, trust-building. Barco ended the peace commissions and created the first institutional peace bodies at the heart of the government administration. They were called the Center for Reconciliation, Normalization, and Rehabilitation (CRNR) and the

Commission on the Study of Violence (CSV), the main participants of which were influential Colombian scholars (López Hernández 2016, 357).

The CSV had an essential role in objectively clarifying the causes of violence and reestablishing trust in Colombia's most violent regions. Their innovative work marked a precedent in the national effort to understand conflicts, the insurgencies' needs and priorities for negotiations, and related mediation activities. Barco's mediation strategy conceived peace talks as a means to improve reincorporation conditions for former combatants. A historical agreement was achieved with the M-19 by guaranteeing their security and political participation and creating a new political party in the new Colombian demobilization and reintegration scenario, the Democratic Alliance M-19. "This successful mediation process to achieve the demobilization and disarmament of various insurgency groups became the main reference to negotiate with the Revolutionary Workers Party, the Quintín Lame Armed Movement, the Popular Liberation Army (EPL), and Ernesto Rojas Commands" (López Hernández 2016, 360).

With reference to the first hypothesis and as demonstrated in Table 3.1, structured mediation processes through institutional arrangements began in Colombia 25 years before the signature of the peace agreement with the FARC-EP. The table summarizes the irregular groups' participation in the mediation processes occurring between 1991 and 2016. Accordingly, primary DDR recipients were part of the United Self-Defense forces of Colombia and the Revolutionary Armed Forces of Colombia-People's Army. In 2006, many former combatants participating in disarmament and demobilization programs were reintegrated into civil life. Those who instead withdrew from the peace agreement terms joined new ANSA groups operating in underground economies.[12] This fact holds the third hypothesis of the chapter, referring to the need for a more comprehensive understanding of the complexity and uncertainty of ongoing multiscale conflicts in Colombia.

Toward Institutional Capacity Building (ICB) Within Complexity and Uncertainty

The preceding section identified the High Commission for Peace (HCP) as the third institutional benchmark of Colombia's mediation processes. During Ernesto Samper Pizano's presidency (1994–1998), the HCP

[12] Information gathered during the fieldwork conducted by the author in March 2020.

Table 3.1 Irregular groups participating in mediation processes 1991–2016

Armed nonstate group	*Year*	*Number of disarmed people*	*Current status*
Popular Liberation Army (EPL)	1991	2256	Active dissidence
April 19 Movement (M-19)	1990	900	Political participation
Revolutionary workers party	1991	200	Civil organizations (research and actions in human rights)
Quintín Lame Armed Movement (MAQL)	1991	157	Demobilized
Ernesto Rojas commands *the urban arm of the EPL*	1992	25	Demobilized
Socialist renewal group	1994	433	Demobilized
Militias	1994	650	Active dissidence in other ANSAs
Francisco Garnica Front	1994	150	Political participation
Revolutionary Independent Movement	1998	171	Civil organizations (research in armed conflict)
Guevarista Revolutionary Army (ERG)	2008	45	Demobilized
United Self-Defense Forces of Colombia (AUC)	2006	31,671	Reintegration
Revolutionary Armed Forces of Colombia-People's Army (FARC-EP)	2016	13,000	Reincorporation

Source: López Hernández (2016), Red Paz—Universidad Nacional de Colombia (2020)

became a permanent institution with only one head, occupied by a public official. A complete bureau with counselors dedicated to advising the high commissioner gathered highly trained experts in negotiation, mainly from outside of Colombia. This position was occupied by recognized mediators who have had experience in peace processes in Colombia and abroad. Carlos Holmes Trujillo[13] was officially named the first high commissioner for peace.

The institutionalization process created by subsequent governments since the National Front was not enough to achieve negotiations with the

[13] Minister of Defense until his death on January 26, 2021, after contracting the COVID-19 virus. Carlos Holmes Trujillo previously held important diplomatic and political positions, including as interior minister and foreign minister.

FARC-EP. The complex situation related to Medellin's and Cali's drug cartels, led by Pablo Escobar and the Rodriguez Orejuela brothers, demanded urgent state responses and shifted the government's priorities regarding the insurgencies. This complexity prepared the country's institutions to deal with a proliferation of ANSAs withdrawing from their original structures after the disarticulation of cartels and joining other illegal activities such as mineral mining, arms trafficking, and extensive networks of other underground economies powered by globalization during the 1990s.

In 1998, under Andrés Pastrana's presidency, a national agenda was established and signed with the FARC-EP as a necessary prestep to begin the peace talks. The agenda included 12 points that were important for the negotiations: (1) a political solution to the insurgency; (2) human rights protection; (3) a holistic rural policy; (4) conservation and sustainable use of natural resources; (5) focus on economic and social structures; (6) justice reform and the fight against corruption and trafficking; (8) state reform; (9) an International Humanitarian Law agreement; (10) the Army; (11) foreign relations; and (12) democratic agreements (Arias et al. 2010, 12).

Withdrawing from the negotiations and returning to war has been a recurrent action of FARC-EP combatants. The recognition of the group's belligerency and its increasing presence in the national territory gave the insurgency unprecedented power, allowing them to impose the demand to negotiate in an exclusive space—the so-called distension zone. For the first time in Colombia's history, a part of the territory was given to an insurgent group. In a territory with an extension of 42.000 km^2, the FARC-EP was able to find the time and space to strengthen its military forces. After the failure of the peace talks, the distension zone operated between 1999 and 2002 (Kline et al. 2021). From a theoretical perspective, this event demonstrates that the conflict was not ripe enough for a resolution, direct negotiation, arbitration, or mediation.

The creation of the special commissions during Belisario Betancur's presidency (a benchmark to reinforce ICB, as the second hypothesis states) was informed by the principle to include civil society representatives within its members. A diverse representation of political forces, civil society, and belligerent actors marked the beginning of the first national trial to create a shared peacebuilding agenda (Fig. 3.1). Aligned with the international literature on peace processes, the term *peacebuilding* appeared as a goal and policy tool for the Colombian government. Despite the peace talks'

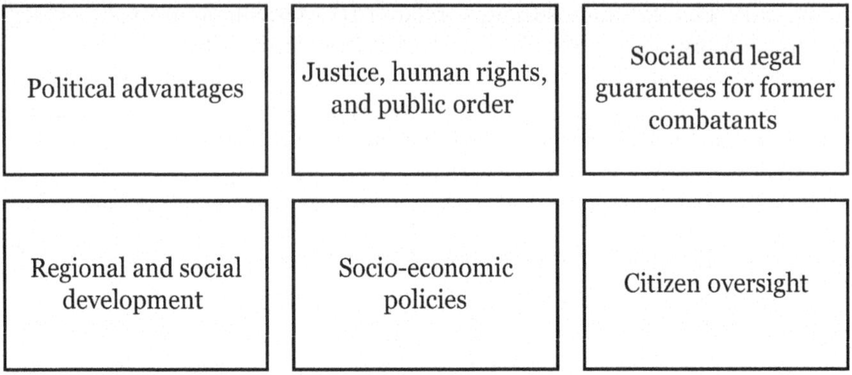

Fig. 3.1 Main drivers of mediation processes with irregular groups in Colombia (Source: García-Durán 2004)

failure to achieve DDR, Colombia was able to foster a remarkable group of mediators, who played key roles in negotiations with the AUC and the FARC-EP in 2016 (Villaveces 2003).

Although mediation is a fundamental tool to negotiate peace, Colombia's case has revealed that the FARC-EP negotiations were challenging even for the most experienced mediators. Anxiety and exhaustion, following so much effort and without positive results, undermined civil society's confidence in the government strategies. This experience brought Colombia the opportunity to concentrate its efforts on a new strategy that combined the Army's modernization to fight the insurgency during the Pastrana and Alvaro Uribe presidencies and with a permanent effort to develop a new constitutional agenda for peace talks during Juan Manuel Santos presidency (Santos Calderón 2014).

Alongside the new mediation strategy that involved political and private actors, a counterinsurgency plan was deployed during the first presidency of Alvaro Uribe (2002–2006), enabling the AUC's demobilization. This negotiation featured adaptive characteristics, as—unlike the previous processes with the FARC-EP—it did not pursue a common agenda such as the objective of a final peace agreement or the parties' commitment beyond the demobilization process. Official speeches and communications were nevertheless accessible to the public. The mediation process was headed by a Special Peace Commission, which was in charge of writing a report with recommendations to be followed by the government (Villaveces 2003).

The negotiation process with the AUC was quite particular as there was no recognition of mutual interdependence. Analyzing this process from Andrew Mack's theory perspective (see Chap. 2) reveals it to be more like the aftermath of an agreement on no-peace-no-war, which left unresolved the sources of conflict but at the same time saved lives.

At this stage, the accumulated mediation experience of Colombia resulted in various levels of adaptiveness: within the state, with international mediators, and with local communities. As a result, more than 31,000 former combatants participated in a DDR process for the first time. A national agency for reincorporation was created based on past experiences to reintegrate former combatants. The fieldwork conducted by the author in February 2020 included interviews with reincorporated combatants who are participating in community work experiences in this context. They supported the peace process with the FARC-EP and felt committed to participating in local initiatives where they have served as communitarian mediators to avoid new violence and sources of conflict (Former Combatant Sources 2020a).

The counterinsurgency strategy eliminated the most influential and senior guerrilla leaders of Latin America: Raul Reyes, Alfonso Cano, and Mono Jojoy were reported dead after Colombian Army military operations. Therefore, Colombia gained a vital tool to negotiate with the FARC-EP after its experience with the AUC, and the conditions were finally established to begin peace talks in 2012. To arrive at this configuration, a critical adaptive mediation process was handled by a secret commission mandated by President Juan Manuel Santos in 2010. As the failed mediation process in the "distention zone" created a precedent of mistrust in the Colombian society, to succeed in this new effort, effective military results against the FARC-EP allowed reestablishing contacts for future negotiation, this time outside Colombia.

A joint agreement between the parties set Cuba to hold a first secret contact to establish a more feasible agenda to end the armed conflict. On February 24, 2012, and for six months following, representatives from the Colombian national government and the FARC-EP held 69 talks in 10 formal sessions before signing the official document "Final Agreement to End the Armed Conflict and Build a Stable and Lasting Peace" (Santos Calderón 2014).

The "exploratory meetings" that led to the joint agreement were held in La Habana (Cuba). However, the first contacts took place on the border between Colombia and Venezuela, with active participation from the former Venezuelan president, Hugo Chavez. In the border meetings, the parties selected Cuba and Norway as "guarantor countries." The FARC-EP delegation accepted the mediation of the International Red Cross to guarantee the traveling safety of their delegation chief to Venezuela. The first meeting with mediators in Venezuela allowed for the discussion of mediator Sergio Jaramillo's agenda, which included roles and tactics for future negotiators of the peace agreement. The mediators were supported by the international experts' advice to assist in outlining and organizing the Colombian government's objectives to end the armed conflict without negotiating a model for the Colombian economy or national armies' status. The motto was that nothing is agreed between the parties until all parties agree on all points of the common agenda.

The final peace agreement with a common agenda was signed in 2016 after four years of negotiations based on six points: (1) completing a comprehensive rural reform, (2) increasing political participation, (3) securing a cease-fire, (4) presenting a solution to the problem of illicit drugs, (5) bringing the rights of the victims to the center of negotiations, and (6) developing implementation and verification mechanisms. Government representatives from Norway, Cuba, Chile, and Venezuela participated as guarantors of the negotiation process but not as mediators; the key practice in this experience was to open a national dialogue that would converge into a national agenda, where victims of the armed conflict and the civil society could participate in the process. During this period, the victims of the armed conflict were very active in the peace talks for the first time in Colombia, and many related commissions were established in the La Habana negotiations (Academia Source 2020b).

The 2016 final peace agreement gave rise to an innovative transitional justice system under the name of Special Jurisdiction of Peace (JEP[14]) that determinates crimes based on reports, audiences, and research by special commissions, victims, academia, and NGOs. This seals the mediation process with the FARC-EP as one of the most successful processes based on evidence and effectiveness. It was able to stop the hostilities and develop a DDR process with over 13,000 combatants. The JEP is, without a doubt, one of the most significant achievements of the mediation process to contribute to ICB as the first hypothesis suggests: in the aftermath of the peace agreement's signing, the first imputations against the former

[14] Spanish acronym for *Jurisdicción Especial para la Paz.*

FARC-EP members were pronounced on January 28, 2021 (Jurisdicción Especial para la Paz 2021), four years after the end of hostilities.

Crucial local mediation initiatives were also initiated in the Territorial Spaces of Capacitation and Reincorporation (ETCR),[15] as an example of bottom-up ICB. One example of this is the ETCR Silver Vidal Mora (department of Chocó), where the first theater, built in the middle of the jungle, offers training in mediation with the participation of local communities and sometimes international organizations (Carvajal 2020).[16] An adaptive approach based on the creation of key institutions, support for the mediation and peacebuilding process, and the inclusion of local actors, as well as their self-organization capabilities and resilience, has been crucial to sustaining peace in Colombia's complex and uncertain context.

Conclusion

The dynamic and adaptive nature of mediation applied to various protracted and complex armed conflicts in Colombia was achieved by establishing a common and flexible agenda. From the first trials and errors to the founding of a genuine way to integrate former ANSAs combatants, this chapter introduced the main strategies, pluralities, and connections used by the Colombian government, the ANSAs, and mediators, during 12 long negotiation processes from 1991 to 2016.

During the last three decades, Colombia gained relevant mediation experience through these 12 peace processes, involving the state and various ANSAs and offering relevant lessons learned to mediators around the world. With reference to the first hypothesis and as pointed out in the first section, from the negotiation with the Popular Liberation Army (1991) until the peace agreement with the FARC-EP (2016), various mediation experiences have encompassed diverse strategies that combined standard and adaptive practices, which resulted in successful cease-fires that contributed to more performant DDR processes and that saved people's life.

Hence, flexibility and adaptiveness became the two main concepts that informed effective mediation structures in Colombia. As an essential aspect of peacebuilding efforts, the Colombian case reveals that these

[15] Spanish acronym for *Espacios Territoriales de Capacitación y Reincorporación*.

[16] In an interview conducted on December 11, 2020, Johana Carvajal, researcher at the ETCR Silver Vidal Mora, described the cultural experience of theater as one of the most constructive to rebuild links in a community marked by violence.

mediation processes contributed to further Institutional Capacity Building for more effective peacebuilding actions (Bercovitch and Kadayifci 2002). In this regard, the Special Jurisdiction of Peace (JEP in Spanish) is a relevant benchmark not only to ICB but also to other Transitional Justice Systems all over the world where protracted conflicts tend to be solved, as the first hypothesis suggests.

However, new sources of conflict have surfaced and jeopardize the process, particularly in the case of ANSAs' network with international crime organizations, local political parties, and local community leaders. Although this evidence may suggest an endless circle of ongoing protracted intra-state conflicts in Colombia—similar to Johan Galtung's definition of "negative peace"—the country has achieved remarkable peace gains resulting from mediation in at least the most recent AUC and the FARC-EP processes (Academia Source 2020a).

From this point of view, the variety of ANSAs and their interactions with the state brought a complex and uncertain nature to these mediation processes. The hostilities between the state and its opponents were not reduced to rebel groups but related to a more complex and changing reality which reflected the dynamics of internal conflicts in Colombia since the 1980s, as it stands in the third hypothesis: illegal groups financed by drug trafficking and a vast network of illegal and flexible business drivers. The arrival of narcotrafficking as a source of finance for the conflict marks a shift in Colombian society's thinking, morals, behaviors, and values. These were not related to the ideology of guerrilla groups such as the FARC, the ELN, and the EPL, the last group still active in Venezuela, particularly after 2015 when the political and economic situation in the country became detrimental (NPO Source 2020). These facts stress the need for a more comprehensive understanding of the complexity and uncertainty of ongoing multiscale conflicts in Colombia.

International relations scholars have been developing a promising paradigm for framing violent ANSAs under a different lens, that is, competitive authoritarianism (Thomas et al. 2005). The author's doctoral research also suggests that the dynamic of ANSAs transforms the paradigm of the monopoly of violence, as well as the taxation and justice by the state (Penagos 2022).

After examining the impact of ANSAs in Colombia's armed conflicts and related mediation experiences, three critical findings stand out: (1) In long mediation processes, standard and adaptive meditation practices will coexist among many attempts to bring the parties to the negotiating table.

(2) The high level of complexity of the context and the variety of armed nonstate actors involved is continuously challenging to mediation and peacebuilding actions.[17](3) The flexibility and adaptiveness in Colombia's experience of mediation give evidence of a mature guideline that has resulted in remarkable achievements in three key sustaining peace aspects: (1) DDR, (2) institutional capacity building, (3) and bottom-up communitarian participation.

In an unprecedented event, the Colombian Congress, during the Juan Manuel Santos presidency (2010–2018), enacted the Law 1908 for Organized Armed Groups (GAO).[18] The Law 1908 developed a unique judicialization process based on two stages: (1) collective talks inside GAOs to decide if they wish to be under Law 1908 and (2) 13 points or conditions that lead to judicialization of the GAOs. The National Government was in charge of the first phase, and the General Attorney Office of the second one. This Law showed GAOs' relevance in the national context of violence and the need to create a special procedure to break up these structures under the general justice system rather than the special transitional justice system (Congreso de Colombia 2018).

At this stage, the accumulated mediation experience of Colombia resulted in various levels of adaptiveness: within the state, with international mediators, and with local communities. In the first level, a National Agency for Reincorporation (ARN) was created based on past experiences to reintegrate former combatants. As a result, more than 31,000 former combatants participated in a DDR process for the first time. The ARN is the state agency in charge of the comprehensive, sustainable, and transitory social and economic reincorporation at two stages: early and long-term reincorporation (ARN 2017). The Reincorporation Route is the roadmap or the agency and contains the general guidelines agreed between the delegates of the former combatants, the National Reincorporation Council and the ARN, a permanent adaptive mediation process.

The fieldwork conducted by the author in February 2020 included interviews with reincorporated combatants who are participating in community work experiences in this context. They support the peace process with the FARC-EP and felt committed to participating in local initiatives

[17] From 281 prioritized municipalities after the signing of the peace agreement with the FARC-EP, 123 are controlled by ANSAs (Fundación Paz y Reconciliación (Pares) 2019).

[18] Spanish acronym for *Grupos Armados Oganizados*.

where they have served as communitarian mediators to avoid new violence and sources of conflict (Former Combatant Sources 2020b).

A second level of adaptiveness is related to international mediators that can be summarized in multiple NGO's as well as international organizations that support the implementation of the peace process. The Final Peace Agreement signed between the Colombian government and the FARC-EP established a complex accompaniment mechanism that include international observers and scholars: "the international community can in different ways help to guarantee the implementation (…). In the area of verification, [the] model (…) has an international component comprising those countries that through the process has acted as guarantors and observers, plus two international spokespersons. The technical aspects are (…) supported by the (…) Kroc Institute for International Peace Studies at the University of Notre Dame" (Colombia 2016).

By May 2021, the Kroc Institute had produced five comprehensive reports and created the Peace Agreement Matrix (PAM) research tool. The reports included interviews with civil society, governments, think tanks, NGOs, and International Organizations (Kroc Institute for International Peace Studies, Iniciativa Barómetro, and Matriz de Acuerdos de Paz 2020). Finally, at the local level—with national impact—several reports were produced and published by independent think tanks such as the *Fundación Ideas Para La Paz* (FIP) and *Fundación Paz y Reconciliación* as a result of the fieldwork in local communities. In this regard, periodical reports suggest a more comprehensive strategy toward sustaining peace. For example, one of the scenarios proposed by FIP researchers is to reinforce technical skills for former combatants. These researchers also discuss new regional dialogues promoting trust to articulate public policy, private initiatives, and local needs, mainly in those regions where civil war has deeply impacted society (FIP 2019).

Colombia's experience contributes to the understanding of how mediation processes are conceived and developed through a process based on an alternative approach that advocates for cooperation and recognizes the communities' role as the key to developing common agendas to rebuild their societies, that is, a process that focuses on self-organization and resilience. The peace agreement's expectations with the FARC-EP—the most senior guerrilla in Latin America—contrast with the endless activities of illicit economies (drug trafficking and illicit mining mainly). The combination of unaddressed root causes of conflict, corruption, and inequality, and strong civil society resistance against the reincorporation process in major cities, presents a new national challenge to developing communitarian mediation processes. Further research on adaptive approaches to structure and implement local and national mediation initiatives in Colombia will address the remaining challenges and enhance peacebuilding programs in territories with recurring or protracted armed violence and social conflicts.

References

Academia Source. 2020a. Interview with Professor Stephen Launay in February, conducted by Lina Penagos.

———. 2020b. Exchange with Professor Maria Emma Will, the Advisor to the Chair of National Center for Historical Memory in the Department Administrative Office of the President of Colombia, during the online colloquium "Sortir de la violence," in November, at La Fondation Maison des Sciences de l'Homme (FMSH), Paris.

Arias, Gerson Iván, Carlos Andrés Prieto, and Milena Peralta. 2010. *¿Qué quieren las FARC? Agendas de negociación en los procesos de paz [What do the FARC want? Negotiation agendas in peace processes?]*. Serie Informes No. 11. Bogota: Fundación Ideas para la paz.

ARN. 2017. *Social and Economic Reincorporation: Update*. Agency for Reincorporation and Normalization (ARN). http://www.reincorporacion.gov.co/en/reincorporation/Documents/Social_and_Economic_Reincorporation_Handbook.pdf.

Baron, Ilan Zvi, Jonathan Havercroft, Isaac Kamola, Jonneke Koomen, Justin Murphy, and Alex Prichard. 2019. Liberal Pacification and the Phenomenology of Violence. *International Studies Quarterly* 63 (1): 199–212. https://doi.org/10.1093/isq/sqy060.

Bercovitch, Jacob, and Ayse Kadayifci. 2002. Exploring the Relevance and Contribution of Mediation to Peace-Building. *Peace and Conflict Studies* 9 (2): 21–40. https://doi.org/10.46743/1082-7307/2002.1025.

Carvajal, Johana. 2020. Interview with Johana Carvajal, researcher at the ETCR Silver Vidal Mora, conducted by Lina Penagos in France.

CISAC. 2021. *Mapping Militants*. Center for International Security and Cooperation. Stanford: Freeman Spogli Institute for International Studies. https://cisac.fsi.stanford.edu/mappingmilitants/mappingmilitants.

Colombia. 2016. *Final Agreement to End the Armed Conflict and Build a Stable and Lasting Peace*. http://especiales.presidencia.gov.co/Documents/20170620-dejacion-armas/acuerdos/acuerdo-final-ingles.pdf.

Congreso de Colombia. 2018. *Ley 1908 de 2018 [Law 1908 of 2018]*. Congreso de Colombia.

de Coning, Cedric. 2021. *Adaptive Mediation. Chapter 2 in This Volume.*

FIP. 2019. *La Reincorporación de Las FARC Tres Años Después. Desafíos y Propuestas [The Reincorporation of the FARC Three Years Later. Challenges and Proposals].* Fundación Ideas Para La Paz (FIP). December 6. http://empresaspazddhh.ideaspaz.org/documento/la-reincorporacion-de-las-farc-tres-anos-despues-desafios-y-propuestas.

Former Combatant Sources. 2020a. Interview with an anonymous source (former combatant) on February 25, conducted by Lina Penagos at the ETCR Icononzo in Tolima.

———. 2020b. Interview with anonymous sources (former combatants) in February and March, conducted by Lina Penagos at the ETCR Icononzo (Tolima, Colombia), El Oso (Tolima, Colombia), Tierra Grata (Cesar, Colombia) and Monterredonto (Cauca).

Fundación Paz y Reconciliación—Pares. 2019. *Más sombras que luces, un análisis de seguridad en Colombia [More Shadows Than Lights, a Security Analysis in Colombia].* Fundación Paz y Reconciliación. August 28. https://pares.com.co/2019/08/28/mas-sombras-que-luces-un-analisis-de-seguridad-en-colombia/.

García-Durán, Mauricio. 2004. *Alternativas a La Guerra: Iniciativas y Procesos de Paz En Colombia [Alternatives to War: Initiatives and Peace Processes in Colombia].* Accord No. 14. London-Bogota: Conciliation Resources-Accord,Centro de Investigación y Educación Popular Cinep. https://www.c-r.org/resources/alternativas-la-guerra-iniciativas-y-procesos-de-paz-en-colombia.

Herbolzheimer, Kristian. 2016. *Innovations in the Colombian Peace Process.* NOREF Report. The Norwegian Peacebuilding Resource Centre.

Jurisdicción Especial para la Paz. 2021. *La JEP imputa al antiguo Secretariado de las Farc-Ep crímenes de lesa humanidad y crímenes de guerra por secuestros [The JEP Accuses the Former Secretariat of the FARC-EP of Crimes Against Humanity].* https://www.jep.gov.co:443/Sala-de-Prensa/Paginas/La-JEP-imputa-al-antiguo-Secretariado-de-las-FARC-Ep-cr%C3%ADmenes-de-lesa-humanidad-.aspx.

Kline, Harvey F., Clemente Garavito, James J. Parsons, Robert Louis Gilmore, and William Paul McGreevey. 2021. Colombia—La Violencia, Dictatorship, and Democratic Restoration [Colombia—The Violence, Dictatorship, and Democratic Restoration]. *Encyclopedia Britannica.* July 13. https://www.britannica.com/place/Colombia.

Kroc Institute for International Peace Studies, Iniciativa Barómetro, and Matriz de Acuerdos de Paz. 2020. *Tres Años Después de La Firma Del Acuerdo Final de Colombia: Hacia La Transformación Territorial [Three Years After the Signature of the Final Agreement of Colombia: Towards Territorial Transformation].* Informe 4. Bogotá: Universidad de Notre Dame. http://peaceaccords.nd.edu/wp-content/uploads/2020/06/Cuarto-Informe-Final-with-Annex-Link.pdf.

López Hernández, Claudia. 2016. *¡Adiós a las Farc! ¿Y ahora qué? [Goodbye to the Farc! And now what?]*. Bogotá: DEBATE.

NPO Source. 2020. Exchange with Jeremy McDermott, the Executive Director of InSight Crime, During the Online Seminar of "COVID & Crimen Organizado," in December.

Penagos, Lina-Maria. 2022. *Zonas Grises y Economías Subterráneas: Transposición Burocrática y Relaciones de Poder En La Arquitectura Del Estado Contemporáneo. El Caso de La Frontera Colombo-Venezolana [Grey Zones and Underground Economies: Bureaucratic Transposition and Power Relations in the Architecture of the Contemporary State. The Case of the Colombian-Venezuelan Border]*. PhD Dissertation, Université Gustave Eiffel.

Red Paz—Universidad Nacional de Colombia. 2020. *Sesión 6: Avatares de Los Procesos de Paz En Colombia (1990–2020) [Session 6: Avatars of the Peace Processes in Colombia (1990–2020)]*. https://www.youtube.com/watch?v=a-PLd80wX40&list=PL8UrtW_7N9APkl5NV27hQu8azdILBhexr&index=11.

Sánchez Gómez, Gonzalo. 1988. Rehabilitación y Violencia Bajo El Frente Nacional [Rehabilitation and Violence under the National Front]. *Análisis Político* 4 (May): 21–42.

Santos Calderón, Enrique. 2014. *Así Empezó Todo : El Primer Cara a Cara Secreto Entre El Gobierno y Las Farc En La Habana / Enrique Santos Calderón [This Is How It All Began: The First Secret Face to Face Between the Government and the Farc in Havana / Enrique Santos Calderón]*. Primera edición. Bogotá: Intermedio.

Señal Memoria. 2017. Radio Nacional: Un discurso para la memoria en la voz de Belisario Betancur [National Radio: A Speech for the Memory in the Voice of Belisario Betancur]. *Señal Memoria*. February 3. https://www.senalmemoria.co//articulos/radio-nacional-un-discurso-para-la-memoria-en-la-voz-de-belisario-betancur.

Thomas, Troy S., Stephen D. Kiser, and William D. Casebeer. 2005. *Warlords Rising: Confronting Violent Non-State Actors*. Lanham, MD: Lexington Books.

Universidad del Rosario. 2016. *Conmemoración Bicentenario de La Pacificación 1816 [Bicentennial Commemoration of the Pacification 1816]*. Universidad del Rosario. https://www.urosario.edu.co/Pacificacion/Inicio2/.

Villaveces, Juanita. 2003. Why Peace Process Fail or Move Forward? Negotiations in Colombia with FARC and AUC (1998–2003). *Borradores de Investigación En Economía* 35. https://repository.urosario.edu.co/bitstream/handle/10336/10887/3781.pdf.

CHAPTER 4

Peacemaking from Within: Adaptive Mediation of Direct Dialogue in Mozambique's New Peace Process (2013–2019)

Rui Saraiva

Introduction

Mozambique has faced several cycles of violent conflict since the independence war against Portuguese rule (1964–1974), followed by a long civil war (1977–1992) between FRELIMO (Mozambique Liberation Front) and RENAMO (Mozambican National Resistance), and its recent recurrence (2012–2019). Decades of peace negotiations have followed, resulting in three main peace agreements: the 1992 General Peace Agreement (GPA), the 2014 Cessation of Military Hostilities Agreement (CMHA), and the 2019 Maputo Accord for Peace and Reconciliation (MAPR). After the 1992 GPA, numerous peacebuilding programs have been implemented by various actors, ranging from traditional international donors

R. Saraiva (✉)
JICA Ogata Sadako Research Institute for Peace and Development, Tokyo, Japan
e-mail: Farosaraiva.Rui@jica.go.jp

C. de Coning et al. (eds.), *Adaptive Mediation and Conflict Resolution*, Sustainable Development Goals Series,
https://doi.org/10.1007/978-3-030-92577-2_4

such as the G19 group[1] to donors that have emerged in the last 15 years, for example China, Brazil, India, Vietnam, and the Gulf Countries (de Carvalho, Rozen, and Reppell 2016, 11).

From 1992 to 2012, Mozambique's peacebuilding process was hailed as a successful case of liberal peacebuilding, resulting from a successful mediation process led by a faith-based mediator, the lay Catholic association Community Sant'Egidio. However, recent events challenged more than 20 years of peacebuilding outcomes, with numerous factors contributing to the relapse of violence in the country. In 2012, the country saw a small-scale resurgence of conflict emerging between the Mozambican government and RENAMO due to tensions between both groups during peacetime (Vhumbunu 2017). The recurring conflict was characterized by a series of small-scale attacks in Mozambique's central and northern regions. Despite their limitations, the logistics and number of victims of the attacks were comparable to other intrastate conflicts, significantly impacting the peace prospects in the country and reopening the possibility of civil conflict. The failure of the disarmament, demobilization, and reintegration (DDR) process had been at the heart of RENAMO's concerns. Many of RENAMO's ex-combatants remained ineligible for pensions, which could have allowed them to maintain their dignity and provide for their basic needs. Young RENAMO recruits, many of whom were relatives of ex-combatants, concluded that resorting to arms was the only way to achieve a more effective peace agreement (Wiegink 2015). Therefore, RENAMO has been claiming for more decentralization, provincial autonomy, equal state resources allocation, and more opportunities to hold sufficient political power, while the objective of the Mozambican government has been the total disarmament of RENAMO's residual forces and the complete cessation of hostilities (Government Source 1 2020; Academia Source 1 2020).

The impact of the small-scale civil war worsened over time. By March 2016, the UNHCR reported over 10,000 Mozambican refugees fleeing to Malawi and a considerable increase in the number of internally displaced persons (IDPs) (Shimo 2016). Other events added layers of complexity to the Mozambican peace and development context. In 2016,

[1] Traditional peace and development donors in Mozambique include the UN, the African Development Bank, the World Bank, the EU, Portugal, Japan, Germany, Austria, Denmark, Portugal, Canada, Denmark, Finland, France, Ireland, Italy, Norway, the UK, Sweden, Switzerland, Belgium, Spain, the US, and the Netherlands.

Mozambique's public debt crisis prompted international partners, including the International Monetary Fund (IMF), the World Bank, and several bilateral development agencies, to suspend their assistance (Cascais 2018). Since the suspension of foreign aid, which directly supported a considerable part of the national budget, a heavy negative impact was felt across the economy and in the Mozambican taxpayers' pockets (Academia Source 2 2020). Mozambique has also been prone to natural disasters, such as floods, droughts, and cyclones, which have only aggravated the economic, peace, and security crises. In 2019 alone, Cyclones Idai and Kenneth affected more than 2.8 million people in Mozambique (International Federation of Red Cross and Red Crescent Societies (IFRC) 2019).

As if all these events were not enough, an Islamic insurgency[2] in Northern Mozambique emerged in 2017, with the goal of establishing an Islamic state in the Cabo Delgado province (Faleg 2019). Violent extremism of this nature erupted for the first time in October 2017, in Mocímboa da Praia, when militants attacked a police station and government buildings. The violence has been centered in Mozambique's northeastern province bordering Tanzania—the least-developed region in the country (Matsinhe and Valoi 2019, 8). The attacks followed tensions between the extremist sect and other segments of the local community, who had been fighting over social and economic grievances, religious intolerance, and dissatisfaction with the local Frelimo-led authority. At the time of writing, insurgent attacks in Northern Mozambique have thus far caused nearly 4000 deaths and forced over 700,000 people to flee their homes (ACLED 2021; UNHCR 2021). Cabo Delgado remains a fertile ground for violent extremism, aggravated by an increased presence of government forces in the region, predominantly following hard-security approaches to address this crisis. President Filipe Nyusi admitted that the situation in Cabo Delgado could potentially jeopardize peace prospects in the country, including the ongoing DDR process with RENAMO (Rodrigues 2020).

Since 2012, a complex environment with serious challenges to peace and security in Mozambique has prompted international cooperation for sustaining peace in the country through various mediation initiatives, humanitarian aid, peacebuilding, development assistance, and security responses. A large number of RENAMO militants in the center and northern provinces of Niassa, Tete, Nampula, and Inhambane, including those

[2] Two active groups have been named in the literature and interviews: Ansar-al-Sunna or Al-Shabab and the Islamic State of Iraq and the Levant (ISIL/ISIS).

who are now linked with the Military Junta, are the first factor within the complex environment. The second is the ongoing Islamic insurgency in Cabo Delgado, a Muslim-majority province rich in natural resources and agricultural potential on the northeastern border with Tanzania. As a result, there is now a widespread perception of insecurity among Mozambican political elites and the population in general. Many consider Mozambique to be facing not one but two armed conflicts occurring simultaneously (Civil Society Source 2 2020). The Mozambican people's general perception is that the peace achieved in 1992 has been suddenly lost (Civil Society Source 3 2020).

Addressing a Mozambican changing context became a key priority for mediation efforts between 2012 and 2019. Peacemaking solutions often involved a sense of urgency due to the complex and uncertain environment described above. The recent peace process involved multiple stakeholders and featured three mediation stages addressing the RENAMO insurgency. Both conflict parties and several domestic and external mediation actors, such as individuals, states, international organizations (IOs), and nongovernmental organizations (NGOs), attempted to find new solutions to the conflict and participated directly or indirectly in the mediation process. The distinctive mediation styles, methods, and approaches are described here in three main sections. The first section focuses on domestic mediation with no external process facilitation, the second on standard high-level international mediation, and the third on adaptive mediation as the facilitation of direct dialogue between both parties. Although this chapter distinguishes between mediation styles and their respective efficacy, it is essential to recognize that all stakeholders involved in the peace process, especially the Mozambicans that worked tirelessly in the various stages of the mediation process, tried their best to achieve peace and improve the lives of their compatriots.

This chapter also attempts to answer two main research questions within the context of the 2013–2019 peace process in Mozambique: (1) What are the key characteristics of standard and alternative mediation practices employed to reach the 2019 MAPR? (2) How were mediators able to adapt to uncertainty and complexity during the negotiations? By answering these questions, this chapter attempts to offer relevant lessons for mediators and peacebuilders around the world facing increasing challenges to their activities, including not only peace and security risks but also human security threats, such as natural disasters and the spread of infectious diseases. It also attempts to validate, through the case study of

Mozambique, that "adaptive mediation" is more effective than standard mediation approaches in complex and recurring armed conflicts. After initial failed mediation attempts by domestic mediators that favored more assertive mediation techniques, the mediation process welcomed high-level international mediation and a large group of external mediators. They focused on determined-designed mediation techniques that excessively dominated the mediation agenda, leading both parties to look for a new paradigm in terms of peace negotiations in Mozambique. Thus, the final mediation stage of the recent Mozambican peace process was flexible, adaptive, and pragmatic in style, addressing the failures and ineffectiveness of previous mediation endeavors. The mediators concentrated on encouraging the self-organization of both parties and ensuring national ownership of the peace process. They accomplished a new peace agreement in August 2019 by facilitating direct negotiations between the two main parties' leaders, as well as incorporating representatives from both parties in the mediation team. An adaptive mediation strategy established an enabling environment for Mozambicans on both sides of the conflict to genuinely collaborate in developing a long-term pathway to peace.

This study is the result of fieldwork conducted in Mozambique, between January and February 2020, employing methods such as semi-structured interviews and participant observation, initially meant to cover the reformulation of peacebuilding programs after the signature of the 2019 MAPR, but opening an avenue of research on peacemaking initiatives that led to the signature of the new peace agreement.[3] In addition, content analysis of online news coverage between 2012 and 2019 (mainly in Portuguese) and discourse analysis of the main stakeholders involved in the peace process shed light on formal and informal mediation activities that sustained significant peace gains and offered new pathways for peace in Mozambique.

[3] Previous data collection, between March and August 2015, in Maputo, Mozambique, was supported by the Japan Society for the Promotion of Science's Africa *Zuno-Junkan* Program. The author would like to thank Prof. Toshiya Hoshino and Prof. Virgil Hawkins' support and guidance at Osaka University.

Domestic Mediation Without External Process Facilitation

Between April 2013 and August 2015, 114 rounds of talks between RENAMO and the Mozambican government—led by the president at the time, Armando Guebuza—were facilitated by five mediators, four of them related to religious organizations and one from academia (Mozambique Information Agency 2015). At this point, Afonso Dhlakama, the RENAMO leader, retired to an uncertain location in the Gorongosa Mountains in Sofala province. RENAMO's initial requirement as of the eighth round of negotiations was for external international mediators to join the process, including the former South African president, Thabo Mbeki, the Italian bishop, Dom Matteo Zuppi, and other key figures from the United Nations (UN), the Southern African Development Community (SADC), the European Union (EU), the African Union (AU), and the US. However, RENAMO gave in to Guebuza's preference to keep external involvement aside and relied on five domestic facilitators: (1) the Catholic priest Fr. Felipe Couto, (2) the Anglican Bishop Dinis Sengulane, (3) the Methodist Pastor Anastácio Chembeze, (4) the Muslim cleric Sheikh Saide Habibo, and (5) the academic Lourenço do Rosário. They formally joined the mediation process at the 33rd round of negotiations in Maputo on February 12, 2014 (Mozambique Media Online 2013; MediaFax News 2014).

The five mediators often shared their vision for the peace negotiations during their interactions with the media. The dean of the Polytechnic University in Maputo, Lourenço do Rosário, highlighted the need to address the failed disarmament and reintegration of RENAMO men in the Mozambican armed forces (*Forças Armadas de Defesa de Moçambique* (FADM) and in the police (*Polícia da República de Moçambique* (PRM)). Together with decentralization, this was a policy issue that has not been addressed effectively by peacebuilding programs during the past 20 years. On the other hand, Rosário's position on revising the electoral law was that this was an issue to be addressed in the parliament, implying that this was not necessarily a priority of the mediation process (Carlos 2013).

Dinis Sengulane, the Anglican bishop for the region of Pequeno Limbobo, was previously involved in the 1989 Nairobi negotiations that preceded the 1992 Rome Peace Process. He often collected relevant inputs for the mediation process from Sofala and other provinces with strong RENAMO influence. Sengulane's vision for peace rested on three main pillars: (1) engaging in formal and informal dialogue, (2) addressing issues of social character, and (3) progressively eliminating the instruments of war while recognizing that there is still a long way toward sustainable peace in Mozambique (Silva 2015, 113).

The Methodist minister Anastacio Chembeze, besides becoming one of the five domestic mediators, was appointed as the interim executive director of the Mozambican Electoral Observatory (MEO) to ensure an adequate monitoring of the October 15, 2014, elections. Chembeze was trained at the Mozambican peacebuilding NGO Justa Paz, created after the 1992 GPA, and at a sister institute, the Africa Peacebuilding Institute, located at the time in Mindolo, Zambia (Lofton 2014). The MEO was a coalition of religious and civil society groups that have been monitoring the elections since 2003. The members of the coalition included a vast number of observers and experiences rooted in local perspectives. In November 2013, the MEO observed municipal elections in Mozambique and later deployed 742 observers for the 2014 census (Hanlon 2014).

One of the main representatives of the Muslim community in Mozambique, Sheik Saide Habibo, underlined his intention to work with people in good faith to promote harmony and social, spiritual, and economic well-being for all Mozambicans in order to maintain long-term peace in the country. He added that peace actions should not be limited to national reconciliation but should also include activities to continuously promote ethics in civil society. As part of his mediation style and peace vision, Habibo supported the creation of the "Religious Network for Reconciliation and Peace," a group of religious nongovernmental organizations that intended to support the realization of free, fair, and transparent elections in Mozambique. All five mediators would engage with various initiatives that directly or indirectly supported the peace process, since peace in Mozambique was conceived in the mediators' mind to be a national project in which everyone should have the opportunity to participate (Horizonte 2014, 6; Jornal de Notícias Newspaper 2014).

The five domestic mediators received support from the Center for Humanitarian Dialogue (HD), an NGO based in Geneva, Switzerland, which provided technical know-how. The HD organized training retreats to support the national mediators' skills in strategic thinking and communication. The HD also organized a religious leaders' forum to promote a broader dialogue about reconciliation throughout Mozambique (Centre for Humanitarian Dialogue 2016, 10). Subsequently, the mediation agenda in this first stage of the peace process highlighted four main issues:

First, the focus on reforming the electoral system resulted in changes to the electoral law and allowed for political nominations and party control over electoral bodies. Despite these changes, RENAMO was unable to offer qualified staff to facilitate the election process for the 2014 national elections, which resulted in the relative failure of these negotiations. Second, the process highlighted security and defense issues, which led to the signing of an agreement to end hostilities. The 2014 CMHA represented another formal attempt to reintegrate RENAMO members into the Mozambican Armed Forces and the Police. Third, the mediators also attempted to draw attention to issues such as the state's politicization and, fourth, to the need for equal redistribution of wealth (Bertolaso-Krippahl 2013).

The 2014 CMHA established a Team of Military International Observers on the Cessation of Military Hostilities (*Equipa de Observação da Cessação das Hostilidades Militares* (EMOCHM) with 23 foreign military officers[4] and 70 Mozambican officers[5] to monitor the process of disarmament and the social reintegration of RENAMO's residual forces (Government of Mozambique 2014). The work of the EMOCHM required the Mozambican government to spend more than 540.2 million Mozambican meticais to cover expenditures related to the monitoring mission, that is, accommodation, food, subsidies and allowances, consumables, fuels, communication equipment, training, and so on. The EMOCHM purchased a total of 59 vehicles and additional materials to accommodate the residual forces including tents, beds, lockers, generators, water tanks, stoves, refrigerators, and kitchen and bathroom supplies. The allocated budget was also spent on the salaries of international and national observers (Folha de Maputo Newspaper 2015). However, the mission was considered both ineffective and costly, as 20 percent of the reintegration budget was allocated alone for the needs of the EMOCHM. In the end, the Mozambican government was uncomfortable with the idea of external observers monitoring what was understood as a strictly "domestic" problem and, therefore, a problem that could be solved without the involvement of foreigners (Jornal Notícias Newspaper 2015).

In 2015, with the election of a new Mozambican president, Filipe Nyusi, the mediation process progressed with two rounds of bilateral talks

[4] From Botswana, Zimbabwe, South Africa, Kenya, Cape Green, Portugal, Italy, Great Britain, and the US.

[5] Half from RENAMO and the other half from the FRELIMO government.

between Nyusi and Dhlakama. In April 2015, the meetings between both leaders resulted in the draft of a new law on autonomous provincial governments, which would be later rejected by the parliament. In July 2015, a constitutional amendment concerning the revision on provincial governors' appointment was submitted by RENAMO, but it would also be rejected in the parliament. As the FRELIMO majority in the parliament kept politically sanctioning the result of the negotiations between both leaders, RENAMO would resort again to armed violence, with several attacks occurring mainly in the Tete province. In response, on September 25, 2015, Afonso Dhlakama saw his residence in Beira invaded by the Rapid Intervention Unit (*Unidade de Intervenção Rápida* (UIR)) and the Special Operations Group (*Grupo de Operações Especiais* (GOE)) of the PRM. Behind the scenes, the domestic mediators and Dhlakama's close advisers worked to schedule a meeting between Nyusi and Dhlakama. The mediators were able to persuade the RENAMO leader to leave his hideout and travel to Beira with them and a group of journalists on October 8, 2015. Dhlakama's home in Beira, however, was attacked the next day in a large military operation, his bodyguards were detained, disarmed, and only subsequently released, and the opposition leader was placed under house arrest. As a result, Dhlakama retook refuge in the Gorongosa Mountains, completely withdrawing from the mediation structure with no intention of negotiating with Mozambique's government (Botequilha 2015).

The trust between the five mediators and Dhlakama was severely weakened following the October 8 incident. This operation not only undermined confidence in the national mediators but also led to an abrupt interruption of the 2014 CMHA. A new cycle of uncertainty and military confrontation began, at a time when the country could hardly afford another conflict and the 2014 CMHA had lost its raison d'être. According to Maria Ivone Soares, the head of RENAMO's parliamentary group at the time, the main conditions for RENAMO to resume high-level talks with the Nyusi government were the inclusion of new mediators and a clearer mediation agenda that would allow the negotiation of issues related to autonomous provinces (Weimer and Carrilho 2017, 129–30). Accordingly, RENAMO requested the domestic mediators' removal, arguing that the Catholic Church and the South African president Jacob Zuma should assume the role of mediators instead (Júnior 2015). As a response, the five mediators underlined that their role in the political dialogue had been minimal since mid-2015. From that moment in time, the direct involvement of the domestic mediators in the peace process became more difficult due to dynamics resulting from an administration change. FRELIMO had become divided between the "hardliners" supporting Guebuza's confrontational approach and the "softliners" welcoming Nyusi's policy of direct dialogue promotion (The Economist 2015).

The five mediators highlighted that one of the main causes for the failure of the peace negotiations was the ineffectiveness of the EMOCHM. However, speaking on behalf of the mediators, Fr. Filipe Couto argued that only two people would have the solutions to overcome the remaining challenges, that is, both Nyusi and Dhlakama. As a way to seal the conclusion of this mediation stage, President Nyusi publicly criticized "the intermediaries who, due to the importance they have intended to gain in the dialogue process, sometimes they have not faithfully transmitted the messages of both parties" (Filipe Nyusi in Matias 2015). It was not confirmed whether Nyusi was referring to the five mediators or other mediation team members; however, this statement confirmed that both parties believed the mediation structure and strategy would have to change to become more effective.

The domestic faith-based and civil society mediation structure without external process facilitation allowed for 114 negotiation sessions at the Joaquim Chissano Conference Center in Maputo. The mediation strategy was sufficient to achieve an amnesty law, followed by the 2014 CMHA and a new electoral law that enabled national elections in 2014 without much objection from RENAMO before the voting took place. However, this stage of the mediation process was not effective enough to avoid further conflict recurrence, and it failed to address grievances that had remained since the signature of the 1992 GPA. In October 2015, Lourenço do Rosário suggested that the disagreement between politicians and the military created obstacles to the negotiations. In addition, both RENAMO and FRELIMO remained internally divided between "doves" and "hawks," that is, one faction looking for military confrontation (hawks) and the other political dialogue (doves) (Weimer and Carrilho 2017, 156).

Despite the good offices and the genuine commitment of the five national meditators, given the above context, this mediation structure was unable to adapt to a complex environment and emerging uncertainties. The trust was lost between both parties and the mediators because of the impact caused by several key events: the failure of the 2014 CMHA, the ineffectiveness of the EMOCHM, claims of fraud in the 2014 elections, and various police and military operations threatening Dhlakama's life and safety. The mediation team also could not effectively build trust with the new Mozambican administration and find solutions to address the divide between Gebuza's and Nyusi's supporters inside FRELIMO. Finally, this mediation structure confirmed that domestic solutions without external process facilitation might result in significant deadlocks and the peace process's breakdown. As mentioned by De Coning (Chap. 2), "External influence has many advantages, including bringing leverage, encouraging accountability, opening political space, and encouraging more inclusive processes." However, instead of opting for external facilitation of direct dialogue, both parties first sought an external solution focused on a standard international mediation structure, which turned out to be determined-designed in nature instead of adaptive to an increasingly complex environment. In this stage, the peace process was handed over to external mediators in the hopes that both sides would agree on a version of the solutions they would design, leaving an excessive amount of deliberation and agenda-setting power in the hands of international mediators.

Standard High-Level International Mediation

President Nyusi has consistently aspired for continued dialogue with Dhlakama and aimed at holding the third round of talks with a new mediation team. In May 2016, the RENAMO leader agreed to discuss how to reestablish formal negotiations with the government. In this regard, a "Joint Commission"[6] was formed in Maputo, initially preparing the meetings between both leaders within a four-point agenda to guide the formal negotiations. Each party selected two of these four items for the mediation agenda: (1) the decentralization and provincial autonomy of six provinces, and appointment of governors by RENAMO; (2) the end of military

[6] FRELIMO members: Jacinto Veloso (former minister of security); Alfredo Gamito (former minister of state administration and former member of parliament); Benvinda Levy (former minister of justice); Alves Muteque (president's office); António Boene (lawyer); and Eduardo Chiziane (professor of law, University Eduardo Mondlane). RENAMO members: José Butters (member of parliament); Jeremiah Pondeca (former member of parliament); André Magibire (member of parliament); Eduardo Namburete (member of parliament, professor of communication sciences, University Eduardo Mondlane); Maria Joaquina Inácio (party's senior staff); Leovilgildo Buanancasso (Council of State). Both FRELIMO and RENAMO nominated the international mediators who would later integrate the "Joint Commission."

hostilities; (3) the disarmament of RENAMO' combatants; and (4) the integration of RENAMO unarmed soldiers in the FADM, the PRM, and the Mozambique's State Security and Intelligence Services (*Serviços de Informação e Segurança do Estado* (SISE) (Vines 2019, 19).

The Mozambican government started by sending requests to the European Union (EU), the Catholic Church, and South Africa to join the new mediation team. Nyusi and Dhlakama reinforced the idea that, at this point, the way forward in the mediation process would be to seek international mediation, as this was the successful mediation strategy that led to the 1992 GPA (Lusa News Agency 2016c). The Mozambican government nominated the following mediators: Ketumile Masire, former president of Botswana, linked to the Global Leadership Foundation (GLF), along with Robin Christopher; Jakaya Kikwete, former president of Tanzania, represented by Ibrahim Msambaho; and the African Governance Initiative (AGI), linked to former British prime minister Tony Blair, represented by Jonathan Powell of InterMediate (UK). RENAMO appointed three mediators, namely the EU, which was represented by Mario Raffaelli (former mediator in the 1992 peace process) and Monsignor Ângelo Romano (Community of Sant'Egidio); the Vatican, represented by the Apostolic Nuncio in Maputo, Monsignor Edgar Pena, and the secretary of the Episcopal Conference of Mozambique, Auxiliary Bishop of Maputo, Dom João Carlos Hatoa Nunes; and the South African president Jacob Zuma, represented by Mandlenkosi Memelo and George Johannes of the Ministry of Foreign Affairs. Forty-seven sessions of negotiations were held by the Joint Commission and the international mediators in the five-star "Avenida Hotel" in Maputo (Reis 2017; Lusa News Agency 2016b; Hanlon 2016; Weimer and Carrilho 2017, 137).

By August 2016, the international mediation team's leader, Mario Raffaelli (representing the EU), noted the lack of immediate progress, as both parties were just "discussing … discussing … discussing" with no practical achievement, denoting an environment of extreme uncertainty after few rounds of international mediation. The head of the RENAMO's delegation at the time, José Manteigas, mentioned that one of the most contentious issues on the negotiation table was the appointment of RENAMO provincial governors in six provinces. In this context, the international mediation team decided to set up two subcommittees. One would prepare a legislative package on decentralization to be ready before the 2019 elections, and the other would focus on military issues (Matias 2016).

The work of the decentralization subcommittee was extensive. It aimed at supporting the process of revising the Mozambican Constitution and a number of different laws: (1) the law related to the reform of the state, (2) the law on provincial assemblies, (3) the basic law of the organization and functioning of public administration, (4) the law empowering local district authorities, (5) and the approval of the law of governing bodies and the (6) law of provincial funding. This set of new laws was meant to pave the way for a peaceful electoral process. However, the timing of this ambitious decentralization agenda was not ripe for a concrete agreement between both parties. RENAMO submitted a reform package to the subcommittee, but the lack of internal party consensus resulted in the failure of FRELIMO to submit a complimentary or alternative proposal to the Joint Commission. Therefore, the package of legal revisions mentioned above was not welcomed in all FRELIMO circles (Lusa News Agency 2016d).

Another challenge to this mediation framework was the lack of coordination between the two subcommittees on matters related to procedures, contents, and calendars, as well as the large presence of mediators, many of them non-Portuguese speakers, which slowed the progress of the negotiations. Finally, the exclusion of civil society organizations from the mediation process, including the third major party in the Mozambican parliament, the Democratic Movement of Mozambique (*Movimento Democrático de Moçambique* (MDM)), did not allow for an alternative, more open format of negotiations, for example through the creation of national committee for the revision of the constitution (Weimer and Carrilho 2017, 138–39). As the subcommittee's work was being developed, an escalation of attacks took place, possibly a strategy by RENAMO to strengthen its position during the negotiations (Fabricius 2016). This event hindered the negotiations between both parties, proving that some mediation initiatives might, in fact, result in more violence instead of more positive outcomes.

The next step suggested by the international mediation team was to seek an immediate ceasefire and to create a demilitarized corridor that would allow the mediators to meet with Afonso Dhlakama. Subsequently, a specific working group and the mediators would attempt to establish the conditions for a permanent ceasefire. Once both parties respected the suspension of hostilities and all types of violence, the working group would submit a new timetable to the joint commission to continue with the peace process (Lusa News Agency 2016a). In addition to working toward a ceasefire agreement, the international mediation team introduced a new draft proposal on decentralization in October 2016. The mediators attempted to harmonize the document as much as possible, including both parties' demands, but they could not reach a final draft by the November 2016 deadline to submit the document to the Mozambican parliament ("O Século de Joanesburgo" Newspaper 2016). At this point, Mario Raffaelli changed his mediation strategy. Instead of negotiating new decentralization laws with both parties, the mediator sought to reach a negotiated agreement on the general principles of decentralization reform and leave it to the Parliament to transform it into law. This change in method was not very well received by the FRELIMO leadership, who felt that the Mozambican head of state and the RENAMO leader were being ignored in the process and that too much power was left in the hands of international mediators (Weimer and Carrilho 2017, 139).

As the issue of decentralization became the most contentious in this mediation stage, Nyusi stressed the need to create a specialized working group to discuss the decentralization package without political distinction or the international mediators' presence. The Joint Commission's work would end in December 2016 without any agreement on the decentralization package, and the international mediators abandoned Maputo, saying that they would only return if requested again by both parties (Lusa News Agency 2016d). Although it was impossible to meet RENAMO's requirement to govern in six provinces, the mediation style implemented by the international mediation team paved the way for the revision of the constitution on matters related to decentralization and provincial elections. However, the timing and conditions were also met for a rapprochement between Nyusi and Dhlakama.

After more than 200 rounds of negotiation, both Mozambican leaders surprisingly decided to engage in direct dialogue, abandon the high-level international mediation structure, and permanently dissolve the joint commission (Vines 2019, 20–21). This decision stands out as a clear example of local resilience, with both parties reclaiming ownership of the peace process through an adaptive approach. In this case, it is possible to argue that ineffectiveness was found in the standard international mediation structure, and effectiveness was found instead in the adaptiveness, resilience, and self-organization capacity of both FRELIMO and RENAMO, which, as demonstrated by complexity theory, are components of a complex system that is ever evolving.

During this stage of the mediation process, external mediators failed to effectively recognize the Mozambican context and its complexity, unpredictability, and uncertainty. Both leaderships acknowledged that there was not enough motivation for international mediators to reach an effective agreement, as they earned expensive salaries, and through dozens of meetings attempted to justify their efforts without any practical achievements. Both Dhlakama and Nyusi became increasingly frustrated by the intrigues within their negotiating teams. Some felt that the international mediators who had been involved with the 1992 GPA and returned as mediators in 2016 were too concerned with protecting the legacy of the Rome agreement and exposed their opinions in an excessively public way (Reis 2019a; Civil Society Source 3 2020). The 1992 GPA mediation formula was based on the role of international mediators in supporting confidence-building between both parties and conducting effective power diplomacy. In fact, it was power diplomacy that guaranteed that political arrangements under the GPA were not imprecise or broadly undefined and ensured that enough political and economic incentives were provided to promote a democratic system in the context of a newly emerging post–Cold War liberal order. Third parties, superpowers, and international and bilateral donors, were willing to provide assistance and shoulder the necessary expenditures, allowing consensus to be formed and maintained for the implementation of the 1992 GPA (Gentili 2013). However, a standard high-level international mediation formula 20 years later, and under a different systemic and domestic context, would be condemned to remain ineffective.

As a result of the determined-designed process and directed-mediation employed by international mediators, the leaders of both parties decided to talk directly over the phone, something that had never happened in recent Mozambican history. Also, over the phone, both leaders agreed that a mediation model with a "long table" of negotiation and with many external mediators would not lead to an effective mediation outcome. At this point, both parties understood their interdependence and the importance of collaborating to reach a mutually acceptable agreement. Both Nyusi and Dhlakama hoped for a mediation framework that would foster a process through which the content of the agreements comes from within rather than from excessive input from external mediators or an external normative framework. Therefore, there was an increased perception among the Mozambican political elites that the pathway for a successful agreement would arise instead through direct dialogue between the leaders of both parties supported by an adaptive mediation model that would not be heavily influenced by external interests, predetermined international standards, or the history and examples of past negotiations.

Adaptive Mediation as Process-Facilitation of Direct Dialogue

Beginning in December 2016, a small mediation team of four members was led by the Swiss ambassador to Mozambique, Mirko Manzoni. The other team members were Neha Sanghrajka, mediation advisor at the Centre for Humanitarian Dialogue; Jonathan Powell, director at Inter Mediate; and Eduardo Namburete, senior lecturer at Eduardo Mondlane University and member of parliament for RENAMO between 2005 and 2010 (Reis 2019b). This mediation team focused on facilitating direct dialogue between the Mozambican government and RENAMO, while promoting both parties' self-organization and resilience and responding in adaptive ways to the challenges that arose during the negotiations. More importantly, this mediation style was not conditioned by past 1992 GPA mediation practices, and it was fully committed to a nationally owned peace process.

The new stage of negotiations highlighted issues related to power-sharing, decentralization, and the demobilization and reintegration of RENAMO residual armed forces. Many RENAMO combatants and former combatants continued to demand further reintegration in the armed and police forces, generating a continuous climate of tension between both parties. RENAMO also highlighted the need for reintegration in the SISE and the need for equal redistribution of revenue from natural resources, as one of the world's largest gas reserves was discovered in Mozambique in 2012 (Academia Source #2; Academia Source #3).

After President Nyusi requested Manzoni to become the lead mediator of the peace process, the first challenge was to travel to the mountainous region of Gorongosa to meet with Dhlakama. Manzoni underlined that this implied not staying in five-star hotels but instead in the middle of the forest or the bushes. Maputo's journey to Gorongosa spanned over 1000 km and required taking several flights, riding four-wheel vehicles and bikes, and simply walking for long periods of time (Crawford 2019). Showing this level of effort was an important step to build trust with the RENAMO leader. Manzoni explained the genuine efforts of the small mediation team in this key initial moment of this mediation stage: "The rebels always came to pick us up on foot in the same place, but then we never took the same path. We had to hurry to have a few hours of discussions and be back in the jeep before dark. At first, I thought that Dhlakama would end up coming to Maputo. (…) This has never happened, and we have been to the Gorogonsa mountains 35 times" (Petite 2020).

Besides the immediate positive impact of new mediation methods and a new strategy, the peace process was mainly centered on the direct communication between the two leaders, first via phone and at a later stage meeting in person. Direct dialogue emphasized the idea that the peace process needed more Mozambican control and to emerge from within instead of from the outside. Therefore, the mediation team's initial stance was to focus on working as process facilitators of a direct and continuous dialogue between the two Mozambican leaders. The rapprochement between both leaders and the new mediation model quickly resulted in a ceasefire announced in December 2016. This ceasefire lasted initially for one week, then another 60 days after that, followed by another month, and then was extended permanently and without a deadline. This initial achievement allowed the two leaders to speak face to face in August 2017. The fact that President Nyusi traveled to the Gorongosa Mountains to meet Dhlakama was a clear sign of reconciliation and that the peace process was now in the hands of both leaders. As a result, the Manzoni mediation team and related mediation outputs were well evaluated by the two parties, who underlined the effectiveness and discretion of the mediators, as well as the ability to create an environment of trust (Reis 2019b). According to Manzoni, the small size of the mediation team and the soft skills of the mediators, such as discretion and humility, were fundamental to the effectiveness of the mediation process (Crawford 2019). In this regard, Manzoni said, "the peace process was deadlocked, and I believe the government appreciated my discretion. When I had criticisms, I communicated directly to those concerned rather than giving paternalistic lessons in the media" (Petite 2020).

After consultations with the RENAMO leader, President Nyusi announced on February 3, 2017,[7] the redefinition of the mediation architecture, based on the regular contact and coordination of procedures and

[7] On February 3, the Day of Mozambican Heroes, Mozambique commemorates the thousands who fought and died in the country's independence war against Portugal. The date is based on the assassination of Eduardo Mondlane, a prominent independence leader in the country's history.

the monitoring of progress between the Mozambican head of state and the RENAMO leader, leading to a much greater degree of trust-building. The mediation team expanded the architecture of the peace process by establishing two working groups of six people each: one working on decentralization and the other on military issues (i.e., disarmament, demobilization, and reintegration). In May 2017, an eight-person "Monitoring and Evaluation Team" was established and mandated to monitor the ceasefire. Additionally, on March 6, 2017, the Swiss ambassador established a "Contact Group" with six other ambassadors from the US (the co-chair), Botswana, China, the EU, Norway, and the UK. The Contact Group avoided the pitfalls of the previous international mediation stage, and these external stakeholders were able to gain both parties' trust due to Manzoni's focus on fostering direct dialogue with an attitude of discretion and encouraging the same within the structure of the Contact Group (Vines 2019, 21).

The progress of the negotiations continued during the second half of 2017. Nyusi confirmed that the mediation process would remain centered on four key points: (1) regular contacts between top leaders; (2) the work of two technical working committees on decentralization and military issues; (3) the supervision provided by the international contact group; and (4) information sessions with other Mozambican political parties and the public in general. In February 2018, Nyusi and Dhlakama met for a second time in central Mozambique. At this meeting, both leaders welcomed the reports elaborated by the working committees, and later Nyusi publicly announced the submission of a new draft law on decentralization to the Mozambican parliament, with the consensus of both leaders resulting from the direct dialogue initiative (Institute for Multiparty Democracy 2019, 2–3).

Unexpectedly Dhlakama passed away on May 3, 2018, due to complications related to diabetes. The RENAMO leader's unforeseen demise resulted in a significant setback for a peace process that was at last on the road toward a final agreement. Manzoni and the mediation team were unexpectedly shaken by his death, which represented the height of complexity and uncertainty in an already-fragile peace process. In Manzoni's own words, this event was a "mediation blackhole": "When after more than two years of negotiation he died, honestly it was a blackhole as if everything was lost. Even now, I feel the emotion, because he was a strong man, and you could not expect him dying like that" (Mirko Manzoni in Crawford 2019). The negotiations stalled for months as RENAMO adjusted to the loss of its leadership and prepared to choose a successor. Shortly after that, Ossufo Momade, a former lieutenant general (until 1992) and secretary-general of RENAMO (between 2005 and 2012), became the interim leader of RENAMO and was later elected as the effective leader at a party congress on January 17, 2019 (Henriques 2019).

RENAMO's leadership transition significantly delayed the pace of negotiations, caused in part by Momade's refuge in a safe haven in Gorongosa and the emergence of internal disputes inside RENAMO after Dhlakama's death. As a result of the mediation team's effort, Momade met with Nyusi for the first time in the city of Beira on July 11, 2018, which allowed for the continuation of previous negotiations and paved the way for the signing of an important Memorandum of Understanding (MoU) on military issues in August 2018. The MoU represented an essential milestone in the peace process and the achievement of a clear consensus between both parties on DDR issues. Immediately after that, the mediation team and both parties created an institutional framework with four bodies to support the MoU's implementation: (1) the Military Affairs Commission with six members; (2) the Joint Technical Framework Group (*Grupo Técnico Conjunto de Enquadramento* (GTCE)) with four members; (3) the Joint Technical Group for Disarmament Demobilization and Reintegration (*Grupo Técnico Conjunto de Desarmamento, Desmobilização e Reintegração* (GTCDDR)) with six members; and (4) the Monitoring and Verification Group (*Grupo de Monitoria e Verificação* (GMV)) with eight members (Institute for Multiparty Democracy 2019, 4). The latter included an additional international team made up of senior military advisers that would provide technical assistance and ensure the DDR process's credibility. The nine international observers were appointed by Germany, India, Ireland, Norway, Switzerland, Tanzania, the US, and Zimbabwe and were led by Javier Antonio Pérez Aquino, an Argentinian expert on DDR issues in Colombia (Forquilha 2020, 73).

The 2018 MoU broke the deadlock on military issues and fostered decisive steps toward reaching a new peace agreement. The process facilitation of direct dialogue continued with two rounds of direct talks between Nyusi and Momade in early 2019. In March 2019, Cyclone Idai caused extensive damage, killing several people in Mozambique. This event indirectly impacted the negotiations. The two conflicting parties took this key moment to demonstrate national unity, offering a sign of hope that it was still possible to reach an agreement during these challenging times. This is also the case with the national unity in Mozambique to address the Islamic insurgency in the north of the country. The mediators identified these aspects as a significant change in the mindset of both conflicting parties, which were then making national interest a priority (Jaberg 2019). Subsequently, in June 2019, another meeting between the two leaders took place in Chimoio, in Manica province, during which they provisionally agreed to a definitive peace agreement (Vines 2019, 22).

The MAPR was signed on August 6, 2019, by the Mozambican president and FRELIMO leader, Filipe Nyusi, and by the RENAMO leader, Ossufo Momade. Two weeks later, on August 21, 2019, the agreement was cast into legislation by the Parliament, with 236 votes in favor and 14 abstentions from the smallest opposition party, the MDM. Both parties described this as being the final in a series of three agreements. The first agreement was the GPA signed in Rome on October 4, 1992, by President Joaquim Chissano and the late RENAMO leader, Afonso Dhlakama, which ended 16 long years of civil war between FRELIMO and RENAMO. The second was the CMHA, signed on September 5, 2014, by President Armando Guebuza and Dhlakama, which ended temporarily the armed conflict that had resurged in 2012, allowing for the October 2014 general elections. The new peace agreement attempts to address two critical issues that had failed after more than 20 years of the 1992 GPA implementation: the demobilization and reintegration of RENAMO fighters and the decentralization of political power in Mozambique. The new agreement represents a new milestone for peace and reconciliation. However, uncertainty and peacebuilding challenges remain in Mozambique.

The results of the 2019 national elections in Mozambique and the related post-electoral violence confirm that issues related to DDR, decentralization, and power-sharing remain to be addressed and that volatility and uncertainty remain on the Mozambican horizon. Besides, at the time of writing, the division of RENAMO into two groups, the political branch led by Ossufo Momade and the "Military Junta" led by Mariano Nhongo, is threatening to destabilize the implementation of the peace agreement. As Manzoni (Radio Télévision Suisse 2019) highlighted, providing support for the implementation of the peace accord is as important as reaching the peace accord, as well as having the UN and all the international cooperation partners' support to achieve definitive peace in Mozambique. Despite the remaining peacebuilding challenges, peacemaking gains were possible due to the pragmatism and adaptive approach of the mediation team led by Manzoni, from which it is possible to highlight some lessons learned: "We should try to learn from what was done. I think it can be replicated because it was done in a very simple manner, not with big machinery, just a lot of goodwill. (...) We remained very discreet until the very last minute, and this was one of the keys to the success of the process" (Mirko Manzoni in Crawford 2019).

Neha Sanghrajka, a former chief mediator of the Kenyan peace process in 2007 and a member of the mediation team led by Manzoni, also underlined that Mozambique offers many lessons for other peacemakers and peacebuilders involved in contemporary armed conflicts. Sanghrajka mentioned that the last stage of the mediation process was all about "national ownership," when in other "standard" styles of mediation, this concept is often not internalized by international mediators. One of the main points of learning from the Mozambican process was that peace could never be imposed from the outside, but instead must be led by the people of the affected country. In contrast to the usual emphasis by external mediators on statistics, numbers, and indexes, effective mediation processes should be nationally and locally inclusive, incorporating local perspectives as much as possible: "Peace is not just log frames, indicators, words on a piece of paper. It is actually the combatant who is worried that his child will not recognize him after such a long war. It is the woman that cannot do business on the side of the road because there is a conflict" (Neha Sanghrajka in Chatham House 2020).

In terms of national ownership of the peace process, both parties should be acknowledged as the main key actors and stakeholders. Amid the uncertainty generated by its historical leader's sudden death, RENAMO remained firmly committed to achieving peace rather than resorting to violence. Besides, the Mozambican government also had a vital role in the mediation process's most uncertain moment. Filipe Nyusi, the Mozambican president, was present at Dhlakama's funeral in Beira and delivered a eulogy recognizing the historical importance of Dhlakama for peace in Mozambique, generating a spontaneous moment of reconciliation on that occasion. Finally, it is important to note that all working teams involved during the last mediation stage were composed by Mozambicans from both sides of the conflict. They excelled working together and with the mediators during the negotiations: "It was this silent unity and resilience of the Mozambican people themselves that really pushed this process forward. We (the mediators) were just lucky to be able to help in whatever way we could" (Neha Sanghrajka in Chatham House 2020).

Conclusion

Addressing the failures and ineffectiveness of previous peace negotiations, the final round of the new Mozambican mediation process was adaptive and pragmatic in style. It privileged the process facilitation of direct dialogue between both parties—the Mozambican government and RENAMO—in the context of a nationally owned peace process. This effective style of mediation was focused on three main pillars: (1) self-organization and national ownership, which put the leaders of both parties and many Mozambicans from both sides at the center of the architecture of negotiations, to work together during the peace process; (2) an understanding of mediation as a synonym of process facilitation, with a small mediation team of four members working discretely and unassumingly amid challenging conditions; (3) an adaptive and pragmatic approach that enabled the mediators to deal more effectively with complexity and uncertainty during the negotiations, for example the sudden death of RENAMO's leader. An adaptive mediation structure, style, and methods allowed first for a permanent ceasefire in 2017, which led to the signature of the 2018 MoU on military affairs and, finally, the Maputo Accord for Peace and Reconciliation in 2019.

This case seems to indicate that in contemporary complex and recurrent armed conflicts, the effectiveness of the mediation process depends first on the resilience and adaptiveness of both parties in the conflict, as well as the local communities and all domestic stakeholders involved in the peace process. Second, it also depends largely on the mediators' mindset and the ability of the external mediators to listen to domestic actors while focusing on understanding the culture and context of the conflict-affected situation. A mindset of discretion and humility, and a smaller number of external mediators involved in the peace process, contributes to building trust among all parties. Third, when this mindset is allied to a pragmatic and adaptive approach, this will enable the mediators to face complex and uncertain environments more effectively.

In the Mozambican case, the collected data revealed that through an adaptive process facilitation of direct dialogue, both parties decided to pursue a peaceful resolution to the recurrence of conflict instead of resorting to violence. Dhlakama's sudden death was the most unexpected event occurring during the negotiations, but this "mediation blackhole" was mitigated by the adaptive approach of the mediation team and both parties. There is enough evidence to confirm that the most effective mediation structure has emerged from within Mozambique, that is, from adaptive process facilitation of direct dialogue between both leaders instead of an externally determined-designed mediation initiative. Therefore, the implementation of the 2019 MAPR and related peacebuilding actions should also remain nationally owned and adaptive in nature while adequately supported by international cooperation partners. After the signature of the new peace agreement in 2019, Mirko Manzoni was appointed as the personal envoy of the UN secretary-general for Mozambique. The personal envoy's primary function is to deepen the dialogue between the Mozambican government and RENAMO and assist in implementing the MAPR. Using an adaptive approach applied to peacebuilding, Manzoni and both parties have made significant progress in consolidating early gains by advancing DDR activities first and expecting to progress on decentralization and reconciliation later. However, the post-conflict peacebuilding environment presents relevant implementation challenges, and peacebuilders should be careful to avoid past mistakes and strive to continue operating under a peacebuilding framework focused on flexibility, adaptiveness, and institutional learning.

At the time of writing, Mozambique continues to face an ongoing conflict in Cabo Delgado with extreme violence perpetrated by armed non-state actors. In addition, RENAMO's Military Junta, led by Mariano Nhongo, might resort to violence if better conditions for reintegration are not met during the implementation of the 2019 MAPR. Finally, the impact of climate change, frequent natural disasters, and the spread of infectious diseases, such as the SARS-CoV-2, might aggravate the fragility of the Mozambican context. Therefore, adaptive mediation and adaptive peacebuilding should be seen as an ongoing process and a long-term endeavor in Mozambique. Mediators and peacebuilders should continue to promote the self-organization and resilience of Mozambique's society through adaptive, pragmatic, and context-specific peace initiatives in order to effectively address emerging new peace threats, risks, and challenges, and ultimately sustain peace in Mozambique.

References

Academia Source 1. 2020. Interviewed by Rui Saraiva in Maputo, Mozambique.

Academia Source 2. 2020. Interviewed by Rui Saraiva in Maputo, Mozambique.

ACLED. 2021. Cabo Ligado Weekly: 15–21 February 2021. February 24. https://acleddata.com/2021/02/23/cabo-ligado-weekly-15-21-february-2021/.

Bertolaso-Krippahl, Cristina. 2013. *Governo moçambicano propõe novas conversações à RENAMO [Mozambican Government Proposes New Talks to RENAMO]*. Deutsche Welle. https://www.dw.com/pt-002/governo-mo%C3%A7ambicano-prop%C3%B5e-novas-conversa%C3%A7%C3%B5es-%C3%A0-renamo/av-17184308.

Botequilha, Henrique. 2015. *Polícia invade casa de Dhlakama na Beira [The Police Invades Dhlakama's House in Beira]*. Diário de Notícias. https://www.dn.pt/mundo/policia-invade-casa-de-dhlakama-na-beira-4825406.html.

Carlos, João. 2013. *Moçambique ainda não vive 'cenário de guerra civil', assegura mediador [Mozambique Still Does Not Live 'Civil War Scenario', Says Mediator]*. Deutsche Welle. https://www.dw.com/pt-002/mo%C3%A7ambique-ainda-n%C3%A3o-vive-cen%C3%A1rio-de-guerra-civil-assegura-mediador/a-17196432.

Carvalho, Gustavo de, Jonathan Rozen, and Lisa Reppell. 2016. *Planning for Peace: Lessons from Mozambique's Peacebuilding Process*. Institute for Security Studies (ISS). https://issafrica.org/research/papers/planning-for-peace-lessons-from-mozambiques-peacebuilding-process.

Cascais, Antonio. 2018. *Mozambique's Debt Crisis: Who Will Pay the Bill?* Deutsche Welle. https://www.dw.com/en/mozambiques-debt-crisis-who-will-pay-the-bill/a-45105639.

Centre for Humanitarian Dialogue. 2016. *The Centre for Humanitarian Dialogue in 2015*. https://www.hdcentre.org/wp-content/uploads/2016/06/Annual_Report_-_The_Centre_for_Humanitarian_Dialogue_in_2015.pdf.

Chatham House. 2020. *Mozambique's Peace and National Reconciliation Agreement: One Year On*. https://www.youtube.com/watch?v=T0XBOVlt_zE.

Civil Society Source 2. 2020. Interviewed by Rui Saraiva in Maputo, Mozambique.

Civil Society Source 3. 2020. Interviewed by Rui Saraiva in Maputo, Mozambique.

Crawford, Julia. 2019. *'Quite an Adventure': How the Swiss Brought Peace to Mozambique*. SWI Swissinfo.Ch.2019. https://www.swissinfo.ch/eng/good-offices-_-quite-an-adventure%2D%2D-how-the-swiss-brought-peace-to-mozambique-/45260124.

Fabricius, Peter. 2016. *Mozambique: Devolution or Revolution?* ISS Africa. https://issafrica.org/iss-today/mozambique-devolution-or-revolution.

Faleg, Giovanni. 2019. *Conflict Prevention in Mozambique. Can There Be Peace after the Strom?* European Union Institute for Security Studies.

Folha de Maputo Newspaper. 2015. *EMOCHM custou 540 milhões de meticais [EMOCHM Cost 540 Million Meticais]*. Folha de Maputo. http://www.folhademaputo.co.mz/pt/noticias/nacional/emochm-custou-540-milhoes-de-meticais/.

Forquilha, Salvador. 2020. *Desafios Para Moçambique 2020 [Challenges for Mozambique 2020]*. Maputo: IESE. https://www.iese.ac.mz/wp-content/uploads/2020/12/Desafios-2020_online.pdf.

Gentili, Anna Maria. 2013. *Lessons Learned from the Mozambican Peace Process*. Istituto Affari Internazionali (IAI). https://www.jstor.org/stable/resrep09785.

Government of Mozambique. 2014. Projecto de Lei de Memorando de Entendimento [Draft Law Memorandum of Understanding]. https://peacemaker.un.org/sites/peacemaker.un.org/files/MZ-143508-MozambiqueCeasefire_1.pdf.

Government Source 1. 2020. Interviewed by Rui Saraiva in Maputo, Mozambique.

Hanlon, Joseph. 2014. Novo director do Observatório Eleitoral [New Director of the Electoral Observatory]. https://www.open.ac.uk/technology/mozambique/sites/www.open.ac.uk.technology.mozambique/files/files/Elei%C3%A7%C3%B5es_Nacionais_31-24deJulho_Observat%C3%B3rio_Eleitoral.pdf.

———. 2016. Talks with Mediators Yesterday and Today. https://www.open.ac.uk/technology/mozambique/sites/www.open.ac.uk.technology.mozambique/files/files/Mozambique_332-21July2016_Mediation-begins.pdf.

Henriques, Liliana. 2019. *A Renamo elegeu Ossufo Momade como seu novo líder [Renamo Elected Ossufo Momade as Its New Leader]*. RFI. https://www.rfi.fr/pt/mocambique/20190117-renamo-elegeu-ossufo-momade-como-seu-novo-lider.

Horizonte. 2014. Líderes religiosos criam Rede de Reconciliação e Paz [Religious Leaders Create Network of Reconciliation and Peace]. *Horizonte—Electronic Daily of General Information*, September 12.

Institute for Multiparty Democracy. 2019. *Implementação do Memorando de Entendimento sobre Assuntos Militares. Avanços no Desarmamento, Desmobilização e Reintegração [Implementation of the Memorandum of Understanding on Military Issues. Advances and Challenges in Disarmament, Demobilization and Reintegration (DDR)]*. http://imd.org.mz/index.php/component/edocman/policy-brief-2-2019-implementacao-do-memorando-de-entendimento-sobre-assuntos-militares-avancos-e-desafios-no-desarmamento-desmobilizacao-e-reintegracao.

International Federation of Red Cross and Red Crescent Societies (IFRC). 2019. *Operations Update, Mozambique: Tropical Cyclones Idai and Kenneth*. IFRC.

Jaberg, Federico Franchini, and Traduit de l'italien par Samuel. 2019. *Mirko Manzoni, l'artisan suisse de la paix au Mozambique [Mirko Manzoni, the Swiss Peace Artisan in Mozambique]*. SWI swissinfo.ch. https://www.swissinfo.ch/fre/m%C3%A9diation_mirko-manzoni%2D%2Dl-artificier-suisse-de-la-paix-au-mozambique/45210874.

Jornal de Notícias Newspaper. 2014. *Criada Rede de Reconciliação e Paz [Peace and Reconciliation Network Created]*. https://jornalnoticias.co.mz/index.php/politica/22967-eleicoes-2014-criada-rede-de-reconciliacao-e-paz.

Jornal Notícias Newspaper. 2015. Fracasso da EMOCHM: Desmilitarização da Renamo pode se arrastar por muito tempo [Failure of EMOCHM: Demilitarization of Renamo Can Drag on for a Long Time]. *Jornal Notícias*. https://www.jornalnoticias.co.mz/index.php/politica/37719-com-o-fracasso-da-emochm-desmilitarizacao-da-renamo-pode-se-arrastar-por-muito-tempo.

Júnior, Alfredo. 2015. *Mediadores moçambicanos repudiam pedido de afastamento do processo da Renamo [Mozambican Mediators Repudiate Renamo's Request to Withdraw from Process]*. VOA. https://www.voaportugues.com/a/mediadores-mocambicanos-repudiam-pedido-de-afastamento-do-processo-da-renamo/3117372.html.

Lofton, Bonnie Price. 2014. *JustaPaz, 1996: Lifting Mozambique from the Rubble of War—Peacebuilder Online*. https://emu.edu/now/peacebuilder/2015/07/justapaz-1996-lifting-mozambique-from-the-rubble-of-war/.

Lusa News Agency. 2016a. *Observadores internacionais para cessar-fogo em Moçambique? [International Observers in Mozambique for a Ceasefire?]* DW.COM. https://www.dw.com/pt-002/observadores-internacionais-para-cessar-fogo-em-mo%C3%A7ambique/a-19503402.

———. 2016b. Mario Raffaelli é mediador-chefe da União Europeia para paz em Moçambique [Mario Raffaelli is the EU's Chief Mediator for Peace in Mozambique]. *MOZREAL* (blog). https://mozrealblog.wordpress.com/2016/07/14/mario-raffaelli-e-mediador-chefe-da-uniao-europeia-para-paz-em-mocambique/.

———. 2016c. *Governo moçambicano anuncia pedidos de mediação do conflito militar [Mozambican Government Announces Request for Mediation of Military Conflict]*. Observador. https://observador.pt/2016/06/21/governo-mocambicano-anuncia-pedidos-de-mediacao-do-conflito-militar/.

———. 2016d. *Moçambique. Negociações de paz voltam a terminar em silêncio [Mozambique. Peace Negotiations End in Silence Again]*. Observador. https://observador.pt/2016/12/15/mocambique-negociacoes-de-paz-voltam-a-terminar-em-silencio/.

Matias, Leonel. 2015. *Mediadores negam qualquer conivência na invasão à casa de Dhlakama [Mediators Deny Any Complicity in the Invasion of the Home]*. DW.COM. https://www.dw.com/pt-002/mediadores-negam-qualquer-coniv%C3%AAncia-na-invas%C3%A3o-%C3%A0-casa-de-dhlakama/a-18937687.

———. 2016. *Negociações prosseguem em Maputo entre obstáculos e avanços [Negotiations Continue in Maputo Amidst Obstacles and Progress]*. DW.COM. https://www.dw.com/pt-002/negocia%C3%A7%C3%B5es-prosseguem-em-maputo-entre-obst%C3%A1culos-e-avan%C3%A7os/a-19488934.

Matsinhe, David M., and Estácio Valoi. 2019. *The Genesis of Insurgency in Northern Mozambique*. Institute for Security Studies (ISS).

MediaFax News. 2014. *Moçambique Para Todos: Governo, Renamo e 5 Observadores Tentam Selar 'Consensos Conseguidos' [Mozambique for All: Government, Renamo and 5 Observers Try to Seal ' Achieved Consensus']*. https://macua.blogs.com/moambique_para_todos/2014/02/governo-renamo-e-5-observadores-tentam-selar-consensos-conseguidos.html.

Mozambique Information Agency. 2015. *Mediadores Confiantes No Reatar Do Diálogo Político [Mediators Confident in Resuming Political Dialogue]*. https://www.portaldogoverno.gov.mz/por/Imprensa/Noticias/Mediadores-confiantes-no-reatar-do-dialogo-politico.

Mozambique Media Online. 2013. *Governo aceita presença de Dom Dinis Sengulane e do professor Lourenço do Rosário [Government Accepts the Presence of Dom Dinis Sengulane and Professor Lourenço do Rosário]*. MMO Notícias. https://noticias.mmo.co.mz/2013/12/dialogo-com-renamo-governo-aceita-presenca-de-dom-dinis-sengulane-e-lourenco-rosario.html.

O Século de Joanesburgo Newspaper. 2016. *Mediadores de paz em Moçambique só regressam ao país se forem convocados [Peace Mediators in Mozambique Will Only Return to the Country If They Are Summoned]*. https://www.oseculoonline.com/mediadores-de-paz-em-mocambique-so-regressam-ao-pais-se-forem-convocados/.

Petite, Simon. 2020. *Mirko Manzoni, Le Faiseur de Paix Mésestimé [Mirko Manzoni, the Underrated Peacemaker]*. Le Temps. https://www.letemps.ch/monde/mirko-manzoni-faiseur-paix-mesestime.

Radio Télévision Suisse. 2019. *Interview de Mirko Manzoni, ambassadeur suisse nommé envoyé personnel d'António Guterres au Mozambique [Interview with Mirko Manzoni, Swiss Ambassador Appointed Personal Envoy of António Guterres to]*. Broadcast. rts.ch. July 10. http://pages.rts.ch/la-1ere/programmes/forum/10550329-forum-du-10072019.html.

Reis, Bárbara. 2017. Moçambique, segundo 'round': mais 60 dias à procura da paz [Mozambique, Second Round: 60 More Days in Search of Peace]. *PÚBLICO Newspaper*. https://www.publico.pt/2017/03/03/mundo/noticia/mocambique-segundo-round-mais-60-dias-a-procura-da-paz-1763813.

———. 2019a. Um telefone trouxe a paz a Moçambique e o Papa confirma-a [A Telephone Brought Peace to Mozambique and the Pope Confirms It]. *PÚBLICO Newspaper*. https://www.publico.pt/2019/09/04/mundo/noticia/p24-4-setembro-2019-1885369.

———. 2019b. Moçambique: à terceira é de vez? [Mozambique: Will It Work at the Third Attempt?] *PÚBLICO Newspaper*. https://www.publico.pt/2019/08/06/mundo/noticia/mocambique-terceira-1882224.

Rodrigues, António. 2020. *Nyusi admite que ataques em Cabo Delgado 'podem comprometer' soberania em Moçambique*. PÚBLICO. March 27. https://www.

publico.pt/2020/03/27/mundo/noticia/nyusi-admite-ataques-cabo-delgado-podem-comprometer-soberania-mocambique-1909803.

Shimo, Kelvin. 2016. *Growing Number of Mozambicans Flee to Malawi*. UNHCR. https://www.unhcr.org/news/latest/2016/3/56e91b486/growing-number-mozambicans-flee-malawi.html.

Silva, Fernando. 2015. The Role of the Christian Council of Mozambique in the Colonial War (1964–1974) and in Civil Wars (1977–2014): Christians in Colonial Wars. *Studia Historiae Ecclesiasticae (SHE)* 41 (January). https://doi.org/10.17159/2412-4265/2015/v41n1a8.

The Economist. 2015. *Frelimo Grandees Voice Support for Opposition Dialogue*. http://country.eiu.com/article.aspx?articleid=2002926784&Country=Mozambique&topic=Politics&subtopic=Forecast&subsubtopic=Political+stability&u=1&pid=1622904946&oid=1622904946&uid=1.

UNHCR. 2021. *Cabo Delgado Situation*. United Nations High Commissioner for Refugees (UNHCR). https://reporting.unhcr.org/sites/default/files/UNHCR%20Mozambique%20IDP%20Response%20update%202-15%20April%202021.pdf.

Vhumbunu, Clayton Hazvinei. 2017. *Suppressing the Revival of Conflict in Mozambique through Inclusive National Dialogue*. https://www.accord.org.za/conflict-trends/suppressing-revival-conflict-mozambique-inclusive-national-dialogue/.

Vines, Alex. 2019. *As Perspectivas de um Acordo Sustentável entre as Elites em Moçambique [Perspectives on a Sustainable Agreement Between Elites in Mozambique]*. Chatham House. https://www.chathamhouse.org/sites/default/files/2019-09-04-ElitePerspectivesMozambique-Portuguese.pdf.

Weimer, Bernhard, and João Carrilho. 2017. *A economia política da descentralização em Moçambique: dinâmicas, efeitos, desafios [The Political Economy of Decentralization in Mozambique: Dynamics, Effects, Challenges]*. Maputo: IESE.

Wiegink, Nikkie. 2015. Former Military Networks a Threat to Peace? The Demobilisation and Remobilization of Renamo in Central Mozambique. *Stability: International Journal of Security & Development* 4 (1: Art.56): 1–16. https://doi.org/10.5334/sta.gk.

CHAPTER 5

Adapting from Outsider to Insider Mediation in the Bangsamoro Peace Process, Southern Philippines

Miyoko Taniguchi

Introduction

Peacebuilding in the post–Cold War era is a nonlinear process due to the complexity of protracted conflict and violence involving nonstate groups as well as regional and international actors. Despite the decrease in the number of war deaths since 1946, conflict and violence are currently on the rise, with many conflicts today waged between nonstate actors such as political militias and criminal and international terrorist groups (UN 2020), resulting in a massive scale of forcibly displaced persons. The intermingling factors that have led to these trends lie in weak governance, organized crime, fragmented opposition movements, violent extremism, gender, youth, and natural resource management in conflict settings.

Given the above situation, mediation, understood as preventive diplomatic efforts for peace by the international community, has been

M. Taniguchi (✉)
Japan International Cooperation Agency, Tokyo, Japan
e-mail: Taniguchi.Miyoko@jica.go.jp

C. de Coning et al. (eds.), *Adaptive Mediation and Conflict Resolution*, Sustainable Development Goals Series,
https://doi.org/10.1007/978-3-030-92577-2_5

considered an effective instrument for preventing, managing, and resolving conflicts and developing sustainable peace. The term "mediation" entered the diplomatic arena in 1948 when the UN launched mediation efforts in Palestine. Since then, international mediation, regardless of whether it addresses interstate or intrastate conflicts, has mainly been undertaken by third parties or external actors, especially as the number and intensity of intrastate conflicts have increased since the end of the Cold War.

To encourage effective mediation, the UN issued *The United Nations Guidance for Effective Mediation* in 2012 as an annex to the report of the secretary-general on *Strengthening the role of mediation in the peaceful settlement of disputes, conflict prevention and resolution* (A/66/811, June 25, 2012) (UNSC 2012), identifying key fundamentals[1] based on case studies. However, third-party or external mediation has not always been successful under political transition settings in conflict-affected countries in which society is divided and there is weakened social cohesion and trust. As observed in the cases of Colombia, Myanmar, Syria, Libya, and Yemen, mediation and other forms of third-party involvement appear to be challenging (Baumann and Clayton 2017) and limited in their ability to address the complex and interdependent dynamics of conflicts at the national and local levels.

Reflecting the above, conflict resolution literature has emphasized the roles of international or outsider mediation, while little research has focused on internal or insider mediation. Wehr and Lederach (1991) first developed the concept of "insider-partial" mediators within conflicts who benefit from a certain connectedness to and a high degree of trust from the conflict parties. Svensson and Lindgren (2013) further elaborated the role of insider-partial mediators who bring important indigenous resources to a peace process and can thus complement external mediators by mitigating the bargaining problem of information failure.

Despite the recognition of the importance of insider mediation for sustainable peace, it has not been a focus in academia because it is difficult for outsiders to obtain data and information that are politically sensitive or confidential in a transitional setting in order to understand such a complex process. Most networks, which are considered as the fundamental

[1] Those include preparedness, consent, impartiality, inclusivity, national ownership, international law and normative frameworks, coherence, coordination, and complementarity of the mediation effort and quality peace agreements.

infrastructure of insider mediation, are informal or personal, requiring outsiders to apply an adaptive approach reflecting local power dynamics and social relations among individuals and groups at the national and local levels. In addition to the lack of studies that have examined "insider mediation," it is scientifically or methodologically difficult to prove the outcome and effectiveness of the practice, as peacebuilding itself is a complex and continuous process that has no clear end or stopping point.

To overcome these limitations, this chapter aims to conceptualize the meaning of the term "mediation" and discuss its outcome and effectiveness for sustainable peace, taking up the case of Mindanao, located in the southern Philippines, where separatist rebels have fought over five decades for independence and autonomy in a Muslim-dominated area. To this end, this chapter primarily attempts to answer two main questions within the context of the Bangsamoro peace process: (1) What are the key characteristics of standard and alternative mediation, and formal or informal mediation practices? (2) How did mediators or parties to the conflict adapt or fail to adapt to uncertainty and complexity? By answering these questions, this chapter extracts good practices or lessons learned. It contributes to the existing literature by showing that adaptive mediation approaches, shaped by multilayered mediation with the emphasis on insider mediation, is effective and increases the likelihood of sustainable peace.

Literature Review and Problem Statement

Mediation has been seen as a particularly important aspect of peacebuilding efforts that may be used in different phases of a conflict (Bercovitch and Kadayifci 2002, 21). In this context, mediation is defined as "a process of conflict management where the disputants seek the assistance of, or accept an offer of help from, an individual, group, state or organization to settle their conflict or resolve their differences without resorting to physical violence or invoking the authority of the law" (Bercovitch et al. 1991, 8). Given this definition, the term is synonymous with "international mediation," which is primarily conducted by third-party or external actors, in which it is assumed that the third party is neutral or impartial. Assefa (1987, 22) suggests that there is a general agreement that both neutrality toward the issue in dispute and "independence from all parties to the conflict" are "requisites for the successful mediator." Similarly, Wehr (1991, 51) claims that strict neutrality is necessary, and that a mediator's credibility is contingent upon the absence of a "commitment to any party in the conflict."

With neutrality or impartiality as the central role of a mediator, mediation can efficiently and effectively provide information to the opposing parties that they would have been unable to obtain if the third party had not intervened (Beardsley 2008; Rauchhaus 2006; Kydd 2006; Kleiboer 1996; Bercovitch 1986; Svensson 2007, 2009). Maintaining open lines of communication between or among the parties involved and trading asymmetries in information (Princen 1992), third parties can provide alternative views on issues and identify a set of mutually acceptable agreements, bringing about potential compromises (Regan and Stam 2000). Regan and Aydin (2006, 740) articulate that "outside interventions can provide a more objective view of conditions and possible outcomes of the conflict, which helps adversaries to update their beliefs about the likely outcomes." Absent an outside intervention, the information held by the warring parties is at best asymmetrical, and neither side has a unilateral incentive to honestly convey its intentions.

The roles and functions of mediators can be categorized according to their expected outcome. Beardsley et al. (2006) identify three mediation styles,[2] that is, facilitation, formulation, and manipulation on international crises together with three outcomes: formal agreement, postcrisis tension reduction, and contribution to crisis abatement. The researchers verified the relationship between these mediation styles and outcomes, finding that manipulation has the strongest effect on the likelihood of both reaching a formal agreement and contributing to crisis abatement, while facilitation has the greatest influence on increasing the prospects for lasting tension reduction and the ownership and commitment of both parties involved, ultimately leading to sustainable peace. In practice, these styles can be used in combination to maximize their overall effectiveness, depending on the timing and intensity of the conflict.

In the early 1990s, Wehr and Lederach (1991), widely known in the fields of conflict transformation and peacebuilding, first highlighted the

[2] A facilitative mediator may simply provide the physical space for negotiation, organize the logistics, collect information, set the agenda, and help understand the messages between the parties. A formulative mediator suggests potential solutions to the disputants, highlights common interests, controls timing, helps devise a framework for typical outcome, makes substantive suggestions and proposals, and suggests concession the parties could make. Further, a manipulative mediator keeps parties at the table and provides a substantive contribution to the negotiation, including suggesting potential solutions.

importance of insider-partial mediators in their multidimensional work. They defined a mediator as an actor within the conflict who benefits from a certain connectedness to and a high degree of trust from the conflict parties (Wehr and Lederach 1991, 87). It is likely that these mediators have intimate knowledge of the conflict and unique entry points for mediation through an accumulated trust from all sides and that they reach their greatest potential in combination with the benefits of outsider-neutral and other mediators. In this sense, partiality can be seen as positive in that these mediators share the same social contexts as the parties and are committed to a just and durable settlement, as they must live with the consequences of their work even in the post-negotiation setting.

Svensson and Lindgren (2013) further elaborated upon this argument, emphasizing the importance of specifying the causal mechanisms behind successful mediation and linking third party mediation with insider-partial mediation for sustainable peace, not limited in its success to terminating conflicts and ending violent behavior (Regan and Aydin 2006; Regan and Stam 2000). The results of empirical data analysis suggest that the advantages of insider mediators lie in their access to credible information and indigenous resources and their capacity to understand the context with fewer incentives to exploit it for their own benefit, since they face risks to their reputations over the long term (Svensson and Lindgren 2013, 715–16). Compared to external mediators, especially those who follow manipulative and formulative approaches, insider mediators benefit from the self-organization that that arises from their work to organizing, regulating, and maintaining the peace process without an external or internal managing agent (de Coning 2021, Chap. 2 in this volume).

In light of the limited findings presented in the mediation literature, I address three arguments that attempt to explain why the combination of external and insider mediation can increase the likelihood of reducing multilayered conflict and violence and achieving sustainable peace. First, external mediators can facilitate information exchanges between the parties involved to reach agreements and settlements. Even if tensions becomes high, maintaining an open channel of communication is important to prevent any party from taking military action, as this implies a reputation risk for both sides. Through this process, the parties are expected to develop personal relationships, increase their levels of commitment to settlements, and build some degree of trust.

Second, insider mediators from diverse sectors such as government, media, rebel factions, religious institutions, and civil society organizations

(CSOs) can promote dialogue among their leaders that contributes to self-organization. Outside the confines of a formal peace process, insider mediation can change actors' mindsets and behaviors, build connections and trust, and rebuild or strengthen relationships where the social fabric is weakened or broken (UNDP 2018, 6). Social capital can serve as the foundation for peacebuilding or conflict prevention, especially in transition settings in which resource competition among stakeholders within the society becomes high. After reaching a settlement, the role of the third party will be diminished to monitoring the implementation of the agreement. Alongside the peace negotiations, formal or informal localized conflict resolution and management mechanisms should be developed. This coincides with the notion of adaptive mediation, which requires actors to be resilient and self-organized in order to recognize their interdependence and increase their sense of ownership over agreements (de Coning 2018, 2021, Chap. 2 in this volume).

Third, all multilevel mediation efforts can be made synergistically effective by strengthening the linkages among actors. In contrast to international (external) mediation, which focuses predominantly on high-level negotiations that include top-level state and rebel leaders together with high-ranking officials or diplomats from the international community, insider mediation engages multiple levels of society to address crises and ongoing tensions. Applying the model at three levels for peacebuilding—the top, middle, and grassroots levels of society (Lederach 1997)—insider mediators can be from any level, while those levels are complementary and overlap in terms of both actors and activities (UNDP 2014). In a divided or stratified society in which the root cause of a conflict originates in the divide-and-rule policy undertaken by a colonial government, insider mediation reinforced by outsider mediators can be viewed as an instrument for unifying the society and building sustainable peace in the long term.

Based on the findings of the above studies, I hypothesize that in complex conflict settings, strengthening multilayered mediation linkages increases the likelihood of conflict resolution and peacebuilding. Because it is assumed that insider mediation efforts combined with external technical, financial, or political support can enhance insiders' ownership or self-reliance and capacity through their self-organization, it is expected that even without external mediation, national or local stakeholders can work toward peacebuilding on their own.

Research Design (Method and Analyses)

This study adopts a case study method, taking the case of Mindanao, where Moro[3] rebels (Moro Islamic Liberation Front and (MILF) and Moro National Liberation Front (MNLF)) composed of Muslim and other indigenous peoples launched a separatist movement against the Christian majority state in the late 1960s. This conflict centered on self-determination for independence and autonomy, and is considered to be one of the most protracted in the world. Meanwhile, local clan feuds among the Moros are rampant, and ISIS-affiliated extremist groups have been active in the area since the 2010s. The case of Mindanao deserves analysis, as international and insider mediation efforts have been undertaken on the island over the last 40 years. Further, in 2019, a new autonomous region, called the Bangsamoro Autonomous Region in Muslim Mindanao (BARMM), and the MILF-led Bangsamoro Transition Authority (BTA) were created as a product of the peace process mainly between the Moro rebels and the Government of the Philippines (GPH).

This study addresses the features of outsider mediators in this conflict using three categories of mediation styles: facilitation, formulation, and manipulation. The main argument is that while the Duterte administration has achieved the most success by enacting and ratifying the Bangsamoro Organic Law (BOL) (Republic Act 11054) to create the BARMM and BTA, this "success" can be viewed as the results of incremental peacebuilding processes that strengthened vertical and horizontal relations among the Moros and the Christians that have been undertaken over several decades by diverse stakeholders.

Data on the mediators' roles, approaches and strategies, intervention timing, objectives, and expected outcomes and effectiveness were collected through reviews of the relevant literature and interviews with stakeholders, including the parties involved and other stakeholders in the mediation process between the MILF and the GPH. The collected data were analyzed to (1) identify factors and actors that led to the creation of the new autonomous region through multilayered mediations by broadening the definition of mediation from traditional (international-outsider-predetermined) to innovative (local-insider-adaptive), and (2) elaborate

[3]At present, the terms "Bangsamoro" and "Moro" are used interchangeably to refer to mainly Islamized ethnolinguistic groups of Mindanao. With ethnopolitical connotation, Bangsamoro is used in the MILF peace process to implicitly differentiate it from the Moro of MNLF.

upon adaptiveness at the local level by validating the local context and its role in shaping the peace process.

Rather than using a structured questionnaire, the interviews were designed to be open-ended enough to allow interviewees to narrate the important points that emerged for them regarding mediation in relation to conflict resolution and peacebuilding. Interviews with 36 respondents were conducted in February 2020 and lasted 1–1.5 hours each. These were followed by online interviews due to the COVID-19 pandemic. All of the interviews were recorded, analyzed, and coded for context analysis. To supplement the interviews, I also obtained and utilized data from online articles with direct quotations and statements from webinars without interpretation.

Overview of the Mindanao Context: Conflict, Violence, and the Peace Process

Over the last five decades, the peace process in Mindanao has partly resulted from changes in the government's policies and directions toward peace, influenced by the international and domestic situation. This process started under Marcos (1965–1981) and continued with Aquino (Corazon) (1986–1992), Ramos (1992–1998), Estrada (1998–2001), Arroyo (2001–2010), Aquino III (Benigno Jr.) (2010–2016), on to Duterte (2016–2022). The political reality in the Philippines, which lacks guarantees regarding the continuity of the administration's public policy, has significantly affected the status and protraction of the peace process. In this sense, peacebuilding in Mindanao is by nature a nonlinear process.

In the peace process between the GPH and the MNLF, both parties signed a peace agreement in 1976 in Tripoli that stipulated the establishment of an autonomous government that exercises judicial powers (Sharia) and possesses special security forces and an economic system under the auspices of the Organization of Islamic Cooperation (OIC). As a partial product of the agreement that resulted in the provision in the 1987 Philippine constitution, the Autonomous Region in Muslim Mindanao (ARMM) was officially created in 1990 through a referendum without the participation of the MNLF.[4] However, the armed conflict was reignited

[4]The MNLF disagreed to conduct the referendum, as the peace agreement in 1976 did not specify the requirement of conducting the referendum to create a new autonomous region.

until President Ramos resumed the negotiations. Eventually, the Final Peace Agreement (FPA) was reached in 1996 that led to the election of Nur Misuari, then MNLF chairman, as the governor of the ARMM. In recognition of the incomplete implementation of the FPA claimed by the MNLF and the OIC, a tripartite review process by the GPH-MNLF-OIC started in 2007 and resulted in an agreement that included the so-called 42 consensus points, which has remained unimplemented.

Peace negotiations between the GPH and the MILF started in 1997, immediately after the singing of the FPA. Since then, the negotiation process was interrupted three times in 2000, 2003, and 2008 by outbreaks of high-intensity violence in response to changes in the government's direction and policy toward the peace process. After over 30 rounds of talks, under the Aquino administration, both parties signed the Framework Agreement on the Bangsamoro (FAB) in 2012 and the Comprehensive Agreement on the Bangsamoro (CAB) in 2014 that was planned to replace the ARMM with a new political entity with a larger territorial scope and broader autonomy called Bangsamoro. However, the CAB could not be legislated at the Philippine Congress due to the president's declining influence over the Congress as a consequence of the Mamasapano crash[5] in January 2015 (Franco 2017; Taniguchi 2019).

Under this situation, President Duterte, who came into power in July 2016, brought a new dimension to the Bangsamoro peace process, adopting a more "inclusive approach" that involved the MILF, all factions of the MNLF (except the Misuari-faction), non-Islamized indigenous peoples, and others who could even be viewed as "spoilers" of the peace process. During the Bangsamoro Basic Law (BBL) deliberations in 2017, a five-month-long armed conflict—the Marawi siege—occurred in Marawi, Lanao del Sur, between the government security forces and pro-ISIS militants, who had broken away from the MILF. With the strong initiative of the president himself, BOL was enacted in 2018 and led to the creation of the BARMM and accordingly the BTA in 2019, which is expected to govern the region until 2022 when the Bangsamoro election is planned to be held.

[5] This refers to an incident that occurred during a police operation, which took place on January 25, 2015, at Mamasapano, Maguindanao, by Special Action Force of the Philippine National Police against the Bangsamoro Islamic Freedom Fighters (BIFF) and the MILF. The operation was intended to capture or kill wanted Malaysian terrorist and bomb-maker Zulkifli Abdhir and other Malaysian terrorists or high-ranking members of the BIFF.

In addition to the vertical conflict discussed above, feuds among prominent Muslim clans over political power, land, and resources, called *Rido*, have also been rampant in the region. These horizontal conflicts are characterized by sporadic outbursts of retaliatory violence between families and kinship groups as well as between communities in which the government or central authority is weak (Torres 2014). In a historical sense, the "divide and rule" policy introduced by the US colonial government has prevented the Moros from unifying against the state. The government provided the local leaders, mostly *datu*, with vested interests or official positions to pacify the region. The recent introduction of decentralization enabled local chief executives to directly access national resources through political competition. As a result, clan feuds and political violence have intensified.

Bangsamoro is intrinsically a society divided by diverse affiliations such as kinship (clan), ethnolinguistic groups, and political positions (separatist rebels or state collaborators). Thus, it should be understood that the complexity of the Bangsamoro context lies in vertical and horizontal conflict and violence.

Multilayered Mediation for Bangsamoro

Mediation Under the MNLF Peace Track as Precondition

In the course of peace talks between the MNLF and the GPH, the OIC and the member states have been involved since 1975. In particular, Libya was active in negotiating the 1976 Tripoli Agreement but officially it acted as an OIC representative, while Indonesia was actively involved in crafting the 1996 Final Peace Agreement (FPA) (Lingga 2006, 5).

In response to the MNLF's allegation of genocide toward the Muslims by the GPH, the OIC started to get involved in settling the conflict in 1973. During the Arab-Israeli war, the OIC pressured the GPH to settle the conflict through a political and peaceful solution, threatening an oil embargo, elevating the matter to the UN, and applying economic sanctions (Rodil 2000).

Libyan foreign minister Abdelsalem Ali Treki played a crucial role as mediator, directing both parties to sign a peace agreement. As a result, the MNLF gained autonomy for the Muslims, while the GPH was guaranteed sovereignty and territorial integrity. Two decades later, as the agreement had still not been fully implemented, Indonesia reinstalled talks in 1993, acting under the auspices of the OIC and as chair of the Committee of the Six.[6] Following the noninterference principle of the Association of Southeast Asian Nations (ASEAN), Indonesia required the MNLF to put less weight on the self-determination that led to the singing of the FPA (Santos 1999). However, the FPA again faced challenges with implementation.

Based on the above, the roles of the OIC as the third-party mediator were effective to break the impasse and sign a peace agreement, using leverage as major member states of the OIC and the ASEAN (Indonesia), pressuring the MNLF to abandon its claim for independence, and negotiating for regional autonomy as an alternative. This process lacked an inclusive facilitation process between the parties and among the Moros that would have increased a sense of ownership, and enhanced self-organization. As a result, the agreement has not been sustained, creating a high level of dependency on external actors.

Peacebuilding Architecture Between the GPH and the MILF

Since the start of the peace process in 1997, the peacebuilding architecture utilized by the GPH and the MILF has evolved over time, adapting to the status of the process. However, the overall architecture is composed of the following: (1) the Peace Panel between the GPH and the MILF facilitated by Malaysia (2001) and observed by the International Contact Group (ICG) (2009); (2) the Joint Coordinating Committee on the Cessation of Hostilities (JCCCH) between the GPH and the MILF as a ceasefire coordination mechanism monitored by the Malaysia-led International Monitoring Team (IMT) (2004); and (3) the Third-Party Monitoring Team (TPMT) (2013) as the monitoring mechanism of the implementation of the peace agreements (Fig. 5.1). Unlike other cases of peacebuilding that are mainly initiated by the UN, this case is characterized by its "hybridity"—with international, national, and local actors—and its "multi-layeredness," with diverse international, national, and local (state and nonstate) actors with roles and functions that strengthen the relationships among diverse local actors that have their own constituencies in a divided society.

After the peace process between the GPH and the MILF started in 1997 under the Ramos administration and led to reaffirming the General

[6] Indonesia, Libya, Saudi Arabia, Bangladesh, Senegal, and Somalia.

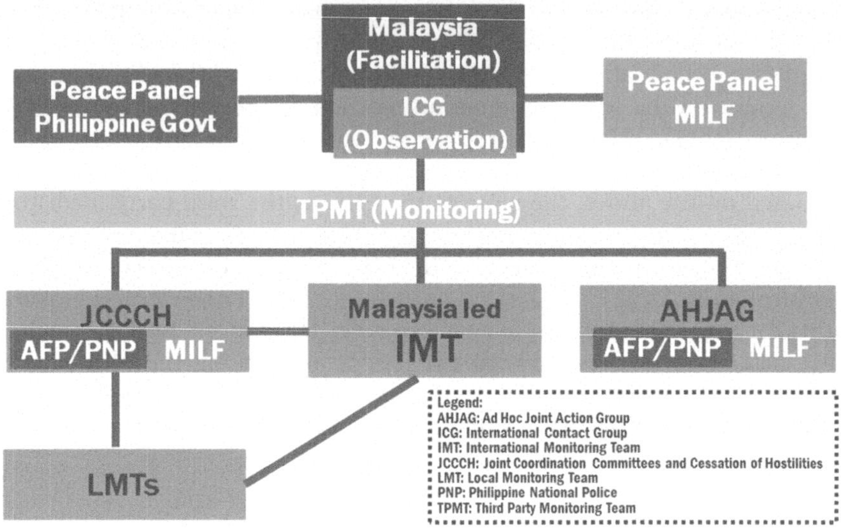

Fig. 5.1 Overall peacebuilding architecture between the GPH and the MILF. (Source: Author)

Cessation of Hostilities in July 1997, peace talks with a focus on establishing and maintaining a ceasefire, known as the JCCCH, were undertaken solely by internal actors. However, these peace talks were disrupted due to a military operation conducted by the Armed Forces of the Philippines (AFP) under the Estrada administration (1998–2001) from March to July 2000. In order to resume peace talks, then president Arroyo, who came into power in January 2001, requested that Malaysian prime minister Mahathir serve as a third-party facilitator to build trust with the MILF. With this facilitation, both parties signed the Agreement on Peace (Tripoli Agreement), which contained the three aspects of security, rehabilitation, and ancestral domain in June 2001.

As a product of the Tripoli Agreement in 2001, the Bangsamoro Development Agency (BDA) was created as the MILF's development arm to determine, lead, and manage rehabilitation and development projects in conflict-affected communities. Similarly, the Bangsamoro Leadership and Management Institute (BLMI) was created in 2009 to develop the capacities of MILF ex-combatants to transform from rebels to government officials. These attempts were planned based on the lessons learned from the experience of the ARMM government that had been considered to be dysfunctional.

In response to the OIC's proposal for a peacekeeping force, the Malaysia-led IMT—composed of 60 members from Malaysia (withdrawn in 2008 and returned in 2010), Brunei, Libya (withdrawn in 2011)—was officially deployed in Cotabato City in October 2004, and was later joined by Japan (2006), Norway (2010), the European Union (2010), and Indonesia (2012).Upon the request from the JCCCT and the Local Monitoring Teams (LMTs), the IMT is responsible for ceasefire monitoring, humanitarian and rehabilitation efforts, and development. In order to reduce the AFP's threat to local citizens, the Civilian Protection Component was included in 2009 with the assignment of one expert from the EU and three from local NGOs. Except for some isolated cases, the presence of the IMT as a third party contributed to dramatically reducing ceasefire violations (from 689 cases in 2002 to 7 cases in 2007) (Lingga 2008), preventing them from escalating armed conflict, and building trust between the parties (Abubakar 2006; Gündüz and Torralba 2014; Lingga 2008).

The failed signing of the Memorandum of Agreement on Ancestral Domain (MOA-AD) in August 2008, following the Supreme Court ruling that it was unconstitutional, resulted in ceasefire violations, increased hostilities, and the displacement of around 750,000 people by the end of 2008. Backchannel diplomacy by the UK government, the Center for Humanitarian Dialogue (CHD) (Swiss), and the Asian Foundation (TAF) (the US) brought a one-year impasse that led to the creation of new mechanisms to include the international community in the peace processes (Rood 2016). In response to desires from both parties, the ICG, comprised of four countries—Japan, the UK, Turkey, and Saudi Arabia—and four international NGOs—Muhammadiyah (Indonesia), TAF, the CHD, and Conciliation Resources (the UK)—was established in 2009 to rebuild trust between the parties and act as a guarantee mechanism for the MILF (Tengku 2017). Importantly, this was the first-ever formal hybrid mediation support initiative (Herbolzheimer and Leslie 2013).

In 2012, the FAB, a preliminary peace agreement, was signed under the Aquino administration and ultimately reached the CAB in 2014, calling for the creation of an autonomous political entity named Bangsamoro to replace the ARMM. Based on lessons learned from the MNLF track, both panels agreed to establish a Third-Party Monitoring Team (TPMT) composed of five members from local NGOs, international NGOs,[7] and the EU to monitor, review, and assess the implementation of all signed agreements. It should be highlighted that the peace negotiation can be terminated upon the signing of an "Exit Document" by both parties with the Malaysia facilitator, the TPMT, upon the confirmation of the full implementation of all agreements.

If one traces the development of all these new mechanisms, from the JCCCH, the IMT, the ICG, to the TPMT, then one can see how they are adaptations of what has been tried before, based on the lessons that were identified from previous successes, stalemates, and failures (Zartman 2001). In comparison to the MNLF-GPH track, the mechanism involved more local actors to reflect the local context. For instance, the IMT, together with JCCCH, has direct linkages with local communities to obtain security status that is shared with the ICG members. Further, the ICG members from international NGOs linked with local NGOs to ensure concerns and needs on the ground were reflected in the peace talks. Similarly, the TPMT relied on local NGOs to collect the information needed to monitor the implementation status of the agreement. Likewise, the third-party engagement, which diversified the actors and their roles, synchronized the peace talks, and monitored the ceasefire and implementation, is more effective to ensure a timely and appropriately response for conflict resolution and prevention. The next section focuses on how mediations transitioned from third-party actors to insiders, building confidence and trust among the stakeholders.

From Third-Party to Insider Mediation

Third-Party Mediation

Peace Panel: Malaysia Facilitator

With the ASEAN principles of mutual recognition, acceptance, nonintervention, and respect, the facilitator has taken significant roles in moving forward peace talks and bringing both parties to the peace table since 2001, despite impasses along the way (Shea 2017). From the beginning, there were no terms of reference (TOR) for the facilitator. In fact, the

[7] Turkish the Foundation of Human Rights and Freedoms and Humanitarian Relief and the TAF.

Aquino administration attempted to write the TOR, but the MILF and the Malaysian facilitation team essentially asserted that formality was unnecessary since informality had worked well and provided for flexibility (Rood 2016, 86).

Informality can be explained in the context of Malay culture known for its "quiet diplomacy" (Taya et al. 2018). Traditionally, third-party facilitators or mediators serving as go-betweens avoid embarrassment by using indirect language, and decision-making is based on consensus to avoid any hard feelings (Tengku 2017). Underlining this notion, in the beginning, the facilitator played a significant role as a peace broker in bringing both parties to the negotiation table through shuttle diplomacy, traveling to Manila and Cotabato to meet the panels and their principles, listening, discussing, and identifying points of disagreement when the two conflicting parties were stuck in their formal negotiation. This was intended to lower tensions and encourage direct interaction in the form of negotiation that can be viewed as conciliation (Taya et al. 2018).

Under the Aquino III administration, however, Tengku Dato' Ab Ghafar Tengku Mohamed, who had served as the facilitator from 2001 to 2002, was replaced by Datuk Othman bin Abdul Razak, who had been perceived as biased to the MILF by the GPH since the Arroyo administration (ICG 2009; Apandi et al. 2018). Together with the diplomatic tensions between Malaysia and the Philippines caused by the failure of the MOA-AD that led to the withdrawal of Malaysia from the IMT in 2008 (return in 2010), no substantial peace talks were conducted at the beginning of the Aquino administration (Rood 2016). In order to break this deadlock, the chairperson of the GPH peace panel requested that Japan host high-level talks between top leaders, President Aquino and Chairman Murad of the MILF, which resulted in great success in confidence- and trust-building between the leadership groups (Lam 2008). This historical event became a game changer for the progress of the Bangsamoro peace process.

Against this background, the next facilitator, Tengku, who served from 2011 to 2016, prioritized trust- and confidence-building, which resulted in the garnering of trust from both parties (Tengku 2017). In general, the actual roles that the facilitator played during the negotiation were: (1) presiding over the talks as a referee in case of misunderstanding; (2) helping bridge differences by shuttling between the parties; and (3) administering the discussion. Over the years, Malaysia's role in the peace process has strengthened, as the country has gradually earned the trust of both parties. Accordingly, the facilitator's role has transformed from facilitator to mediator and negotiator, with these three roles becoming increasingly interchangeable (Leslie 2013).

Peace Panel-International Contact Group

With the participation of diplomats and International NGOs, the ICG was established in 2009 mainly as a compromise to the MILF's desire to internationalize the peace talks and the government's aversion to external interference in domestic affairs. The overarching purposes of the ICG were to: (1) accompany and mobilize international support for the peace process; and (2) exert proper leverage and sustain the interest of the parties and maintain a level of comfort that restores mutual trust (Herbolzheimer and Leslie 2013).

The members were carefully selected by both parties with consideration of: (1) the strength of the support given by the state and relevant experience of the International NGO to peace in Mindanao; (2) recognized expertise in the field of conflict transformation; (3) the desire to include both Western and Muslim participants; (4) the government's reluctance to include big powers and multilaterals; and (5) the MILF's reluctance to consider countries that provided military aid to the AFP such as the US and Australia (Herbolzheimer and Leslie 2013). In fact, all members selected were persons or organizations that had worked toward conflict transformation or peacebuilding in Mindanao.

At the start, there were no official terms of reference (TOR), but they were eventually formulated and attached to the FAB to formalize their tasks and status. The official roles were translated into practice and stipulated that: (1) members meet before negotiations to share information and expectations; (2) members quietly observe negotiations, and if requested by the parties or the facilitator, they comment on an issue or produce draft documents for the discussion; and (3) if talks reached an impasse, members meet with the facilitator and shuttle between both parties to identify common grounds or other solutions for breaking the deadlock (Leslie 2013; Rood 2016).

The relationship between the facilitator and the ICG members evolved over time. While the facilitator has never been in a directive position to the members, all members shared the ideas to form a consensus toward the same direction. In this sense, the ICG is conceived as a collaborative and complementary mechanism among the members who have specific expertise and diplomatic status, or a hub of international and domestic stakeholders to network and build wider relationships, providing technical, financial, information, and administrative assistance for both parties, as needs arise.

The ICG took on the role of providing technical input for negotiations when the panels were working on four annexes of a final agreement: transitional arrangements and modalities; wealth sharing; power sharing; and normalization. The ICG members were allowed to participate and provide the technical working groups with direct technical inputs during the groups' working sessions, while all outputs from each group were shared among them, discussed, and finalized (Rood 2016). Upon the request of the parties, each ICG member provided technical input and assistance in the crafting of the annexes. For instance, the UK shared lessons from Northern Ireland; Conciliation Resources provided analyses of the draft documents from the panels and discussion papers on transition, normalization, and the devolution of policing; TAF forced on strengthening governance; and CHD brought in high-profile experts to provide input on topics such as power-sharing and wealth sharing (DPI 2014).

In the process, the ICG members extended to outside official talks, maximizing their own designations and capacities based on their expertise promoting peace in Mindanao. Embassies (Japan and the UK) regularly met with lawmakers and local politicians from Mindanao to listen to their concerns and suggestions and exert diplomatic leverage in support of the peace negotiations. On the other hand, NGOs have worked with local civil society and on the promotion of cross-community dialogues, providing technical and financial support to local NGOs or CSOs, and sharing lessons learned with other stakeholders, including the business and security sectors, the media, and academia.

Hybrid mediation is considered to be innovative in that the facilitator and the ICG members took facilitation roles: in (1) easing tensions and building confidence and trust between the parties by creating an environment that was conducive to exchanging ideas, dispelling misunderstanding, and clarifying consensus points; (2) building formal and informal or vertical and horizontal networks and social capital in a historically divided society and strengthening the ties between the state and civil society; (3) synchronizing all the efforts to bring about synergetic effects on peace talks, ceasefire, and distribution of peace dividends in an inclusive manner; and (4) mobilizing any forms of support from the international community from peacemaking, peacekeeping, and humanitarian and socioeconomic development.

Looking through the lens of adaptive mediation (de Coning 2021, Chap. 2 in this volume), the facilitation process led by the facilitator and the ICG members enhanced the capacity of both parties and stimulated self-organization among the parties through negotiating over agendas, finding consensus, and stipulating them into the agreement. In the beginning, the TOR of the ICG were purposely not specified to adapt their strategies and approaches to the changing political environment or the security status on the ground. At the same time, as the process reached a deadlock, backchannel diplomacy was conducted at a meeting as usual in Kuala Lumpur, Malaysia, and also in Manila and Cotabato, in the Philippines to transmit necessary information and resolve misunderstandings between the parties in order to get back to the negotiation table.

It is expected that all of the above can contribute to: (1) increasing both parties' sense of ownership and commitment for the implementation of the agreement through a transparent process in the international community; (2) nurturing norms and values for conflict resolution through democratic means on the basis of consensus; and (3) increasing resilience to cope with uncertainty, setbacks, and shocks, when attempting to facilitate such complex social change processes.

Insider Mediation: Insider Mediation Group (IMG)

The signing of ceasefire and peace agreements by both parties does not ensure peace. In contrast to third-party mediation, insider mediation by the parties involved in the peace process as well as diverse groups within Moro society is a new attempt to increase the likelihood of sustainable peace in a divided society shaped by complex, protracted conflict and violence.

Around the signing of the CAB in 2014, new attempts were undertaken for advocacy, and informal dialogues and consultations were established around the enactment of the BBL in Congress (Kumar 2017). As a track-two form of advocacy, "Friends of Peace" was formed with the initiative of Cardinal Orland Quevedo, the Archbishop of Cotabato and a highly respected public figure in the Philippines where the Catholic Church is influential in politics (Cartagenas 2010; Pinches 1997). The Cardinal, who has also been engaged in promoting peace in Mindanao over the last few decades (Asiones 2019; Abreu 2008), identified public figures, including a leading historian, a prominent female journalist, a drafter of the 1987 Philippine constitution, influential members of the private sector, and academics. In the aftermath of the Mamasapano encounter, these figures were engaged in conducting public advocacy and providing legislators with legal advice to move forward (Kumar 2017). Despite all of these efforts, the incident eventually led to the failure of the BBL to be passed.

Under the Duterte administration, this group has evolved to adopt roles and functions related not only to promoting social harmony and interfaith dialogue but also to unifying Moro society including its fragmented leadership (MILF-MNLF and the factions), ethnolinguistic groups, non-Muslim indigenous groups, faith-based leaderships, and advocates. Most of its members are professionals or senior advisers to leadership such as lawyers, engineers, civil servants, and government officials related to the Moro leaderships, influential clans, and CSOs. With the support from the EU and the UNDP, the members were trained to enhance their capacity around mediation and negotiation skills at the Clingendael Institute in the Netherlands and the Philippines (mostly in Davao City in Mindanao) from 2016 to 2017.

In the course of the training, the participants organized themselves into informal task forces, named the Insider Mediation Group (IMG). Working closely with the MILF-led Bangsamoro Transition Commission (BTC)[8] tasked with drafting the BBL, some of them were formally appointed as commissioners, and the task force for engaging in the Congress took on a significant role in building a wider consensus among stakeholders or interest groups among the Bangsamoro on the passing of the BBL during the last administration, calling for unity among the Moros and leaders. One of the biggest achievements was the group's lobbying and provision of legal advice to Christian legislators during the deliberation of the bill so that the proposed BBL by the BTC that complies with the CAB would not be watered down.

At present, the IMG has been expanded within the Moro and between the Moro and Manila, and members have evolved their roles and applied to run the interim government, mediating and building consensus within and outside government. In the BTA, 10 out of 80 members of parliament (MP) are IMG members, while some are Cabinet members and a few are

[8] Under Executive Order No. 120, the BTC, composed of 15 members (8 from the MILF and 7 from those selected by the GPH involving diverse sectors, was constituted primarily in 2015 to draft a BBL under the Aquino administration after the FAB was signed. Under the Duterte administration stipulated in Executive Order No. 8, the BTC was reconstituted to strengthen and expand the functions of the Commission with the total of 21.

high-ranking officials. On the basis of the trust and confidence built among them during the legislative process, the members are now mediating interests and building consensus among diverse stakeholders inside and outside organizations (Arguillas 2019). Some concrete examples regarding the engagement are presented in the following paragraphs.

The IMG has played a pivotal role in strengthening vertical and horizontal ties. One mediator is a lawyer by profession and a former high-ranking government officer of the ARMM regional government. As a legal advisor on the MILF side, he has been engaged in peace talks between the MILF and GPH and was also assigned to serve as a member of the Joint Normalization Committee. During the legislative process of the BBL, he had been a legal advisor for Senator Juan Miguel F. Zubiri from Bukidnon (Mindanao), who was the chairman of the subcommittee on BBL, to ensure the spirit and intent of the CAB. After the creation of the BTA, he has been addressing issues of local governance as the minister of the local government and now delivers emergency services as a member of Bangsamoro Inter-Agency Task Force on COVID-19, coordinating with other ministers and local government executives.

Another mediator is associated with the religious aspect of the mediation process. Despite his upbringing in an influential clan in local politics, he has been engaged in religious dialogues, community engagement, and conflict resolution on the ground. He only stepped into the political mainstream in 2016 when he was appointed as a member of BTC and now serves as an MP in the BTA parliament. His exposure to a multicultural environment during his stay at Ateneo de Davao University (Jesuit) helped him realize the importance of interreligious dialogue (Lidasan 2020). In 2011, he was appointed as the head of the newly created Al Qalam Institute, which is an institute for Islamic Identities and Dialogue at the University, by Fr. Joel E. Tabora, S.J, the president of the University. Interacting with the mediator, Fr. Tabora has come to deeply understand the historical and cultural background of the conflict and has worked for peace and justice in Mindanao, as proven by the push for the passage of the BTC-drafted BBL.[9] In this sense, Davao became a hub of insider

[9] During deliberations under the Aquino and Duterte administrations in 2016 and 2018, respectively, Father Tabora took the initiative that the presidents of the all the Ateneo universities in the Philippines called for the passage of the proposed BBL that was drafted by the MILF-led BTC, putting the statement on national and local newspapers.

mediation between the Moro and Christian communities outside the Bangsamoro.

One mediator on the MNLF side, who is a lawyer by profession, a former member of the BTC, and the present MP in the BTA, pointed out that the role of mediators has become more important and relevant, given the intertwining, conflicting interests of diverse groups within the Bangsamoro, in order to enact necessary laws such as electoral and local government code (Sema 2020). As such, in a transitional setting in which formal institutions or organizations are being developed, this type of informal network within the Bangsamoro and within the Philippines can fill in the gaps until a formal institution can be effectively established. It also functions as a mechanism to prevent conflicts over resource allocation caused by changes in power relations in the formation of a new political order.

Over time, the number of mediators has increased from 30 in 2016 to more than 100 in 2020, involving more diverse groups or sectors in the newly created political entity. With the confidence and trust that has been constructed since the last administration, even mediators outside the BTA have been actively engaged in supporting the functioning of the BTA, in academia and CSOs, national and local governance. Importantly, keeping collaborative efforts with the national government is considered as key to success, as many contentious issues, which are not clarified, should be shared and solved between the BTA and the national government.

As shown above, the IMG is conceived as a platform for the Bangsamoro that works toward a political settlement, adjustment, and reconciliation among diverse interest groups. Through continuous processes, the actors in a conflict can understand and respect their differences, exchange ideas, build a consensus, modify their norms and values, and build confidence and trust through informal dialogues. In other words, the whole process can be viewed as the formation of a new political order, expansion of the public sphere, and creation of a new "political community" shaped by new norms and values under a new identity as the Bangsamoro. In this sense, insider mediation is also viewed as a binding and healing process engaged in by a historically divided or fragmented society. Thus, all the efforts conducted through the IMG to strengthen vertical and horizontal relations with trust can contribute to more sustainable peace by increasing the society's resilience to violent conflict.

From the adaptive mediation perspective, insider mediation contributed to increasing the level of interdependency between the parties and within the Moro society, and lessoning the roles of outsider mediators that would increase the likelihood of self-organization and resilience to cope with uncertainty, setbacks, and shocks in the longer term. During the implementation stages of the peace agreement, the Bangsamoro government has to be engaged in negotiating with the national government and adjusting the interests among diverse sectors of people within the Moros or the Bangsamoro. Achieving that aim requires the rebels to acquire those political skills and maneuvers in order to transform from rebels to government officials. In that sense, learning from the process of adaptive mediation, including insider mediation prior to the signing of peace agreement, would greatly help for the parties to sustain the agreement.

Conclusion

Based on the findings presented above, four advantages of an adaptive mediation approach can be identified from the Bangsamoro peace process. First, the model of third-party mediation based on impartiality has been shaped by consensus (not confrontation) by both parties, which resulted in nurturing trust, norms, and values for conflict resolution through democratic means. Second, adaptive mediation approaches utilizing innovative, flexible, inclusive, and transparent approaches allowed the local context to be considered in the decision-making process during negotiation through a collaborative and complementary mechanism at the national and local levels. This type of adaptive mediation increases both parties' level of acceptance, commitment, and ownership regarding the implementation of the signed peace agreement. Third, while the inclusion of diverse stakeholders in the peace process is key to the successful unification of people in a historically divided society, norms and values should be shared in order to develop respect for differences and build a consensus through dialogue. Fourth, shifting from the negotiation to implementation stages, the roles and functions of third parties change from providing input to ensure an agreement toward monitoring the status of implementation. As peace talks progress, insider mediators can gradually increase their levels of involvement for trust and consensus-building and the adjustment of conflicting interests among diverse stakeholders. The Bangsamoro experience has shown that incremental and adaptive efforts will contribute to developing resilience to conflict and violence and ultimately to sustainable peace.

References

Abreu, Lualhati M. 2008. Ancestral Domain- The Core Issue. In *The Moro Reader: History and Contemporary Struggles of the Bangsamoro People*, ed. Bobby M. Tuazon. Quezon City: CenPEG Books.

Abubakar, Ayesah. 2006. Keeping the Peace: The International Monitoring Team (IMT) Mission in Mindanao. http://www.eprpinformation.org/wp-content/uploads/5656-v-Keeping_the_Peace__The_International_Monitoring_Team__IMT__Mission_in_Mindanao.pdf.

Apandi, Laila Suriya, Rusdi Omar Ahmad, and Abdul Rahim Anuar. 2018. An Honest Peace Broker? Malaysia as a Third Country Facilitator of Peace Building Process in the Southern Philippines. *International Journal of Engineering & Technology* 7: 576–580.

Arguillas, Carolyn O. 2019. Insider Mediators inside the BARMM: Mediating Groups, Mediating Interests. *MindaNews*, April 15. https://www.mindanews.com/bangsamoro-insider-mediators/2019/04/insider-mediators-inside-the-barmm-mediating-groups-mediating-interests/.

Asiones, Noel G. 2019. The Task and Ministry of Peacemaking in Mindanao: Understanding a Peacemaker's Recipe for Peace. *Humanities and Social Science Research* 2 (4): 22–33.

Assefa, Hizkias. 1987. *Mediation of Civil Wars: Approaches and Strategies: The Sudan Conflict*. Boulder: Westview Press.

Baumann, Jonas, and Govinda Clayton. 2017. Mediation in Violent Conflict. Ed. Christian Nünlist. *CSS Analyses in Security Policy*, 211 (June).

Beardsley, Kyle C. 2008. Agreement without Peace? International Mediation and Time Inconsistency Problems. *American Journal of Political Science* 52 (4): 723–740.

Beardsley, Kyle C., David M. Quinn, Bidisha Biswas, and Jonathan Wilkenfeld. 2006. Mediation Style and Crisis Outcomes. *Journal of Conflict Resolution* 50 (1): 58–86.

Bercovitch, Jacob. 1986. International Mediation: A Study of the Incidence, Strategies and Conditions of Successful Outcomes. *Cooperation and Conflict* 21 (3): 155–168.

Bercovitch, Jacob, and Ayse Kadayifci. 2002. Exploring the Relevance and Contribution of Mediation to Peace-Building. *Peace and Conflict Studies* 9 (2): 21–40.

Bercovitch, Jacob, J. Theodore Anagnoson, and Donnette L. Wille. 1991. Some Conceptual Issues and Empirical Trends in the Study of Successful Mediation in International Relations. *Journal of Peace Research* 28 (1): 7–17.

Cartagenas, Aloysius. 2010. Religion and Politics in the Philippines: The Public Role of the Roman Catholic Church in the Democratization of the Filipino Polity. *Political Theology* 11 (6): 846–872.

de Coning, Cedric. 2018. Adaptive Mediation. *ACCORD*. https://www.accord.org.za/conflict-trends/adaptive-mediation/.
———. 2021. Adaptive Mediation and Conflict Resolution: Peace-making in Colombia, Mozambique, the Philippines and Syria. ed. Cedric de Coning, Ako Muto, and Rui Saraiva. Palgrave Macmillan.
DPI. 2014. *Briefing: International Contact Group for the Southern Philippines Peace Process*. London: Democratic Progress Institute.
Franco, Joseph. 2017. Uncertainty in Duterte's Muslim Mindanao. In *Southeast Asian Affairs 2017*, ed. Daljit Singh and Malcolm Cook, 297–312. ISEAS–Yusof Ishak Institute.
Gündüz, Canan, and Raul Torralba. 2014. *Evaluation of the Nonviolent Peaceforce Project with the Civilian Protection Component of the International Monitoring Team in Mindanao, Philippines*. European Forum for International Mediation and Dialogue, Initiatives for International Dialogue.
Herbolzheimer, Kristian, and Emma Leslie. 2013. *Innovation in Mediation Support: The International Contact Group in Mindanao*. Practice Paper, Conciliation Resources, London.
ICG. 2009. The Philippines: Running in Place in Mindanao. *Asia Briefing* 88, International Crisis Group, Jakarta and Brussels.
Kleiboer, Marieke. 1996. Understanding Success and Failure of International Mediation. *Journal of Conflict Resolution* 40 (2): 360–389.
Kumar, Chetan. 2017. *Track-Two Initiatives of Nationally-Led Peace Processes: The Case of the Philippines*. Issue Brief: Practices from Peace and Development Advisors 5, UNDP, UNDPA, Norwegian Institute of International Affairs.
Kydd, Andrew H. 2006. When Can Mediators Build Trust? *American Political Science Review* 100 (3): 449–462.
Lam, Peng E.R. 2008. Japan's Peace-Building in Mindanao: Partnering Malaysia, the Philippines and the Moro Islamic Liberation Front. *Japanese Studies* 28 (1): 45–57.
Lederach, John Paul. 1997. *Building Peace: Sustainable Reconciliation in Divided Societies*. Washington, DC: United States Institute of Peace Press.
Leslie, Emma. 2013. Widening the Table: Hybrid Support Groups in Conflict Mediation. *World Politics Review, Feature Report: Getting to Peace: New Approaches to Ending Conflict*, 9–13.
Lidasan, Mussolini S. 2020. Interview with Mussolini S. Lidasan by Author Conducted in Cotabato City. 25 February.
Lingga, Abhoud Syed M. 2006. *Role of Third Parties in Mindanao Peace Process*. Occasional Paper 2006–01, Institute of Bangsamoro Studies, Cotabato.
———. 2008. *Malaysia's Pull-out from the International Monitoring Team: Implications to Peace Process in Mindanao*. Institute of Bangsamoro Studies Discussion Paper 2008–01, Institute of Bangsamoro Studies, Cotabato.

Pinches, Michael. 1997. Elite Democracy, Development and People Power: Contending Ideologies and Changing Practices in Philippine Politics. *Asian Studies Review* 21 (2–3): 104–120.

Princen, Thomas. 1992. *Intermediaries in International Conflict*. Princeton: Princeton University Press.

Rauchhaus, Robert W. 2006. Asymmetric Information, Mediation, and Conflict Management. *World Politics* 58 (2): 207–241.

Regan, Patrick M., and Aysegul Aydin. 2006. Diplomacy and Other Forms of Intervention in Civil Wars. *Journal of Conflict Resolution* 50 (5): 736–756.

Regan, Patrick M., and Allan C. Stam. 2000. In the Nick of Time: Conflict Management, Mediation Timing, and the Duration of Interstate Disputes. *International Studies Quarterly* 44 (2): 239–260.

Rodil, B. R. 2000. *Kalinaw Mindanaw: The Story of the GRP-MNLF Peace Process, 1975–1996*. 1st AFRIM. Davao City, Philippines: Alternate Forum for Research in Mindanao.

Rood, Steven. 2016. The Role of International Actors in the Search for Peace in Mindanao. In *The Long Journey to Peace and Prosperity*, ed. Paul D. Hutchcroft, 62–95. Mandaluyong City: Anvil Publishing, Inc.

Santos, Soliman M. 1999. Islamic Diplomacy: Consultation & Consensus. *Accord: International Review of Peace Initatives* 6: 20–28.

Sema, Omar. 2020. Interview with Atty. Omar Sama by Author Conducted in Cotabato City. 26 February.

Shea, Nathan. 2017. Regionalism and Islam: Malaysia Peacemaking Strategy. In *State Support for Peace Processes: A Multi-Country Review*, ed. John Langmore, Tania Miletic, Aran Martin, and Nathan Shea. Melbourne: The University of Melbourne, Australian Government.

Svensson, Isak. 2007. Mediation with Muscles or Minds? Exploring Power Mediators and Pure Mediators in Civil Wars. *International Negotiation* 12 (2): 229–248.

———. 2009. Who Brings Which Peace? Neutral Versus Biased Mediation and Institutional Peace Arrangements in Civil Wars. *The Journal of Conflict Resolution* 53 (3): 446–469.

Svensson, Isak, and Mathilda Lindgren. 2013. Peace from the Inside: Exploring the Role of the Insider-Partial Mediator. *International Interactions* 39 (5): 698–722.

Taniguchi, Miyoko. 2019. Rethinking 'Liberal Peacebuilding': Conflict, Violence, and Peace in Mindanao. *Social Transformations Journal of the Global South* 7 (1): 165–193.

Taya, Shamsuddin, Rusdi Omar, Che Mohd Aziz Yaacob, and Abdul Lantong. 2018. Peacebuilding Model of Third-Party Mediation in the Philippines: Comparing Malaysia and the OIC. *The Journal of Social Sciences Research* 6: 1151–1157.

Tengku, Abdul Ghafar. 2017. *Beyond the Peace Tables: Reflections on the GPH-MILF Peace Process*. Ed. Ab Kabir Shahpur Tengku, Karen Simbulan, and Laurens Visser. Siem Reap, Cambodia: The Centre for Peace and Conflict Studies.
Torres, Wilfredo Magno, III. 2014. Introduction. In *Rido: Clan Feuding and Conflict Management in Mindanao*. Quezon City: Ateneo de Manila University.
UN. 2020. *A New Era of Conflict and Violence*. United Nations. https://www.un.org/en/un75/new-era-conflict-and-violence.
UNDP. 2014. *Supporting Insider Mediation: Strengthening Resilience to Conflict and Turbulence*. New York: United Nations Development Programme and European Commission.
———. 2018. *Engaging with Insider Mediators: Sustaining Peace in an Age of Turbulence*. 2nd ed. New York: United Nations Development Programme.
UNSC. 2012. Strengthening the Role of Mediation in the Peaceful Settlement of Disputes, Conflict Prevention and Resolution: Report of the Secretary-General. A/66/811, United Nations Security Council (UNSC). https://peacemaker.un.org/sites/peacemaker.un.org/files/SGReport_StrenghteningtheRoleofMediation_A66811_0.pdf.
Wehr, Paul. 1991. *Conflict Regulation*. Boulder: Westview Press.
Wehr, Paul, and John Paul Lederach. 1991. Mediating Conflict in Central America. *Journal of Peace Research* 28 (1): 85–98.
Zartman, I. William. 2001. The Timing of Peace Initiatives: Hurting Stalemates and Ripe Moments. *Global Review of Ethnopolitics* 1 (1): 8–18.

CHAPTER 6

Exploring Mediation Efforts Amid Systemic and Domestic Constraints: The Case of the Syrian Conflict

Ako Muto

Introduction[1]

Complex, protracted, and recurring intrastate conflicts remain one of the biggest contemporary threats to global peace. They increasingly require pragmatic and context-specific peace actions—peacemaking, peacekeeping, and peacebuilding—to be implemented and effectively coordinated at all stages of the conflict cycle. Any external actor involved with peace initiatives in such a complex context is increasingly asked to recognize the context and embrace adaptiveness in interventions as well as to support, as much as possible, the inclusion of national and local actors in the peace process.

[1] Disclaimer: The views and interpretations expressed in this chapter are the result of the author's analysis and do not necessarily represent those of the organizations or persons mentioned.

A. Muto (✉)
JICA Ogata Sadako Research Institute for Peace and Development,
Tokyo, Japan
e-mail: Muto.Ako@jica.go.jp

C. de Coning et al. (eds.), *Adaptive Mediation and Conflict Resolution*, Sustainable Development Goals Series,
https://doi.org/10.1007/978-3-030-92577-2_6

The issue of context recognition is particularly relevant to the case of international cooperation for peace in Syria, one of the most challenging political and humanitarian crises since World War II. Mediation in the context of the Syrian conflict has been described as a mission impossible, during which some of the world's most experienced mediators could not achieve a comprehensive ceasefire, and the context-specific humanitarian ceasefires that were agreed could not be sustained for long. Moreover, a comprehensive contextual analysis of the Syrian conflict, not only from the international and national perspectives, which are contested and changing, but also from the local perspective within Syrian borders, is crucially significant.

The preconditions necessary for mediation to work are introduced by de Coning in Chap. 2 and are as follows: (1) the parties are willing to accept a negotiated solution; (2) they are ready to choose mediation as the method of negotiating a ceasefire or peace agreement and accept a neutral third-party mediator; (3) the parties can negotiate without the negative influence of international pressure or interventions. This chapter reflects on these assumptions, specifically their relevance and applicability in the Syrian conflict. The study is based on data collected via semi-structured interviews conducted with the Syrian people and International NGOs (INGOs) involved in the Syrian platforms, and media analysis on topics related to mediation of armed conflicts, complemented by empirical evidence that explains the mediation dynamics and outcomes during the period from 2011 to 2019.

The chapter is divided into three main sections. First, it demonstrates how the disagreement between the permanent member states (P5) of the United Nations Security Council (UNSC) and the mediation process initiated by the League of Arab States (LAS) affected the activities of the first and second UN Special Envoys. Second, it reveals the domestic constraints in addition to further systemic constraints, which conditioned the activities of the third and fourth Special Envoys; as the fourth Special Envoy is still active at the time of writing, this chapter covers only the period up to the establishment of the Syrian Constitutional Committee in September 2019. Third, it analyzes the contributions of other nonstate actors, specifically civil society and INGOs, to the mediation efforts in Syria during the conflict.

Based on these examinations of both systematic and domestic constraints, the chapter reveals how external actors got involved in the Syrian conflict shortly after the start of the unrest and how the four Special

Envoys appointed by the UN attempted to adapt to such context in facilitating mediation among domestic parties. Hence, it argues that international factors have affected the Special Envoys' mediation efforts in the Syrian conflict. Moreover, the profusion of non-state armed groups added an unavoidable element of complexity that needs to be taken into consideration by mediators and peacebuilders. It also asserts the complex effects of the absence of a concrete agreement on the practices of mediation or a compromise at the international and national levels. In conclusion, the chapter sheds light on the significance and challenges of contextualized and adaptive approaches that will have the potential to promote further contacts among Syrian citizens and open the pathways for mediators to deal more effectively with the conflict.

Systemic Constraints and the Challenges of Establishing a Syrian Transitional Government

This section describes the factors that undermined conventional and high-level mediation efforts during the first four years of the conflict. It examines the different parties involved and their conflicting priorities to reveal how the responses by the international community developed in this complex context and the challenges of establishing a transitional government. The Syrian conflict began in March 2011 with the civil demonstrations in Dara'a, a city in the Southern region of the country, and it became internationalized only a month later. The P5 could not develop a unified response to end the conflict, recreating similar systemic challenges as those presented by the Cold War era. In the UNSC meeting in April 2011, Russia strongly supported the Syrian government, and China followed the same position. France, the UK, and the US supported the opposition (UNSC 2011a). There was no consensus among the P5 over who was responsible for the violence. Thus, it was not the UN but the LAS which was the first to attempt mediation within this context. Traditionally, the LAS has had a policy of nonintervention in the sovereignty of its member states (League of Arab States 1945). However, the change of regimes in Tunisia and Egypt in the wake of the so-called Arab Spring[2] and NATO's activities in Libya led the LAS to demand concessions from the Syrian government, holding it responsible for the violence (Küçükkeleş 2012).

[2] The so-called Arab Spring is the political upheaval that began in Tunisia at the end of 2010 and resulted in the ouster of presidents in that country, as well as in Egypt and Yemen.

Among the Syrian government, the conflict was perceived as a domestic political matter from the beginning that did not require international attention. Thus, the mediation activities conducted by the LAS were perceived as not being meaningful, at least for one of the parties: the Syrian government led by Bashar Al-Assad. It first urged the government to stop the violence and engage in dialogue with the opposition. When this did not happen, the LAS suspended Syria's membership in the league and imposed sanctions in November 2011 (Batty and Shenker 2011). It dispatched a LAS Monitoring Team in the next month to end the violence. Later in January 2012, the LAS introduced the "Arab Plan to Resolve the Syrian Crisis," which included forming a national unity government comprised of the existing government and the opposition, operating under a mutually agreed leader within two months of the start of the dialogue. The plan would grant all presidential powers to the vice president to cooperate fully with a national unity government, and it would enable the drafting of a new constitution for approval by referendum (UNSC 2012a). Despite the continued disagreement among the P5 (e.g., UNSC 2011b, 2012b), the LAS pressed for significant concessions, which the government did not accept. The LAS mediation strategy of resolving the conflict included the requirement that the Syrian president delegate his power before the formation of a transitional government, a strategy backed by the United Nations General Assembly (UNGA 2012). However, this method of imposing a demand did not achieve effective results in bringing both sides to the negotiation table.

Later in February 2012, an alternative mediation method was introduced, with the UN and the LAS jointly appointing Kofi Annan[3] as the Special Envoy to Syria. His mediation efforts were partially successful. Considering the challenging situation that resulted from the lack of consensus among the P5, the Special Envoy's main focus was not to resolve the conflict but instead to "reduce the violence first" (Hinnebusch and Zartman 2016, 7). Annan's six-point plan requested all the contested parties to cooperate with the Special Envoy, effectively ending violence and starting "an inclusive Syrian-led peace process to address the legitimate aspirations and concerns of the Syrian people" (UNSC 2012c, 1). According to the UNSC document S/PRST/2012/6, the P5 unanimously supported the six-point plan, and both the Syrian government and

[3] For additional details on Annan's mediation, see Hinnebusch and Zartman (2016) and Lundgren (2016).

the opposition accepted it (Annan 2012). This compromise resulted in the adoption of resolutions 2042 and 2043 (UNSC 2012d, 2012e) to deploy the UN Supervision Mission in Syria (i.e., UNSMIS). However, though violence decreased somewhat following the dispatch of UNSMIS in April 2012 (Hinnebusch and Zartman 2016, 8; Lundgren 2016), it flared up again. The Special Envoy was unable to take effective measures due to the P5 confrontation, and by mid-June the UNSMIS suspended its activities due to the deteriorating security situation (UN News 2012).

Annan tried to sustain the P5 agreement in order to continue his mediation efforts and effectively reduce violence by organizing an international conference. The consensus document of this international conference, later known as the "Geneva Communiqué," became the primary document in the Special Envoys' subsequent mediation strategy. This document seems to have adopted a mix of standard and adaptive mediation approaches. First, it specified the establishment of a transitional government, but it allowed for all government institutions, including the military and security forces, to remain on the condition of gaining "public confidence"(UNSC 2012f). Annan "knew what had to be avoided: the experience of the chaos unleashed by the US invasion of Iraq meant the state had to be preserved and a transition arranged that would avoid its collapse" (Hinnebusch and Zartman 2016, 7). Thus, he called for the withdrawal of heavy weapons by military and security forces in populated areas (UNSC 2012c). This mixed approach presented a promising mediation alternative, leaving Syria's public institutions, which were to some extent effective before the conflict, in the confidence of the people under a transitional government. In addition to mitigating the deep disagreement among the P5, the approach also considered the internal context in Syria. The mediators learned from the first LAS attempt that the Syrian government would not accept any effort that required the president to step down as a precondition. The Special Envoy thus adapted his mediation efforts to one that recognized and involved the Syrian government.

However, the Geneva Communiqué introduced a "creative ambiguity" regarding the transitional government members (Hinnebusch and Zartman 2016, 9). The document mentioned that transitional government members would consist of both the Syrian government and the opposition, determined by mutual consent. Thus, according to Hinnebusch and Zartman (2016, 9), for Russia, the Geneva Communiqué did not presuppose the president's immediate resignation, whereas the US assumed that the opposition would not agree to having the president as a member of the transitional government. Therefore, the Syrian government did not follow the Geneva Communiqué, and the opposition rejected it because it did not require the president's immediate resignation.[4] Consequently, the Geneva Communiqué remained only a "Geneva conference agreement" that was not adopted as a UNSC resolution until a year after the conference. The circumstances led to Annan's resignation, which was also affected by the UNSMIS withdrawal from Syria, its extension being vetoed in the UNSC.

Annan's mediation approach seemed to prioritize the consent of the P5 and ideally create a situation in which both parties would join the peace process; however, the disagreement among the P5 persisted through ineffective negotiations in Geneva. Moreover, most Syrian parties, that is, the government, the opposition, and the civil society, were not invited or could not travel to Switzerland. The fact that neither warring party was part of the negotiations in Geneva added determined-designed characteristics to the mediation process, while adaptive mediation characteristics, such as promoting self-organization and resilience involving both parties, were absent at this stage. Although Annan recognized the importance of the role of the Syrian civil society (Hellmüller and Zahar 2019), he gave priority to addressing the international context and the P5 disagreement in this stage of the mediation process, and failed to focus on Syria's conflict management and resolution.

Mediation methods that prioritized the international context persisted even after Annan's resignation. Like his predecessor, the second UN Special Envoy Lakhdar Brahimi,[5] started by focusing mediation on decreasing conflict rather than initiating a ceasefire. However, this strategy achieved little progress, and Brahimi took time to build relations with the government after mentioning the need for the president's resignation (Hinnebusch and Zartman 2016, 13). On the other hand, he was also having difficulty interacting with the rebels. France, the UK, the US, Qatar, Saudi Arabia, and some other LAS members decided to support the Syrian Opposition Coalition (i.e., SOC) based in Turkey. However, the SOC's effective control was limited to a few areas in Syria, and the coalition failed to unite hundreds of armed opposition groups. Its leadership

[4] Turkey is said to have urged the opposition groups to reject the Geneva Communiqué (Hinnebusch and Zartman 2016, 11).

[5] For additional details on Brahimi's mediation, see Hinnebusch and Zartman (2016) and Lundgren (2016).

was not effective enough (Ṣāyigh 2013). Therefore, it was challenging for mediators to find an opposition leader that fully represented all opposition stakeholders at the negotiation table. For Brahimi, the circumstances were not conducive to the implementation of standard mediation.

In this context, Brahimi's mediation strategy focused on (1) facilitating small-scale ceasefires to implement humanitarian assistance and (2) addressing the international context with the aim of implementing the Geneva Communiqué. First, Brahimi focused on the regional level by involving Iran to seek influence over the government; however, this strategy failed to gain the support of the LAS. Like his predecessor, Brahimi expected to eventually leverage the influence of Russia and the US in the peace process (Hinnebusch and Zartman 2016; Lundgren 2016). However, seeking a consensus between the P5 members was still challenging and did not result in effective mediation outcomes. The "Geneva 2" international conference was held in 2014, but the assembled parties failed to find a path to a ceasefire. Brahimi subsequently resigned. Nevertheless, the Geneva 2 conference produced some positive outcomes: (1) the government and the opposition gathered in the same place for the first time, and (2) they agreed to let women and children evacuate from Homs, a city besieged by the government (UN News 2014).

These outcomes can be seen as a result of Brahimi's mediation focused on small-scale ceasefires and humanitarian assistance. However, it is also important to note that, as was true during the Geneva conference, members of Syrian civil society were not invited to the Geneva 2 negotiations, although Brahimi was aware of the importance of involving them (Hellmüller and Zahar 2019, 86). The civil society lobbied for an inclusive peace process instead of a government versus anti-government dichotomic strategy, which resulted in the creation of "a small diverse group comprised of civil society figures to act as a sounding board of ideas to the Special Envoy" (Turkmani and Theros 2019, 9). The mediation strategy, however, continued to focus on accommodating the challenges posed by systemic constraints due to disagreements among the P5. This made mediation efforts ineffective, and Brahimi's mediation team could not develop a more adaptive mediation structure.

In summary, key systemic constraints presented by the P5 disagreement and, backed by this dispute, the unwillingness of contested parties to seek a negotiated solution challenged three mediation architectures (i.e., the LAS, Annan, and Brahimi) in Syria. The LAS actively took one side.

Following the government's rejection of the LAS mediation strategy, two of the most reputable mediators in the world, Annan and Brahimi, distanced themselves from this precondition (the resignation of the president) and focused on addressing the P5 issue instead. The two UN Special Envoys sought to create an enabling environment for negotiations, seeking to form a transitional government. This resulted in an initial reduction of violence, but a consensus among the P5 was not achieved, similar to the bipolar constraints of the Cold War era (Lundgren 2019). Those external factors clearly affected the efforts of the two Special Envoys for adaptive mediation. As Lundgren (2020) notes, the mediation strategies of both the LAS and the UN, during the first phase of mediation in Syria, were conditioned by its organizational capacities and member state preferences. This conditionality is one explanation for the long-term ineffectiveness of the mediations.

With the support of the external actors, the contested parties believed in defeating the opponents (Hinnebusch and Zartman 2016, 19) and were not ready to join mediation with their initiatives. As argued in Chap. 2, adaptive mediation is an approach "concerned with enhancing the self-sustainability of the agreements reached." To reach a ceasefire agreement, the contested parties are expected to welcome international mediation as a way to resolve the conflict and then accept a neutral third-party mediator. However, in the case of the Syrian conflict, in the initial mediation stage, the LAS was not necessarily neutral or impartial. Thus, the involved parties were not convinced that mediation would be the better solution than fighting or matching their interests. It can be argued that the ineffectiveness of this mediation phase in Syria indicates that it was premature for both parties to engage with mediation activities toward a peace agreement. This Syrian context reveals how an effective mediation process needs to be facilitated through pragmatism and adaptiveness. For instance, Annan's plan to "reduce the violence first" (Hinnebusch and Zartman 2016) and Brahimi's focus on small-scale ceasefires and humanitarian assistance are examples of adaptive steps to address the contextual constraints against mediation in Syria. Such adaptiveness and effectiveness explain how mediation activities could continue despite high levels of uncertainty and complexity.

Domestic Constraints and the Challenges of Addressing a Changing Syrian Conflict Context

This section discusses the changing context of the Syrian conflict, as well as how it affected mediation efforts by the third and fourth UN Special Envoys. It also highlights how the highly dynamic context that is typical of complex conflict systems, as observed in the Syrian conflict, propelled the mediators to continuously explore new adaptive pathways to reach an agreement. The analysis in this section covers the period from when Russia commenced airstrikes on Syrian territory in September 2015, in the wake of the expansion of the so-called Islamic State of Iraq and Levant (ISIL), until the establishment of the Constitutional Committee. Russia was then criticized for targeting US-backed and armed rebels rather than ISIL (Roth et al. 2015), thus turning the conflict's tide in favor of the Syrian government.

The disagreement among the P5 continued during the period of the third UN Special Envoy to Syria, Staffan de Mistura. The conflict situation was effectively reversed to the advantage of the Syrian government, as mentioned in the previous paragraph. In November 2015, 20 countries and institutions, including the P5, some LAS members, and Iran (not invited to either Geneva conference), held a meeting, known as the Vienna Peace Talks for Syria, and agreed to form the International Syria Support Group (ISSG); the ISSG agreed on a framework for a nationwide ceasefire and a parallel peace process in Syria. The US concessions on Iranian participation signaled a clear shift in the peace process (Mohammed and Murphy 2015). Following the ISSG agreement, the UNSC adopted Resolution 2254 (UNSC 2015), which set out the process for implementing the Geneva Communiqué mentioned earlier, and the document became the basis for the peace process initiated in 2016. The compromise between the P5, the LAS, Qatar, Saudi Arabia, Turkey, and Iran urged the Syrian government and the opposition to consider further collaboration to end the conflict. Thus, negotiations between the parties began only after nearly five years of conflict, when they were prompted by external parties.

In this context, Saudi Arabia, one of the supporters of the oppositions, contributed to the coming mediation. It convened a High Negotiations Committee (HNC) following the adoption of UN Resolution 2254 (UNSC 2015), with the task of selecting new members for the peace process. More than 100 opposition groups, including armed groups that had not shown interest in the Geneva conferences, met to coordinate their participation in the overall peace process. Russia could also participate in the HNC selection process (Lund 2015). However, the main Kurdish group and radical armed groups such as ISIL were excluded from it. Also, this process revealed disagreements among opposition groups on the issue of the Syrian president's resignation (Lund 2015) and uncertainty regarding whether the opposition was prepared to unite and genuinely compromise to a negotiated end of the conflict. Similarly, the Syrian government was unlikely to feel the need to compromise, as it had the upper hand in the conflict. In other words, the mediation process could achieve some consensus only at the international level but was not effective enough to enable an agreement between the local parties; influenced by international interventions, the local parties were still not ready to choose mediation as the method of negotiating a nationwide ceasefire or peace agreement.

The lack of commitment of contested parties to end hostilities made the context uncertain for the mediation by de Mistura. Based on the agreement among ISSG members and UN Resolution 2254, he attempted to focus on bringing the Syrian government and the opposition groups to the negotiation table (UNSC 2016a). However, though the contested parties gathered in Geneva in January 2016, face-to-face meetings were not possible, and de Mistura had to continue shuttle diplomacy—traveling between two or more parties that are reluctant to hold direct discussions. His effort ended after a week (BBC News 2016). In response, "the ISSG presented a proposal for a nationwide 'cessation of hostilities', further outlined in a joint statement by Russia and the United States on February 22, 2016, and endorsed by the Security Council in Resolution 2268" (Lundgren 2016, 278; UNSC 2016b). This proposal was agreed upon by the government and more than 40 opposition groups, and the violence sharply declined for the first time in four years (Lundgren 2016, 278). Akpınar (2016) points out that the external actors concerned with the Syrian crisis were neither neutral nor impartial and that this affected the mediation by the Special Envoys, as this chapter has also demonstrated in detail. The few international agreements achieved in this time simplified the complexity and facilitated the cessation of hostilities among the contested parties.

However, the agreements held for at best three months because of both systematic and domestic constraints. Again, the radical armed groups such as ISIL were excluded from the international agreement. Moreover, the issue of the president's resignation resurfaced among the ISSG during this period (Lundgren 2016, 279), and the original political framework with

Russia backing the government and the US backing some of the opposition groups resumed (e.g., see UNSC 2016c; Gordon and Kramer 2016). In the later part of 2016, Russia, in collaboration with Turkey and Iran, established a new direct political dialogue, known as the Astana talks, which included "all conflicting parties in the Syrian Arab Republic (UNSC 2016d)"[6] and worked as a separate framework parallel to the ISSG. Again, a P5 compromise did not last, and divergent perceptions on how to end the conflict, resulting from systemic constraints, continued. A member of the "National Agenda for the Future of Syria" (NAFS)[7] mentioned, "Many agencies and countries have supported the groups of oppositions to strengthen them and enable them to negotiate. However, at the end, I believe such inputs created the oppositions, not for supporting the solution" (Interviewee 2 2020). The rise of a new external framework concerned with the peace process illustrates the increasing complexity of the context of the Syrian conflict.

Some aspects of the Astana talks were similar to mediation efforts undertaken by great powers during the Cold War, as Lundgren argues (2019, 14), particularly the efforts of the US and the former Soviet Union to secure influence on their respective blocs. In the changed conflict context, the talks ensured the Syrian government's superiority in the conflict. Still, the launch of this framework was followed by the Security Council's adoption of a resolution welcoming a tripartite agreement (UNSC 2016e). The agreement was perceived as being pragmatic, and it was expected to improve the devastating humanitarian situation, especially in the besieged areas (UNSC 2017a). The Astana talks, which included "a wider participation of opposition actors with real battlefield influence" (Lundgren 2019, 9) than the Geneva talks that began in 2016 had, realized face-to-face negotiations (Cengiz 2020). Lundgren (2019) and Cengiz (2020) argue that Russia, which led the Astana talks, and Turkey and Iran, which cooperated, were parties to the conflict, and thus were not mediators in the strict sense of neutrality, but rather sponsors, or "guarantor states," of the peace process they initiated. The three countries gave up on ineffective mediation and developed a framework to adapt to the reality that the regime had gained the upper hand in the conflict.

[6] However, for example, some of the Kurdish groups that controlled the northern area weren't invited (France 24 2017).

[7] The next section refers to NAFS.

The UN mediation adaptively responded to an increasingly complex context that was beyond the reproduction of Cold War structures (Lundgren 2019, 10). This also followed the approach of the two former Special Envoys, Annan and Brahimi, to reduce violence and address the deteriorating humanitarian situation through small-scale suspension of violence (Hinnebusch and Imady 2017, 1). In addition, there were mediation attempts to seek collaborations between the government and opposition beyond the scope of humanitarian ceasefires. For example, there was a joint program plan to promote crops and their sales, although it ultimately failed to reach an agreement (Interviewee 1 2000). Such a program further aimed at building trust between the two sides through dialogue and attempted to restore self-organization and resilience in Syria, where the administrative system had managed to function before the conflict.

Another example of adaptive mediation was the UN's welcome of the agreement among Russia, Turkey, and Iran at the Astana conference in May 2017 to establish four de-escalation zones in Syria. There was a hope that this would ensure access to humanitarian assistance deliveries despite the ongoing war and violence (UNSC 2017b). However, the result was not successful while the conflict continued to escalate (UNSC 2018), as the government moved its military forces from the de-escalation zones to fight with ISIL and other armed opposition groups instead. As a result, the government was able to retake three of the four de-escalation zones by mid-2019 (Lundgren 2019, 10). In such areas, some opposition groups kept control after the small-scale and bottom-up cessation of hostilities, but some of these ceasefires converged into surrender to the government (Hinnebusch and Imady 2017). The government clearly regained lost ground, and the mediation context was changed from its initial configuration.

From that point onward, the mediation process focused on the establishment of a constitutional committee, as proposed during the Astana talks and as part of the peace process set out in the Geneva Communiqué. The Constitutional Committee was an attempt to facilitate direct dialogue among contested parties. In January 2018, the Syrian National Dialogue Congress held in Sochi, Russia, approved a list of candidates for the Constitutional Committee (UNSC 2018). The actual establishment of the Constitutional Committee in Geneva was then the subject of intensive mediation by de Mistura, who was succeeded by the fourth UN Special Envoy for Syria, Geir O. Pedersen. The participation of Syrian experts, the civil society, independent organizations, tribal chiefs and women, the government, and the opposition were confirmed in this process (UNSC 2018). The Syrian civil society officially participated in the peace process for the first time. In October 2019, the Constitutional Committee was established with 50 members of the government, 50 members of the opposition, and 50 civilian representatives (UN Special Envoy for Syria 2019). It took a year and a half to finalize the Committee members despite the UN mediation efforts (Lundgren 2019, 7). Moreover, Lundgren (2019) highlights how the framework formed by the guarantor states separate from the ISSG succeeded in removing talks regarding the transitional government and the consequent resignation of the president from its scope. The establishment of the Constitutional Committee may have been a major achievement in adapting to a situation where mediation for a ceasefire had been unsuccessful, and the prospects of achieving its original purpose of resolving protracted conflicts still seemed remote.

This section summarizes the context surrounding the mediation of the third and fourth UN Special Envoys. Insights from complexity science, specifically about how complex systems evolve and respond to pressure, help to understand this context. First, the UN mediation was influenced by the Astana talks. Second, the continuous changes in conflict dynamics forced the mediation process to respond pragmatically. Third, the mediation process and related goals were, for the most part, externally determined. Hence, when the Syrian government gained the upper hand in the conflict in 2015, Russia strengthened this superiority with the Astana talks being led by the guarantor states. This change in the political power over the mediation process led the mediators to prioritize coordination with the government accordingly and adaptively. One of the key dimensions of the complexity of the Syrian conflict rests on nonlinear and emerging relationships between the conflicting parties and components of the system. The parties to the conflict could not sustain the continuous motivation to engage in the mediation.

Despite the challenges posed by disagreements among key actors, and the lack of commitment and coordination, the Special Envoys successfully facilitated the creation of the Constitutional Committee under challenging systemic constraints and a changing conflict context. In addition, de Mistura tried to promote a temporary and area-limited local cessation of hostilities, even though they were not always successful. Akpınar (2016) notes that de Mistura's mediation strategy achieved many positive outcomes, "such as the longest and broadest ceasefire, access to the majority of besieged areas, considerable de-escalation of violence, and commitment among major actors towards a resolution" (Akpınar 2016, 11). Moreover, the UN's continued dialogue with civil society actors paved the way for the participation of the Syrian civil society in the peace process, for more context-specific solutions and a mediation strategy more inclusive of the local context and local narratives.

The Role of Civil Society in Contextualizing the Mediation Architecture

This section details the role and activities of the civil society in contextualizing mediation efforts by the third and fourth Special Envoys. According to Khalaf et al. (2014), it is important to note that before the conflict, most of the nongovernmental organizations (i.e., NGOs) in Syria were engaged in charity (see also Slim and Trombetta 2014). Syrian and Arab culture places great emphasis on generosity (Bosman 2012), and these institutions were able to contribute to the protection of many vulnerable Syrian families. In the 1990s, around 600 organizations were registered with the government, although relatively little is known about them due to the absence of reliable data on their activities. In 2007, a platform for government-registered NGOs was created under the UNDP's auspices (Khalaf et al. 2014). By 2010, the total number of registered NGOs was 1047 (Hellmüller and Zahar 2019). As the country entered the civil war, some of these organizations became inactive, while others, particularly those with a philanthropic background, became more active in humanitarian assistance (Slim and Trombetta 2014, 43). According to a survey conducted by the voluntary organization, "Citizens for Syria," there were 802 voluntary organizations across Syria in the first half of 2015, and some worked in areas other than charity, such as civic engagement and advocacy, media and communications, and development and housing (Citizens for Syria 2015, 13–14). Although details are not available, a variety of civil society organizations are still working for social change in Syria and could offer relevant contributions to contextualize mediation efforts and support the self-organization capabilities of the various components of the Syrian complex system.

As elaborated in previous sections, Syrian civil society actors did not directly participate in the mediation processes headed by Annan and Brahimi. The Syrian people were considered to be on the side of either the government or the opposition (Hellmüller and Zahar 2019), and their interest did not attract international attention. Addressing systemic constraints and focusing on external actors' influence seemed to have dominated mediation strategies until de Mistura expressed a strong desire to allow more civil society participation. Concurrently with the peace talk that was quickly terminated at the beginning of 2016, as described in the previous section, the Special Envoy set up the Syrian "Civil Society Support Room" (i.e., CSSR) in Geneva, where "more than 500 members of Syrian civil society, one third of them women, including Syrian experts and technocrats" participated in the discussions (Turkmani and Theros 2019, 5). While the first few sessions were dominated by expatriate Syrian men supporting the opposition, a more comprehensive range of civil society members who had distanced themselves from the government/opposition dichotomy gradually became involved (Turkmani and Theros 2019; Hellmüller and Zahar 2019). The participants provided the Special Envoy with expertise and information based on the local context, which contributed to his mediation efforts, particularly when considering the challenges presented by the Astana talks (Hellmüller and Zahar 2019, 86). In this regard, it is also important to note the creation of the Syrian Women's Advisory Board to the UN Special Envoy for Syria, established in February 2016 and composed of 12 independent Syrian civil society representatives from diverse backgrounds. The members of this group would share their experiences with the Special Envoy and other stakeholders and contribute to "exploring solutions for lasting peace" (UN Women 2016).

Through the CSSR, the Syrian civil society not only contributed to the peace process but could also strengthen its network by joining this platform. According to the Norwegian Centre for Conflict Resolution (NOREF), the CSSR increased its membership gradually (Interview to NOREF 2021), becoming more diverse with time and including NGOs and CSOs working both internally and externally in the fields of peacebuilding, law, and humanitarian work. It was consisted of "prominent figures, including legal and constitutional experts, university professors, and former government advisors" (Turkmani and Theros 2019, 20). The meeting locations were also extended to Lebanon, Turkey, and Jordan through video conferences for those citizens who could not make it to Geneva[8] (Turkmani and Theros 2019, 9, 24). Some of the CSSR members

[8] On the other hand, Turkmani and Theros pointed out that local actors in Kurdish-controlled areas found it difficult to travel to Geneva, had limited representation, and had

also joined another platform called the "National Agenda for the Future of Syria" (NAFS). The NAFS is a program established by the UN Economic and Social Commission for Western Asia (ESCWA) that includes a platform for technical dialogue which relies on an inclusive network of Syrian experts to develop all the analysis and policy options presented, and is distant from the peace process. The participants consist of Syrian technocrats and experts engaged in research and analysis to prepare essential documents for future state-building (Bymolt 2016).

It is possible to extract several implications from the CSSR's role in the Syrian peace process. First, it strengthened the participants' network beyond the discourses of the dichotomy of government versus the oppositions.

> Civil society from different geographies and perspectives, as opposed to political negotiating delegations, were able to sit down together and discuss important issues, (…) the process of coming together helped to dilute binary narratives, break down stereotypes of the 'other' and expand opportunities for dialogue and networking across lines of conflict. (Turkmani and Theros 2019, 12)

Therefore, the CSSR could serve as a place where people with different opinions met and exchanged perspectives and strengthened existing networks or formed new ones, regardless of where they were based or their backgrounds and positions. The availability to travel to Geneva was not the requirement for participation (Interview with NOREF 2021).

Second, the CSSR discussions had an impact on the peace process and mediation efforts. Hellmüller and Zahar (2019, 86) point out that:

> They [the participants] enable the mediation team to design a more context-sensitive process—whether on urgent local needs and priorities, legal and constitutional issues, elections, detainees, missing persons and abductees, transitional justice, or other topics, this local knowledge and expertise provides important information about the reality on the ground.

In this way, the discussion in the CSSR supplemented the Geneva talks with the perspective of civil society (Hellmüller and Zahar 2019), facilitating potential agreements although the political negotiations were reaching

difficulty sharing information between organizations (Turkmani and Theros 2019, 23–25). They would be excluded from both the Astana and the Geneva talks.

an impasse (Turkmani and Theros 2019). Therefore, the CSSR's effective contribution offered needed contextualization to the UN-led Geneva talks, bringing the mediation strategy and architecture closer to an adaptive mediation approach coexisting in parallel with the Russian-driven Astana talks.

In addition to the CSSR, INGOs played a significant role in the Syrian civil society. For example, the Finnish Evangelic-Lutheran Mission (FELM), in collaboration with the Common Space Initiative (CSI), supported the Syria Initiative (SI) program, which by the end of 2016 had initiated 15 dialogue forums between Syrians inside and outside the country (Lehti 2019). The program aimed at expanding the process of transforming violence into peace through civil society dialogues and connected them with the UN-led peace process. Furthermore, some facilitators who supported the SI were also involved in the negotiations of the Syrian Women's Advisory Board, as introduced earlier (Lehti 2019). Thus, it can be said that the FELM and the CSI were developing bottom-up adaptive mediation. In addition, Tabak (2015) pointed out that the Humanitarian Relief Foundation in Turkey successfully mediated various conflict situations in Syria (e.g., the release of imprisoned and tortured citizens and journalists) (Tabak 2015). The activities of such INGOs have the potential to significantly promote people's aspirations for peace and transform the conflict. On the other hand, Lehti (2019) argued that the free space for private mediators had been curtailed due to the domestic constraints in the conflict, which were also discussed in this chapter. In order to promote effective bottom-up interactive mediation in civil society, it is important for INGOs to link and complement their activities with the high-level adaptive mediation led by the UN.

On the other hand, the CSSR's contribution to the peace process has been limited in practice. Both the government and the opposition feared that civil society would represent different interests and grow into a third party (Hellmüller 2020, 11). According to Turkmani and Theros (2019, 19), the perceptions of CSSR participants on the role of the platform were more comprehensive than forming a third party to the peace process. They included representing the views of the Syrian people, lobbying for international pressure on the armed forces, and providing professional expertise based on the ground. On the other hand, Hellmüller (2020) argues that the positioning of the CSSR as a supporting resource of the Special Envoy limited its contribution to the peace process. Although the participants offered technical expertise based on their diverse backgrounds, the position of the CSSR turned those inputs into mere information or opinions to support some of the meetings in Geneva (Hellmüller 2020). Thus, although the CSSR was a platform that connected the peace process with civil society, it was not able to effectively bring civil society's interests and aspirations into the peace process.

This section analyzed the role of civil society in making contributions to the UN mediation efforts. The third and fourth UN Special Envoys' mediation style attempted to incorporate context-specific solutions and adaptive characteristics by allowing civil society members an active role in the mediation efforts. De Mistura established the CSSR, and Pedersen was able to maintain it, making the participation of civil society in the peace process more visible. The CSSR played a vital role in strengthening context-specific contributions from the Special Envoys and created a network of participants regardless of their physical location. Hence, it demonstrates how the Special Envoys attempted to develop a more contextualized and adaptive mediation structure despite systemic and domestic constraints. The diverse activities of INGOs would also support the development of civil society in Syria. On the other hand, the contributions of the Syrian civil society in the peace process remain limited. The armed conflict continues with the government's dominancy, and the economic and social fabric of Syrian civil society continues to suffer tremendous damage. It is, therefore, a challenge to link high-level mediation initiatives with support for civil society initiatives that lead to fundamental changes at the societal level.

The international and domestic constraints mentioned in this chapter have led to a situation where the peace process has largely neglected endogenous changes in the local communities towards self-organization and resilience. At the time of writing, no effective peace agreement was reached. While the civil society has been linked formally to the peace process through the CSSR and the Constitutional Committee and has been engaged in the NAFS platform for technical dialogue, ongoing mediation efforts have not allowed for civil society actors to play an essential role in the mediation process. While all four Special Envoys understood the need to involve civil society in the peace process, their formal engagement was hampered by rivalry among the P5 and the persistence of systematic and domestic constraints. In other words, the top-down imposition of externally led determined-designed solutions has consistently hampered mediation efforts in Syria.

Conclusion

This chapter attempted to explore mediation efforts within the context of the challenging systemic and domestic constraints of the Syrian conflict. All three prerequisites for a successful mediation activity did not apply to the Syrian conflict. It seemed premature to start standard mediation activities while it was almost impossible to avoid external interventions. Factors such as the P5 dynamics, the opposition groups' heterogeneity and disunity, the emergence of armed Islamist insurgencies (e.g., ISIL), and the current state of the conflict, which is advantageous to the government, appeared to have made the mediation process challenging. Many factors, such as a history of oppression, a precarious and uncompromising balance of power between the parties, and an uncompromising hostility, constitute an increasing complexity and will make it difficult to achieve successful mediation outcomes. There are three key insights for future mediation efforts in Syria that emerge from the mediation challenges mentioned in this chapter.

First, no mediation attempt has achieved a sustainable ceasefire in Syria yet. Systemic and domestic shifts and constraints made it difficult for mediation to result in an unwavering agreement between the contested parties. In this context, the LAS mediation architecture seemed to respond to a liberal order systemic configuration, as well as to the regional developments related to the upheaval of the so-called Arab Spring. On the other hand, the government's rejection of the LAS mediation indicates that there is a different understanding of such liberal international order. Furthermore, the fact that the rejection worked suggests that such a different understanding can function. Mediators have conducted mediation toward the establishment of a transitional government and have achieved some successes, but this has been externally driven based on a determined-designed direction. Then, a shift in the context of the conflict also led to dynamic changes in systemic and domestic constraints. The UN Special Envoys' mediation became subject to de facto mediation by the guarantors. This approach was adaptive in that the Astana talks kept the government's dominancy in the conflict while they involved many rebels in the talks. Nevertheless, so far, they have failed to achieve the ultimate aim of mediation, which was to bring about a sustainable ceasefire. The case of the Syrian conflict has clearly shown that it is challenging to facilitate such a ceasefire without the three premises mentioned at the beginning of this chapter. On the other hand, this case also revealed that even under such constraints it is possible to achieve some results through adaptive mediation, promoting people's participation in the peace process.

Second, given the complexity and current systemic nature of international relations— that is, the change that occurred in recent history from bipolarity to unipolarity, and more recently from unipolarity to multipolarity—it is highly unlikely that determined-designed and liberal approaches to mediation will remain as an effective solution for internationalized protracted conflicts such as the Syrian case where two or more of the P5 have a direct and contested interest. The P5 disagreements detailed in this chapter appeared to be a revival of systemic constraints like those seen during the Cold War era. Both Annan and Brahimi had hoped for US and Russian leverage on both parties, but this did not always work. Applying mediation approaches with liberal values developed after the Cold War to the Syrian context shows that a similar structure to the Cold War may have been untenable (Lundgren 2019, 14). Furthermore, it should be noted that today, more than 30 years after the end of the Cold War, regional powers (e.g., LAS, Qatar, Saudi Arabia, Turkey, and Iran) have gradually increased their international voice and role. Many of these emergent and influential powers are not necessarily in line with the values of the liberal order that emerged under the post–Cold War unipolar structure. The fact that there has been no path for sustainable peace in Syria indicates that no single external power has absolute influence over the Syrian government or the opposition. The emergence of a multipolar structure and the new role of regional powers make it more challenging for the Special Envoys to conduct mediation successfully. Perhaps the competition of the powers to influence the contested parties that they support undermines the adaptive capacity of the mediators and the parties themselves. This is because such powers are powerful enough to impose their positions, and it is almost impossible for the mediators and the parties to resist.

Third, there is the issue of ripeness of the parties to engage in mediation activities, according to Zartman (2001), that is, when did the parties have the intention to engage in mediation activities? In the case of the Syrian conflict, at the very least, it is possible to confirm that even when the parties started the "peace process" in 2016, there were no face-to-face negotiations; the Astana talks brought both sides to the negotiating table, but not by a neutral third party. In light of what has been discussed so far in this chapter, at the time of writing, the Geneva talks are also unlikely to have made progress in negotiating a ceasefire. Hence, the time for negotiations toward peace may not yet mature. After all, all the involved sides discussed in this chapter, that is, France, the UK, the US, LAS, Qatar, Saudi Arabia, Turkey, Russia, and Iran, keep supporting the contested parties, influencing them to continue fighting. There were various moments of opportunity for breakthroughs and agreements as described in the previous sections, but the opportunity was repeatedly blocked by the reintroduction of the president's resignation. Thus, the core conditions necessary for sustainable mediation that motivate the contested parties seem to be absent.

It seems to be unlikely that the currently applied mediation practices will proceed toward a lasting ceasefire in the Syrian conflict. Still, if there is no action, the armed conflict may continue until (and possibly even after) one side wins the war. If peace actions are employed by mediators and peacebuilders, with a consideration of the aspirations of diverse groups of Syrian citizens such as those participating in the CSSR, to enable them to contribute to the peace process and to take important functions, it will serve as a positive mediation outcome of current mediation efforts. Civil society actors have formally participated in the peace process through the CSSR and the Constitutional Committee, and have been involved in the NAFS technical dialogue. However, ongoing mediation efforts have not enabled the Syrian civil society to play a vital role in the peace process. As discussed by de Coning in Chap. 2 of this book, mediation is widely understood as a delicate and complex undertaking and is more likely to fail to achieve its set objectives than to succeed. However, as Andrew Mack argues (in De Coning, Chap. 2), even failed mediations could save lives to some extent.

Adaptive mediation is an approach focused on finding a resolution to the conflict by recognizing its complexity, unpredictability, and uncertainty and by employing a set of tools that help mediators and peacebuilders to cope with setbacks and shocks. The different mediation efforts in the Syrian case give glimpses of what such adaptive mediation may look like in a protracted conflict, including the following: Annan's plan to have the first international conference, which led to the development of Geneva Communique; Brahimi and de Mistura's focus on small-scale ceasefires and humanitarian assistance; the initiation of the Constitutional Committee during the Astana talks; valuable activities of INGOs; and the CSSR approach to bringing the Syrian civil society into the peace process while also strengthening its own network. Adaptive mediation could achieve a number of results. However, as the deterioration of the economic and social foundation resulting from more than ten years of protracted conflict continues, ineffective mediation efforts to only save lives are not enough for the Syrian people. When standard high-level international mediation efforts are ineffective, particularly during the stage when the dominant parties in the conflict and the direction of the ceasefire are unclear, the harm caused by the Syrian conflict to the general population can be mitigated through the coexistence of a combination of determined-designed and context-specific adaptive peace operations to support the resilience and self-organization of Syrian society. It is crucial that mediators make use of institutional learnings from both the positive results accumulated and the unsuccessful attempts of mediation during a decade of conflict and that the coherent international consensus which enables further adaptive mediation efforts is set up.

References

Akpınar, Pınar. 2016. The Limits of Mediation in the Arab Spring: The Case of Syria. *Third World Quarterly* 37 (12): 2288–2303. https://doi.org/10.1080/01436597.2016.1218273.

Annan, Kofi. 2012. *Interventions: A Life in War and Peace*. New York: The Penguin Press.

Batty, David, and Jack Shenker. 2011. Syria Suspended from Arab League. The Guardian, 12 November. http://www.theguardian.com/world/2011/nov/12/syria-suspended-arab-league.

BBC News. 2016. Syria Conflict: UN Suspends Peace Talks in Geneva. *BBC News*, 3 February. https://www.bbc.com/news/world-middle-east-35488073.

Bosman, Marieke. 2012. *The NGO Sector in Syria—An Overview*. INTRAC Briefing Paper 30, International NGO Training and Research Centre, Oxford, UK. https://www.intrac.org/wpcms/wp-content/uploads/2016/09/Briefing-Paper-30-The-NGO-sector-in-Syria.pdf.

Bymolt, Roger. 2016. *Evaluation of the National Agenda for the Future of Syria (NAFS) Program: Executive Summary*. Conducted by Royal Tropical Institute (KIT) Amsterdam and commissioned by UN ESCWA. https://www.unescwa.org/sites/www.unescwa.org/files/page_attachments/nafs-eval-executive-summary.pdf.

Cengiz, Sinem. 2020. Assessing the Astana Peace Process for Syria: Actors, Approaches, and Differences. *Contemporary Review of the Middle East* 7 (2): 200–214. https://doi.org/10.1177/2347798920901876.

Citizens for Syria. 2015. Mapping the Syrian Civil Society Actors: Phase One. *Citizens for Syria*. https://citizensforsyria.org/OrgLiterature/CfS-mapping-phase1-EN.pdf.

France 24. 2017. Syrian Rebels Will Attend Russia-Backed Astana Peace Talks. *France* 24, 16 January. https://www.france24.com/en/20170116-syria-rebels-will-attend-astana-peace-talks.

Gordon, Michael R., and Andrew E. Kramer. 2016. Tension with Russia Rises as US Halts Syria Negotiations. *The New York Times*, 3 October. https://www.nytimes.com/2016/10/04/world/middleeast/us-suspends-talks-with-russia-on-syria.html.

Hellmüller, Sara. 2020. Meaning-Making in Peace-Making: The Inclusion Norm at the Interplay between the United Nations and Civil Society in the Syrian Peace Process. *Wiley Online Library*, October. https://doi.org/10.1111/spsr.12413.

Hellmüller, Sara, and Marie Joëlle Zahar. 2019. UN-Led Mediation in Syria and Civil Society: Inclusion in a Multi-Layered Conflict. In *Navigating Inclusion in Peace Processes*, ed. Andy Carl. London: Conciliation Resources. https://rc-services-assets.s3.eu-west-1.amazonaws.com/s3fs-public/Navigating_inclusion_in_peace_processes_Accord_Issue_28.pdf.

Hinnebusch, Raymond, and Omar Imady. 2017. Syria's Reconciliation Agreements. *Syria Studies* 9 (2): 1–14. https://ojs.st-andrews.ac.uk/index.php/syria/article/view/1558/1193.

Hinnebusch, Raymond, and I. William Zartman. 2016. *UN Mediation in the Syrian Crisis: From Kofi Annan to Lakhdar Brahimi*. International Peace Institute. https://ssrn.com/abstract=2893359.

Interviewee 1. 2000. Interview with NAFS Member. Skype Interview by Ako Muto.

Interviewee 2. 2020. Interview with NAFS Member. Skype Interview by Ako Muto.

Khalaf, Rana, Oula Ramadan, and Stolleis Friederike. 2014. *Activism in Difficult Times:Civil Society Groups in Syria 2011–2014*. Badael Project and Friedrich-Ebert-Stiftung. https://library.fes.de/pdf-files/bueros/beirut/11162.pdf.

Küçükkeleş, Müjge. 2012. *Arab League's Syrian Policy*. Policy Brief No. 56, Foundation for Political Economic and Social Research, Turkey. http://file.setav.org/Files/Pdf/arab-league%E2%80%99s-syrian-policy.pdf.

League of Arab States. 1945. Charter of Arab League. 22 March. https://www.refworld.org/docid/3ae6b3ab18.html.

Lehti, Marko. 2019. *The Era of Private Peacemakers—A New Dialogic Approach to Mediation*. Switzerland: Palgrave Macmillan. https://www.palgrave.com/gp/book/9783319912004.

Lund, Aron. 2015. *Riyadh, Rumeilan, and Damascus: All You Need to Know About Syria's Opposition Conferences*. Carnegie Middle East Center, 9 December. https://carnegie-mec.org/diwan/62239.

Lundgren, Magnus. 2016. Mediation in Syria: Initiatives, Strategies, and Obstacles, 2011–2016. *Contemporary Security Policy* 37 (2): 273–288. https://doi.org/10.1080/13523260.2016.1192377.

———. 2019. *Mediation in Syria, 2016–19: A Tale of Two Processes*. December. https://doi.org/10.2139/ssrn.3507785.

———. 2020. Causal Mechanisms in Civil War Mediation: Evidence from Syria. *European Journal of International Relations* 26 (1): 209–235. https://doi.org/10.1177/1354066119856084.

Mohammed, Arshad, and Francois Murphy. 2015. Kerry Sees New Syria Talks Next Week, Does Not Rule Out Iran Role. *Reuters*, 23 October. Editor's Picks. https://www.reuters.com/article/us-mideast-crisis-talks-idUSKCN0SH1LN20151023.

NOREF. 2021. Interview Between Japan and Norway. Zoom Interview by Ako Muto.

Roth, Andrew, Brian Murphy, and Missy Ryan. 2015. Russia Begins Airstrikes in Syria; US Warns of New Concerns in Conflict. *Washington Post*, 30 September. https://www.washingtonpost.com/world/russias-legislature-authorizes-putin-to-use-military-force-in-syria/2015/09/30/f069f752-6749-11e5-9ef3-fde182507eac_story.html.

Ṣāyigh, Yazīd. 2013. *The Syrian Opposition's Leadership Problem*. The Carnegie Papers, Carnegie Middle East Center, Lebanon. https://carnegieendowment.org/files/syrian_leaderiship_problem.pdf.

Slim, Hugo, and Lorenzo Trombetta. 2014. *Syria Crisis Common Context Analysis. Coordinated Accountability and Lessons Learning (CALL) Initiative*. ISAC Inter-Agency Humanitarian Evaluations Steering Group, New York. https://interagencystandingcommittee.org/system/files/syria_crisis_common_context_analysis_june_2014.pdf.

Tabak, Hüsrev. 2015. Broadening the Nongovernmental Humanitarian Mission: The IHH and Mediation. *Insight Turkey*, 1 July. https://www.insightturkey.com/articles/broadening-the-nongovernmental-humanitarian-mission-the-ihh-and-mediation.

Turkmani, Rim, and Marika Theros. 2019. *A Process in Its Own Right: The Syrian Civil Society Support Room*. London: Conflict Research Programme, The London School of Economics and Political Science. http://eprints.lse.ac.uk/101034/5/A_process_in_its_own_right.pdf.

UN News. 2012. UN Suspends Monitoring Activities in Syria amid Escalating Violence. *UN News*, 16 June. https://news.un.org/en/story/2012/06/413402-un-suspends-monitoring-activities-syria-amid-escalating-violence.

———. 2014. UN-Arab League Envoy Says Russia, US Pledge to Help Unblock Stalled Syria Talks. *UN News*, 13 February. https://news.un.org/en/story/2014/02/461792-un-arab-league-envoy-says-russia-us-pledge-help-unblock-stalled-syria-talks.

UN Special Envoy for Syria. 2019. Opening Statement to the Constitutional Committee by Geir O. Pedersen, United Nations Special Envoy for

Syria. *Relief Web*. https://reliefweb.int/report/syrian-arab-republic/opening-statement-constitutional-committee-geir-o-pedersen-united.

UN Women. 2016. Syrian Women Advisory Board Shares Experience in Exploring Solutions for Peace. *UN Women*, 31 August. https://www.unwomen.org/news/stories/2016/8/press-release-syrian-women-advisory-board-shares-experience-in-exploring-solutions-for-peace.

UNGA. 2012. *Resolution Adopted by the General Assembly on 16 February 2012: 66/253*. The Situation in the Syrian Arab Republic, United Nations General Assembly. https://www.securitycouncilreport.org/atf/cf/%7B65BFCF9B-6D27-4E9C-8CD3-CF6E4FF96FF9%7D/Syria%20A%20RES%2066%20253.pdf.

UNSC. 2011a. *Security Council Meeting Records*. S/PV.6524. United Nations Security Council (UNSC). https://www.securitycouncilreport.org/un-documents/document/syria-s-pv-6524.php.

———. 2011b. *Security Council Meeting Records*. S/PV.6627. United Nations Security Council (UNSC). https://www.securitycouncilreport.org/atf/cf/%7B65BFCF9B-6D27-4E9C-8CD3-CF6E4FF96FF9%7D/Golan%20Heights%20S%20PV%206627.pdf.

———. 2012a. *Letter Dated 24 January 2012 from the Secretary-General Addressed to the President of the Security Council*. S/2012/71. United Nations Security Council (UNSC). https://digitallibrary.un.org/record/720513.

———. 2012b. *Provisional Record 6711th Meeting*. S/PV.6711. United Nations Security Council (UNSC). https://www.securitycouncilreport.org/atf/cf/%7B65BFCF9B-6D27-4E9C-8CD3-CF6E4FF96FF9%7D/Syria%20SPV%206711.pdf.

———. 2012c. *Statement by the President of the Security Council*. S/PRST/2012/6. United Nations Security Council (UNSC). https://www.securitycouncilreport.org/atf/cf/%7B65BFCF9B-6D27-4E9C-8CD3-CF6E4FF96FF9%7D/Syria%20S%20PRST%202012%206.pdf.

———. 2012d. *Resolution 2042 (2012): Adopted by the Security Council at Its 6751st Meeting*. S/RES/2042. United Nations Security Council (UNSC). https://www.securitycouncilreport.org/atf/cf/%7B65BFCF9B-6D27-4E9C-8CD3-CF6E4FF96FF9%7D/Syria%20SRES%202042.pdf.

———. 2012e. *Resolution 2043 (2012): Adopted by the Security Council at Its 6756th Meeting*. S/RES/2043. United Nations Security Council (UNSC). https://www.securitycouncilreport.org/atf/cf/%7B65BFCF9B-6D27-4E9C-8CD3-CF6E4FF96FF9%7D/Syria%20SRES%202043.pdf.

———. 2012f. *Identical Letters Dated 5 July 2012 from the Secretary-General Addressed to the President of the General Assembly and the President of the Security Council*. A/66/865–S/2012/522. United Nations Security Council (UNSC).

https://www.securitycouncilreport.org/atf/cf/%7B65BFCF9B-6D27-4E9C-8CD3-CF6E4FF96FF9%7D/Syria%20S2012%20522.pdf.
———. 2015. *Resolution 2254 (2015): Adopted by the Security Council at Its 7588th Meeting, on 18 December 2015.* S/RES/2254. United Nations Security Council (UNSC). https://www.securitycouncilreport.org/atf/cf/%7B65BFCF9B-6D27-4E9C-8CD3-CF6E4FF96FF9%7D/s_res_2254.pdf.
———. 2016a. *Letter Dated 17 February 2016 from the Secretary-General Addressed to the President of the Security Council.* S/2016/152. United Nations Security Council (UNSC). https://digitallibrary.un.org/record/820392?ln=en.
———. 2016b. *Resolution 2268 (2016): Adopted by the Security Council at Its 7634th Meeting.* S/RES/2268. United Nations Security Council (UNSC). https://www.securitycouncilreport.org/atf/cf/%7B65BFCF9B-6D27-4E9C-8CD3-CF6E4FF96FF9%7D/s_res_2268.pdf.
———. 2016c. *Provisional 7825th Meeting.* S/PV.7825. United Nations Security Council (UNSC). https://www.securitycouncilreport.org/atf/cf/%7B65BFCF9B-6D27-4E9C-8CD3-CF6E4FF96FF9%7D/s_pv_7825.pdf.
———. 2016d. *Letter Dated 29 December 2016 from the Permanent Representative of the Russian Federation to the United Nations and the Chargé d'affaires a.i. of the Permanent Mission of Turkey to the United Nations Addressed to the Secretary-General and the President of the Security Council.* S/2016/1133. United Nations Security Council (UNSC). https://www.securitycouncilreport.org/atf/cf/%7B65BFCF9B-6D27-4E9C-8CD3-CF6E4FF96FF9%7D/s_2016_1133.pdf.
———. 2016e. *Resolution 2336 Adopted by the Security Council at Its 7855th Meeting.* S/RES/2336. United Nations Security Council (UNSC). http://unscr.com/en/resolutions/2336.
———. 2017a. *Provisional 7870th Meeting.* S/pv.7870. United Nations Security Council (UNSC). https://www.securitycouncilreport.org/atf/cf/%7B65BFCF9B-6D27-4E9C-8CD3-CF6E4FF96FF9%7D/s_pv_7870.pdf.
———. 2017b. *Provisional 7955th Meeting.* S/PV.7955. United Nations Security Council (UNSC). https://www.securitycouncilreport.org/atf/cf/%7B65BFCF9B-6D27-4E9C-8CD3-CF6E4FF96FF9%7D/s_pv_7955.pdf.
———. 2018. *Provisional 8181th Meeting.* S/PV.8181. United Nations Security Council (UNSC). https://www.securitycouncilreport.org/atf/cf/%7B65BFCF9B-6D27-4E9C-8CD3-CF6E4FF96FF9%7D/s_pv_8181.pdf.
Zartman, I. William. 2001. The Timing of Peace Initiatives: Hurting Stalemates and Ripe Moments. *Global Review of Ethnopolitics* 1 (1): 8–18. https://doi.org/10.1080/14718800108405087.

CHAPTER 7

Adapting to Uncertainty: What Have We Learned from Mediation and Conflict Resolution in Colombia, Mozambique, the Philippines, and Syria

Cedric de Coning, Ako Muto, and Rui Saraiva

Introduction

In the *Lost Art of Peacemaking*, David Harland traces the history of international mediation since the end of the Cold War. He recounts many of the great successes of international mediation but argues that since 2008 the number of successful mediations has declined (Harland 2018). He lists

C. de Coning
Norwegian Institute of International Affairs (NUPI), Oslo, Norway

African Center for the Constructive Resolution of Disputes (ACCORD), Durban, South Africa
e-mail: cdc@nupi.no

A. Muto • R. Saraiva (✉)
JICA Ogata Sadako Research Institute for Peace and Development, Tokyo, Japan
e-mail: Muto.Ako@jica.go.jp; Farosaraiva.Rui@jica.go.jp

C. de Coning et al. (eds.), *Adaptive Mediation and Conflict Resolution*, Sustainable Development Goals Series,
https://doi.org/10.1007/978-3-030-92577-2_7

a string of failures in Sri Lanka, Libya, Darfur, South Sudan, Yemen, and Syria and points out that the few successful mediations that were achieved over the last decade and a half were mostly mediated by non–United Nations-led efforts (see also Lehti 2020; Paffenholz 2021). Harland argues that a number of developments have significantly disrupted the international mediation space, including geopolitical rivalry, the atomization of conflict, and the internationalization of internal conflicts.

In this volume, we have argued that the developments Harland and others describe have disrupted the mainstream liberal peace approach to mediation. The underlying theory of change that informs the liberal peace approach is a deductive linear causal model, whereby the outcome is assumed to be more or less guaranteed if the liberal peace design is followed, that is, it is a determined-design model (Eriksen 2009). Since at least the 2008 financial crisis, the success of the liberal peace model has been under increasing pressure (Richmond 2015). The global consequences of the negative impact of the growth imperative on the environment; the growing inequality between the superrich and the rest of the world's population, which manifested both within liberal states and between the liberal club and the rest of the world; and the human suffering and chaos introduced by the wars in Iraq, Afghanistan, Libya, Yemen and Syria all contributed to the rapid erosion of the global public trust in the moral superiority and functional efficacy of the liberal peace model. The combined effect of the rise of China and the increasing influence of a number of regional and middle powers, corporations, and nonstate actors with global impact, the reemergence of fascist populism in the West and violent extremism across its peripheries, and the disruptive effect of social media and other new technologies have introduced an unprecedented level of turbulence in an increasingly closely connected global system. While complexity is not new, these developments have accentuated the diversity of actors and variety of factors, and therefore have further increased the uncertainty and unpredictability that would be mediators have to take into account in any attempt to resolve a particular conflict.

With more analysts, policymakers, and practitioners advocating for a new twenty-first-century approach to mediation, it is now increasingly recognized that old methods designed for interstate disputes and subsequently adjusted to intra-state conflicts are insufficient to respond to today's complex transnational armed conflicts (Lehti 2019, 232; Paffenholz 2021). In this book, we have introduced the Adaptive Mediation approach that is specifically designed to cope with uncertainty and that offers mediators an alternative to the linear, staged, normative, and individualistic liberal peace models of mediation (Bagshaw and Porter 2013). Adaptive Mediation is a facilitated process whereby the content of agreements emerges from among the parties to the conflict themselves, informed by the context within which the conflict is situated.

This book has attempted to deepen our understanding of the Adaptive Mediation approach and how it can be practiced by extracting empirical evidence from four diverse case studies—Colombia, Mozambique, the Philippines, and Syria—in an effort to generate insights into how mediators can apply adaptive mediation approaches to resolve and transform contemporary and future armed conflicts. In this concluding chapter, we take stock of what we have learned from the case studies about the concept and practice of Adaptive Mediation. It is important to note that we are retroactively applying the Adaptive Mediation approach to these cases. Adaptive Mediation is a new concept that was not consciously implemented in any of these four cases. However, we analyze these cases to see if there were elements of an Adaptive Mediation approach in the mediation styles applied and to identify lessons from those approaches and the results they have achieved.

The main research question the book attempted to address is how mediators can cope with and adapt to uncertainty and complexity in contemporary armed conflicts. In order to consider this question in a variety of cases, the case study authors have reflected on a number of other questions, including the following: What are the key characteristics of standard or alternative, and formal or informal, mediation practices in each of the cases? How did the mediators or parties to the conflict adapt or fail to adapt to uncertainty and complexity in each case? Which mediation best practices or lessons learned can we extract from the case studies?

Before we consider some of the key lessons that have emerged from the case studies, we present a brief recap of the Adaptive Mediation approach.

Adaptive Mediation

The standard or mainstream mediation method that has emerged after the Cold War can be described as determined-designed thinking. It is based on the assumption that mediation experts have the agency to analyze a conflict, identify its root causes, and design solutions for the conflict based on international norms (liberal peace ideology) and best practices (lessons based on past successes and failures). Mediation in this context is understood as a process through which the parties—relying on the information, analysis, best practices, and options presented by the expert mediators—are led through a facilitated process that ends with the parties agreeing on a version of the solutions presented to them, modestly adapted to reflect local realities and the most important interests of the parties. In practice, most of the limited solutions offered follow a standard range of options, and, as a result, most peace agreements reached over this period share, at their core, a similar logic: a transitional power-sharing period during which state institutions are developed or restored according to liberal peace norms, including in some cases a constitutional review process, followed by democratic elections.

The underlying theory of change of this determined-design model is that democracy leads to good governance, good governance leads to stability, and stability leads to peace and prosperity for all. Unfortunately, electoral politics can—without sufficiently developed formal and informal institutions to manage the tensions, conflict, and greed it generates—foster new waves of violent conflict and political systems in which one set of elites, often linked to whichever ethnic group happened to form the majority of the population, capture and corrupt the state to serve its own interests. As a result, electoral politics often generates violence and democracy has not always improved governance or resulted in stability. The result of these determined-design mediation processes, measured against the extent to which they led to a self-sustainable peace process, seems to be less than 50 percent over ten years (Collier et al. 2003).

The determined-design theory of change is flawed because social systems are empirically complex. Complex systems, including social systems, are highly dynamic, nonlinear, and emergent. This uncertainty is an intrinsic quality of complex adaptive systems, not a result of imperfect knowledge or inadequate analysis, planning, or implementation. This recognition has specific implications for the way we can plan and undertake mediation, one of which is the recognition that what has worked in one setting cannot be replicated in another. This irreproducibility is one of the core characteristics of complex systems.

The Adaptive Mediation approach provides us with a methodology for coping with this complexity, uncertainty, and irreproducibility. Firstly, it recognizes that a conflict analysis should not be developed by experts and presented to the parties to the conflict. Rather, it must emerge from collaborative engagement with the parties to the conflict and from an inductive iterative adaptive engagement with the context. Arriving at a shared understanding of the conflict is the first building block of the adaptive mediation process and a prerequisite for a self-sustainable mediated settlement. Adaptive Mediation also recognizes that such an analysis needs to be an ongoing and iterative process. As the social dynamics that influence the conflict are continuously evolving, so should the analysis informing the mediation.

Secondly, based on such a shared understanding, the parties to the conflict should generate their own potential range of settlement options. This collaborative process builds confidence, educates each of the parties about their respective world views and underlying assumptions, and broadens the scope of potential solutions beyond the narrow range that parties typically enter a negotiation with. Generating future options can also be complemented with associated collaborative and inclusive processes such as national dialogues or other forms of popular consultation. The process of generating and considering options is an iterative adaptive process that utilizes repeated cycles of variety and selection to reduce and ultimately settle on a shared set of agreed future pathways.

Thirdly, Adaptive Mediation recognizes that a mediation process is not limited to one series of talks and one agreement but is instead a transition process that typically spans decades and includes negotiations and agreements on many aspects of the social contract. It thus takes a whole-of-system, relational, and spatial approach that is open-ended, fluid, and flexible. Agreements should thus include mechanisms that anticipate the need for ongoing conflict prevention and resolution.

Lastly, Adaptive Mediation is an approach that shifts the focus of mediation away from the mainstream idealization and fixation on the mediator, the mediation table, and the settlement agreement. Instead, it approaches mediation as a participatory, adaptive, and iterative facilitation process that accompanies a society on its journey from conflict to sustainable peace.

The core principles of the Adaptive Mediation approach can be summarized as follows:

1. A recognition that social systems are complex and thus highly dynamic and nonlinear. This means that their behavior is inherently uncertain and unpredictable.
2. In order to make sense of such complex conflict systems and to influence them—while recognizing that our agency to understand and influence such complex systems is limited—we need to employ an inductive adaptive theory of change that is based in discovery and learning through iterative cycles of experimentation and feedback.

3. As the ultimate aim is to achieve self-sustainable peace, and the aim of peace mediation is to generate self-sustainable peace agreements, the mediation process needs to enable the maximum participation of the parties themselves in the emergence of an agreement. This means the mediators need to limit their role to process facilitation and allow the content of the agreements to emerge from the self-organizing processes of the negotiations among the parties themselves.

Adaptive Mediation thus differs from the mainstream determined-design and directed-mediation model in that it is an approach that is specifically designed to cope with the uncertainty, unpredictability, and irreproducibility inherent in complex social change process. Adaptive Mediation is a process that is aimed at empowering the parties participating in the mediation to generate solutions themselves. For a peace agreement to be self-sustainable, it has to emerge from a collaborative process owned by the parties to the conflict and it has to emerge from an inductive iterative adaptive engagement with the context. The role of the mediator is limited to facilitating the process. Adaptive Mediation is especially concerned with enhancing the self-sustainability of peace agreements and in this context understand the role of the mediator as facilitating a process of emergent self-organization.

When this approach is applied to conflict analyses, planning, monitoring, and evaluation, the ability of mediation processes to navigate uncertainty and adapt to changing dynamics should be enhanced. In order for more resilient and more self-sustainable agreements to emerge, Adaptive Mediation requires mediators to apply a light touch that encourages greater interdependence among the parties and discourages dependence upon the mediator. As a result, utilizing an Adaptive Mediation approach should result in generating peace agreements that are more locally grounded, self-sustainable, and resilient to setbacks and shocks. In this concluding chapter, we assess the four case studies to see if Adaptive Mediation approaches have yielded these results.

Lehti (2019, 96) underlines that the term "adaptive" refers, in de Coning's theory, on the one hand to resilient and self-organizing societies that are adaptive and on the other hand to the peacemakers' approach. Peacemakers must adapt their actions to the ambiguity of complex conflicts and realize that all analytical methods are only provisional and part of a continuously iterative learning process. As a result, mediators and peacebuilders recognize that there is not an absolute and correct solution to complex problems, and that thinking of peace processes in terms of failure and success is meaningless. Lehti (2019, 97) highlights that adaptive peacebuilding opens a new perspective that is also relevant to mediation and dialogue. If mediators combine the conflict transformation approach with complexity thinking, this will offer fresh substance to what Bercovitch (2002) referred to as the basic essence of peace mediation: transforming the parties' perceptions and behavior.

What Have We Learned from Mediation and Conflict Resolution in Colombia, Mozambique, the Philippines, and Syria?

When considering the four cases—Colombia, Mozambique, the Philippines, and Syria—and taking into account the research questions this volume aimed to address, three key comparative advantages of an Adaptive Mediation approach emerge. The main research question the book attempted to address is how mediators cope with, and adapt to, the uncertainty and complexity that is characteristic of most contemporary armed conflicts? In three of the four case studies—Colombia, Mozambique, the Philippines—we have found that several core elements of the Adaptive Mediation approach were critical to the ability of the later mediation processes to generate peace agreements, compared with earlier attempts. And that, thus far, employing Adaptive Mediation approaches has also resulted in these agreements being more sustainable than previous agreements. In the case of Syria, we argue that the conditions prevented the mediators from being able to apply elements of the Adaptive Mediation approach. The three comparative advantages of an Adaptive Mediation approach that have emerged from the four case studies are as follows: first, the ability to cope with uncertainty; second, the value of limiting the role of the mediator to process facilitation; third, the importance of agreements emerging from the parties themselves.

The Role of Adaptive Capacity in Coping with Uncertainty in Mediation Processes

In order to cope with the uncertainty and unpredictability that is characteristic of highly dynamic and complex systems, mediators need to invest in enhancing the adaptive capacity of their mediation processes. By strengthening the adaptive capacity and resilience of the mediation process, the mediators and parties to the conflict greatly enhance the likelihood that the peace process will be able to withstand, adapt, and even transform, despite the guaranteed setbacks and shocks they will experience, one example of such being the sudden death of one the lead negotiators in Mozambique.

In Colombia, 12 mediation processes addressed several armed conflicts between the Colombian government and twelve armed groups. The peace negotiations in the 1990s led to the demobilization of five armed groups, and in 2006 the right-wing militia, the AUC, agreed to cease its activities. More recently, the Colombian government and the FARC-EP insurgents reached a comprehensive peace agreement after almost four years of peace negotiations in Havana. The 12 mediation processes counted on external support but have been essentially a form of direct dialogue between both parties. In the peace negotiations with the FARC-EP, external support was first provided by Cuba, Norway, Venezuela, and Chile, and later by the US, the UN, Germany, and the European Union. International and national experts also played key roles as mediation advisors to the Colombian government. The later stage of the FARC mediation process welcomed civil society engagement with local voices being heard at the peace table for the first time in the history of mediation in Colombia. For three decades, the cumulative mediation experience acquired over these 12 peace process experiences contributed to the adaptiveness, pragmatism, and effectiveness of mediation initiatives in Colombia. The mediation process became more adaptive with time due to lessons learned from the past experiences. This enabled the mediation process between the government and the FARC to cope much better with uncertainty and unpredictability than the earlier processes had. For example, international and domestic mediators had to adapt to the different motivations of those actors motivated by ideology and those by new drivers of conflict like organized crime. The mediators also had to adapt their own style of mediation and give more room to the parties themselves, as will be discussed in the next two sections.

In Mozambique, the mediation process occurred in three stages with different mediators, mediation strategies, and mediation styles. The first stage (2013–2015) was led by five domestic mediators (four related to faith-based organization and one academic), but in this case, domestic solutions without external process facilitation resulted in significant deadlocks. The second stage (2015–2016) was led by high-level international mediators employing standard determined-designed mediation strategies that reduced the agency and space of both conflicting parties and failed to produce an agreement. The third stage (2016–2019) was led by both conflict parties engaging in a direct dialogue facilitated by the Swiss ambassador to Mozambique, Mirko Manzoni, and his small mediation team. They learned from and addressed the failures and ineffectiveness of previous mediation initiatives, and as a result the final mediation process was much more adaptive and pragmatic in style. The mediators focused on process facilitation, stimulating self-organization among the parties, and national ownership of the peace process. This greatly enhanced the adaptive capacity of the process and enabled it to cope with various setbacks and unexpected developments. They did so by facilitating direct talks between the principals of the two main parties at critical tipping points in the process and by including representatives from both parties in the mediation team. This approach provided an enabling environment for both party leaders and Mozambicans from both sides of the conflict to work together and reach a peace agreement.

In the Philippines, a multilayered mediation process involved several third-party mediators, including states, regional organizations, international nongovernmental organizations (INGOs), and Civil Society Organizations (CSOs). Gradually earning the trust of both parties, Malaysia had a key role in facilitating the mediation process. In 2009, the International Contact Group (ICG) also became a key enabler of the mediation process, employing hybrid mediation strategies that promoted vertical and horizontal relationships during the negotiations. The range of actors and relationships greatly enhanced the resilience and adaptive capacity of the process. The ICG also focused on enhancing the capacity of both parties and stimulating self-organization. After the ceasefires and two peace agreements were signed, insider mediation was provided by diverse groups within the Moro society organized under informal task forces. The mediation process in the Bangsamoro has been adaptive and pragmatic in nature. It started by relying on third-party international mediators trusted by all parties to generate consensus and nurture contextualized understandings on how to resolve the conflict. It then progressed to using insider mediators to increase the levels of interdependency and self-organization between the parties and within the Moro society.

In Syria, mediation efforts were first led by the Arab League and later by a number of UN Special Envoys of the secretary-general for Syria, namely Kofi Annan, Lakhdar Brahimi, Staffan de Mistura, and, more recently, Geir O. Pedersen. Given the complexity and uncertainty of the Syrian context, the fragmentation of conflict parties, and the internationalization of the conflict, it was particularly challenging for mediators to develop a mediation strategy that accommodated the preferences of all stakeholders. Up to the point of finishing this book, great power rivalry prevented the parties from reaching any meaningful agreement to end the conflict. However, all the mediators made efforts to adapt their strategies to domestic and systemic constraints, including by focusing on more limited conflict management, for example local humanitarian ceasefires, rather than peace writ-large conflict resolution. With the UN mediation, the Syrian process became more inclusive over time, inviting civil society actors to participate directly or indirectly in the peace process. In addition, the mediation process also became increasingly pragmatic, for example, with the invitation of Iran to participate in the 2015–2016 Geneva talks. The focus, at times, on mitigation and on life-saving assistance and the protection of civilians, rather than achieving an overall peace agreement, revealed the adaptiveness and pragmatism of the mediation initiatives.

All the cases presented in this volume demonstrate how the conflicts in question were influenced by drivers at multiple levels, from local to global. In particular, the Colombia case revealed the degree to which there is variety between different local contexts in one country, and how mediation processes need to be adaptive to the specific needs of different regions, communities, and local contexts. At the other end of the scale, the Syria case demonstrated how international and regional power rivalries undermined the ability of the mediators to forge peace from the bottom-up. In all these cases, the adaptive capacity of the mediation teams, as well as the negotiation teams of the parties to the conflict, was crucial to their ability to adapt the agenda and process considerations of the talks to stay abreast of and co-evolve with new emerging developments.

The Link between Process Facilitation and Self-Sustainable Outcomes

The mediators and the parties involved in any particular conflict have a wide range of potential styles, ranging from directed-mediation to facilitation, that they can employ. It is not possible to predetermine which style will be optimal in each instance, but overall, for a mediation process to end in a self-sustainable agreement, the Adaptive Mediation approach holds there will have to be a progression toward the facilitation end of the scale.

This is because facilitation gives more agency to the parties, allowing them to develop more ownership of the outcome. This, in turn, ensures that the outcome emerges from the context rather than from the mediator. The choice of style will need to be adapted to the context, and in every context a variety of styles could conceivably be employed, depending on the specific state in which the conflict and mediation process is at any point. Employing a mediation style where the mediator plays a more active role in directing the discussion poses a greater risk that the parties may become trapped in tit-for-tat defections, but often parties start off at this end of the scale until a certain degree of confidence in the mediation process has been achieved.

In the four case studies explored in this book, despite the variety of conflict and mediation contexts, there was a general progression over time from directed-mediation in the earlier cases to process-facilitation in the later cases. In Colombia, the lessons learned from the initial mediation experiences showed how a more directed-mediation style limited the willingness of the parties to negotiate. The mediators dominated the agenda in earlier mediation initiatives and that limited the agency and space of the parties to establish a shared understanding of the problem and pathways for resolving it among themselves. This approach changed during the FARC-EP mediation process, particularly following the exploratory meetings of 2011 near the Colombian-Venezuelan border. Since then, the parties themselves led and steered the meetings throughout the Havana negotiations in 2012 and beyond. One of the key mediation practices at the later stage of the process was to facilitate a national dialogue that would converge into a national agenda. Civil society actors and armed conflict victims were very active in the peace talks for the first time in Colombia, and this contributed to the peace agreement reached in 2016.

In Mozambique, after initial failed mediation attempts by domestic mediators that favored more assertive mediation techniques encouraged by the hard-liner Guebuza administration, a new mediation process welcomed high-level international mediation and a large group of external mediators. However, they also employed directed-mediation techniques that excessively dominated the mediation agenda. In the end, the pathway to a successful agreement resulted instead from the facilitation of direct dialogue between the leaders of both parties, supported by an adaptive mediation model that was not constrained by external interests, predetermined international standards, or the history and examples of past negotiations.

In the Philippines, the "multilayered" mediation structure strengthened the interactions between the stakeholders through vertical and horizontal relationships. In general, external mediators privileged facilitation instead of directed-mediation techniques, providing technical, financial, and political support to the mediation process and promoting trust-building between both parties. This was combined at a later stage with insider mediation, which enhanced the self-organization of both parties to deal with subsequent shocks and uncertainty. The "Friends of Peace" group led by the Archbishop of Cotabato and the Insider Mediators Group comprised of various members of the civil society–supported track-two dialogue initiatives in the Bangsamoro. Through their continuous mediation efforts, a growing common understanding was achieved among the various parties to the peace process.

In Syria, the mediation context presented persistent domestic challenges, such as the fractured nature of the opposition, the unwillingness of the parties to engage in constructive negotiations, and systemic challenges, such as the military and political support given by regional and international actors and the excessive interference of great powers in the negotiation process. Despite these limitations, local and international mediators were at times able to negotiate temporary ceasefires to enable humanitarian access and assistance. At the more formal level, UN mediation efforts employed facilitation techniques to try to make the peace process more inclusive of civil society actors, including women. This enabled the creation of the Syrian Constitutional Committee in 2019 with the intent to pave the ground for a national dialogue and a new constitution.

From Adaptive Mediation to Conflict Resolution: The Importance of Agreements Emerging from the Parties Themselves

Those mediation processes that have been the most successful in adapting to changing circumstances are those that have invested in processes that stimulate institutional learning. Institutional learning in this context refers to a process whereby the mediation participants, that is, the parties to the conflict as well as the mediation team, generate knowledge on an ongoing basis from the process that can inform future action. Adaptation requires selection among possible future courses of action based on feedback on the outcomes of previous choices. The more actively the mediation process is geared toward seeking out and processing feedback, the more likely it is that the mediation process will not be overwhelmed by changes in its environment; the more likely it is to be innovative, resilient, and to successfully arrive at a settlement agreement, and the more likely the agreement is to contain elements that will ensure that the implementation of the agreement is equally geared toward preventing and resolving future emerging conflicts.

In the case of Colombia, institutional learning was reflected in the creation of two significant bodies. The office of the High Commission for Peace gave confidence to the parties participating in the mediation process. It was an essential step in the aftermath of the previous peace process where former combatants were murdered after the signature of the peace agreement, as was the case with the Patriotic Union. For the first time, an institution (functioning like a ministry) had as its only mission the achievement of peace talks with belligerent groups. The second body created was the National Reincorporation Agency (NRA). Initially, this agency led the implementation of the National Plan for Reconciliation introduced by the government. Today, the NRA's mission includes the overall economic and social reintegration policy related to former combatants, regardless of their belligerent origin (guerrilla or paramilitary groups). The NRA has become a key institution to address the national policy of reintegration and to guide international cooperation needs based on their agenda. Both the High Commissioner and the NRA served to institutionalize organizational learning that facilitated ongoing adaptation, problem-solving, and conflict resolution.

In Mozambique, the Manzoni mediation team remained small and discreet. The soft skills of the mediators, such as discretion and humility, were a fundamental element in their mediation strategy, creating an environment of trust between the mediation team and the belligerent parties. The mediators were fully committed to a nationally owned peace process and made substantial efforts to travel to the RENAMO headquarters in the Gorongosa Mountains instead of suggesting meetings in the capital as happened in previous mediation stages. For the first time in history, President Nyusi and the RENAMO leader, Afonso Dhlakama, talked via phone, an event that would open doors for several in person meetings throughout the process. Subsequently, the mediators focused on encouraging direct communication between the two leaders, and this new mediation model quickly resulted in a ceasefire announced in December 2016. The same approach was effective even after Dhlakama unexpectedly passed away and Ossufo Momade became the RENAMO leader after a difficult transition. Momade met with Nyusi for the first time in the city of Beira on July 11, 2018, and several rounds of direct talks took place until a new peace agreement was signed in August 2019. The choice to pursue direct dialogue was a result of institutional learning and an understanding that the peace process needed more Mozambican control and the direct involvement of the party leaders, so that an agreement could emerge from within instead of from outside mediation.

While the level of institutional learning and adaptation in the case of the Philippines changed according to the status of the peace process, a new and significant finding from this case study lies in the role that self-organization and capacity development of diverse stakeholders engaged in conflict resolution played. It helped to mitigate tensions among those directly involved as well as the vested interest groups that supported them. It also helped the parties to focus on reconciliation and on accommodating interests among them. They were able to build consensus and trust among themselves while obtaining positive mediation outcomes through vertical networks—Manila to Bangsamoro—and horizontal networks—within Bangsamoro. Even after the signing of the peace agreement, having a framework that relied on insider mediators provided valuable feedback to tackle future challenges emerging from the peacebuilding process in Mindanao.

In Syria, probably the most complex armed conflict today, the institutional learning process is ongoing, as states and international organizations attempt to find ways to contribute to peace negotiations and mitigate the negative impact of the armed conflict. The UN mediation effort has tried to moderate external and domestic constraints and increasingly focused on building trust and bridging divides. The third and fourth UN Special Envoys attempted to switch from focusing excessively on external leverage and instead attempted to incorporate context-specific solutions. However, at the time of writing, the UN mediation initiative and the Astana negotiations had not achieved significant progress toward a political solution. The effectiveness of future mediation initiatives will undoubtedly depend on the ability of the mediators to learn from past experience, adapt to changing circumstances, and develop context-specific pathways to bring the conflict to an end.

Findings and Recommendations

We have argued that a number of developments—including geopolitical rivalry, the atomization of conflict, and the internationalization of internal conflicts—have challenged the mainstream liberal peace approach to mediation and that analysts, policymakers, and practitioners are increasingly calling for a new approach to mediation in the twenty-first century. We have characterized the liberal peace approach as employing a deductive linear causal theory of change, whereby the outcome is assumed to be more or less guaranteed if the liberal peace design is followed, which is why we have referred to it is as a determined-design model. A number of developments, including especially the inability of the liberal peace approach to bring a peaceful end to the wars in Iraq, Afghanistan, Libya, Yemen, and Syria, to name a few, have contributed to the erosion of the global public trust in the moral superiority and functional efficacy of the liberal peace model. These and other developments discussed in this volume and chapter have introduced an unprecedented level of turbulence in an increasingly closely connected global system. While complexity is not new, these developments have further increased the uncertainty and unpredictability that would be mediators have to take into account in any attempt to resolve a particular conflict. The main research question the book attempted to answer was thus how mediators can cope and adapt to uncertainty and complexity in contemporary armed conflicts.

The golden thread throughout the book was that standard mediation strategies have become increasingly ineffective in such complex environments, requiring a shift from determined-designed mediation to adaptive mediation strategies. The book introduced the Adaptive Mediation approach, which is specifically designed to cope with uncertainty and offers mediators an alternative to the linear, staged, normative, and individualistic liberal peace model of mediation. Adaptive Mediation is a facilitated process whereby the content of agreements emerges inductively from among the parties to the conflict themselves, informed by the context within which the conflict is situated.

In this book, we analyzed four case studies of mediation in four distinct armed conflicts: Colombia, Mozambique, the Philippines, and Syria. These four cases demonstrated the extent to which mediation varies according to context, history, and process. For example, one common approach to mediation has been to wait until the parties to the conflict recognize for themselves that they are unable to achieve their gains through violence, that is, the ripeness principle introduced earlier in the book. While this principle seems to have been at work in at least three of the four cases considered in this volume, all three of these cases demonstrated how long this may take and how fragile and dynamic such calculations are. In contrast, the Syrian case demonstrates that in some cases this ripeness may not occur at all, especially when a conflict is fueled and supported by external backers who use it as a proxy for their own rivalries. So, while ripeness is an important factor in how likely agreements reached will be self-sustainable, other considerations such as the harm caused by the ongoing conflict also motivate internal and external mediators and the United Nations Security Council—which has the ultimate responsibility for international peace and security—to make continuous attempts to persuade the parties to halt the conflict, if not from a political ripeness assessment, then at least on humanitarian grounds. We have chosen to include the Syrian case in this volume as a constant reminder of this imperative, and how incredibly difficult it can be to achieve mediated peace agreements in practice.

Some approaches tend to privilege negotiation and dialogue processes that involve multiple international stakeholders, as in the cases of Colombia, the Philippines, and, to some degree, Syria, but as the case of Mozambique has shown, sometimes mediation benefits from small teams that make the effort to gain the trust of the parties with discretion, humility, and perseverance. Three cases, Colombia, Mozambique, and the Philippines, also demonstrate the value of discreet mediation processes, in which the mediators remain largely in the background and parties to the conflict rightfully occupy the foreground. We have explained why, from a complex adaptive systems perspective, it is necessary for the parties themselves to self-organize and generate their own peace agreement, as a prerequisite for self-sustainable peace. These three cases show that a limited process facilitation approach to mediation can enable greater participation in, and ownership of, the emergence of a peace agreement by the parties and that this is a crucial factor that influences the likely self-sustainability of peace agreements.

The cases of Colombia, the Philippines, and Syria demonstrated that the involvement of women's and youth groups, local community leaders, and insider mediators constitutes an essential strategy to enhance national consensus and ownership. In all these cases, international organizations, bilateral partners, and international mediators played an important role in helping build local capacities and providing the resources required to sustain the mediation efforts. However, in each case, national and local actors were decisive at critical moments to move these processes along, and their close involvement throughout the process was crucial to the self-sustainability, adaptive capacity, and resilience of those processes where agreements were reached.

In some conflicts, like in the Syrian case, mediators may face structural challenges and domestic limitations. They may need to rely on foreign states and seek regional powers to help broker deals among the parties. However, the hypothesis presented by this book, and borne out by three of the four cases considered, is that the most effective mediation practices are those that allow and enable peace to emerge from within. In this context the book explored the Adaptive Mediation approach as an alternative to standard determined designed approaches. Adaptive Mediation enables the parties to generate solutions themselves, and the role of the mediator is limited to facilitating the process. The aim is to support and enable the process, but to do so without undermining the ability of the parties to arrive at a self-organized agreement, as that process is seen as critical for the implementation and self-sustainability of the agreement.

The three cases covered in this book that generated peace agreements—Colombia, Mozambique, and the Philippines—have highlighted three comparative advantages of the Adaptive Mediation approach, namely the ability to cope with uncertainty, the value of limiting the role of the mediator to process facilitation, and the importance of agreements emerging from the parties themselves.

In contrast to determined-design approaches, Adaptive Mediation recognizes that our ability to understand complex systems is inherently limited and time-bound. Complex social systems are dynamic, nonlinear, and emergent. This means that both the drivers and consequences of conflict are continuously evolving. An adaptive approach copes with this uncertainty by employing an iterative process that continuously generates new analyses, as well as regular reflection points where mediation teams reflect and make judgments regarding the changes they have identified and their implications for the mediation process. In Colombia, Mozambique, and the Philippines, those mediation processes that were able to continuously learn from, co-evolve with, and adapt to the fluid and changing political dynamics they were dealing were more effective at generating peace agreements, and those peace agreements, so far, have lasted longer and proved to be more self-sustainable than previous agreements.

All four cases studies in this book support the Adaptive Mediation hypothesis that when the aim is a self-sustainable peace agreement, mediators should limit their role to process facilitation, protect parties from external interests and agendas, foster inductive processes that maximize the capacity of the parties to self-organize, and help them generate agreements that are rooted in the local context. The Syrian case demonstrated how external interference disrupted the ability of the parties to self-organize, especially at several critical potential tipping points, and how this undermined the ability of several highly experienced mediators, and the parties themselves, to find ways to settle on a pathway to end the conflict. In contrast, the mediation experiences in Colombia, Mozambique, and the Philippines have shown that the more the parties (or insider neutrals associated with them) participate in generating a shared conflict analysis, identifying options, and exploring pathways to agreements, the more likely the outcome is to reflect indigenous narratives and perspectives relevant to the context, rather than the assumptions, interests, and biases of the external mediators.

Adaptive Mediation regards the emergence of this self-organizing process among the parties participating in the conflict as a crucial precursor for self-sustainable peace. As many of the failed peace agreements discussed in this book have shown, if the parties are dependent on a mediator to generate agreement among themselves, they are also unlikely to find solutions themselves to emerging crises during the implementation phase. A core tenant of the Adaptive Mediation approach is thus that for peace agreements to be self-sustainable, they need to emerge from the parties themselves.

References

Bagshaw, Dale, and Elisabeth J. Porter. 2013. *Mediation in the Asia-Pacific Region: Transforming Conflicts and Building Peace*. Oxfordshire: Routledge.

Bercovitch, J., ed. 2002. *Studies in International Mediation*. London: Palgrave Macmillan.

Collier, Paul, V.L. Elliott, Havard Hegre, Anke Hoeffler, Marta Reynal-Querol, and Nicholas Sambanis. 2003. *Breaking the Conflict Trap Civil War and Development Policy*. Washington, DC: World Bank and Oxford University Press.

Eriksen, Stein Sundstol. 2009. The Liberal Peace Is Neither: Peacebuilding, State Building and the Reproduction of Conflict in the Democratic Republic of Congo. *International Peacekeeping* 16 (5): 652–666. https://doi.org/10.1080/13533310903303289.

Harland, David. 2018. *The Lost Art of Peacemaking*. Geneva: HD Centre for Humanitarian Dialogue.

Lehti, Marko. 2019. *The Era of Private Peacemakers: A New Dialogic Approach to Mediation*, Rethinking Peace and Conflict Studies. London: Palgrave Macmillan. https://doi.org/10.1007/978-3-319-91201-1.

———. 2020. Private Peacemaking and Dialogic Approach to Mediation. In *The Palgrave Encyclopedia of Peace and Conflict Studies*, 1–13. Cham: Springer International Publishing. https://doi.org/10.1007/978-3-030-11795-5_53-1.

Paffenholz, Thania. 2021. Perpetual Peacebuilding: A New Paradigm to Move Beyond the Linearity of Liberal Peacebuilding. *Journal of Intervention and Statebuilding* 15 (3): 367–385.

Richmond, Oliver P. 2015. After Liberal Peace: The Changing Concept of Peace-Building RSIS. https://www.rsis.edu.sg/rsis-publication/rsis/co15272-after-liberal-peace-the-changing-concept-of-peace-building/.

Index[1]

NUMBERS AND SYMBOLS
1992 General Peace Agreement (GPA), 81, 87, 90, 92, 95, 96, 100
2014 Cessation of Military Hostilities Agreement (CMHA), 81, 88–90, 100
2018 Memorandum of Understanding (MoU) (Mozambique), 99, 102
2019 Maputo Accord for Peace and Reconciliation (MAPR), 13, 81, 84, 85, 100, 102, 103

A
Accountability, 45–47, 91
Adaptiveness, 13, 59, 63–67, 71, 73, 75, 76, 94, 102, 103, 118, 137, 144, 172, 174
Afghanistan, 21, 166, 179
African Union (AU), 5, 20, 86
Ahtisaari, Martti, 5
  Martti Ahtisaari Peace Foundation, 5
Al-Assad, Bashar, 140
Amnesty law, 65, 66, 90
Annan, Kofi, 5, 140–144, 140n3, 148, 150, 156, 157, 173
April 19th Movement (M-19), 60, 65, 67
Aquino, 118, 119, 123, 125, 129n8, 130n9
Arab Spring, 139, 139n2, 155
Armed non-state actors (ANSAs), 58–60, 64, 67, 69, 73–75, 75n17, 103
Arroyo, 118, 122, 125
Association of Southeast Asian Nations (ASEAN), 121, 124
Astana, 147–149, 151, 152n8, 153, 155–157, 178

[1] Note: Page numbers followed by 'n' refer to notes.

C. de Coning et al. (eds.), *Adaptive Mediation and Conflict Resolution*, Sustainable Development Goals Series,
https://doi.org/10.1007/978-3-030-92577-2

Authoritarian, 34
competitive authoritarianism, 74
Autonomous Region in Muslim Mindanao (ARMM), 118, 119, 123, 130

B
Bangsamoro
Bangsamoro Autonomous Region in Muslim Mindanao (BARMM), 117, 119
Bangsamoro Basic Law (BBL), 119, 128–130, 129n8, 130n9
Bangsamoro Transition Authority (BTA), 117, 119, 129–131
Bangsamoro Transition Commission (BTC), 129–131, 129n8, 130n9
Best Alternative to a Negotiated Settlement (BATNA), 20
Betancur, Belisario, 65, 66, 69
Bottom-up peacebuilding, 24, 59, 75
communitarian, 59, 75
Brahimi, Lakhdar, 142–144, 142n5, 148, 150, 156, 157

C
Cabo Delgado, 83, 84, 103
Catholic Church, 5, 89, 92, 128
Ceasefire, v, vi, 1, 4, 7, 8, 93, 97, 98, 102, 121–124, 127, 128, 138, 142–146, 148, 149, 155, 157, 158, 173, 176, 177
Centre for Humanitarian Dialogue (HD), 5, 24, 47, 87, 96
Chembeze, Anastacio, 86, 87
China, 82, 98, 139, 166
Civil society
civil society organizations (CSOs), 93, 115–116, 127, 129, 131, 150, 151, 173
Civil Society Support Room (CSSR), 151–154, 157
Climate change, 2, 103
Cold War, v, 21, 36, 60, 112, 139, 147, 148, 156, 165, 167
Colombia, vi, 2, 3, 8, 10, 12, 13, 57–77, 99, 112, 165–182
Commission on the Study of Violence (CSV), 67
Complexity
complex systems, 11, 22, 24–33, 35–39, 42, 43, 46, 48–51, 149, 150, 168, 169, 171, 181
science, 26, 149
Conciliation Resources, 123, 127
Conflict
analysis, 9, 10, 14, 30, 37–41, 47, 50, 59, 168–170, 182
complex, vi, 51, 59, 116, 137, 145, 169, 170
inter-state, 14, 112, 166
intra-state, 8, 14, 74, 82, 112, 137, 166
management, 2, 4, 7, 19, 23, 24, 59, 61, 111, 113, 116, 142, 174
protracted, v, vi, 8, 10, 13, 58, 59, 73, 74, 111, 128, 137, 149, 156–158
recurring, 10, 82, 85, 137
resolution, vi, vii, 1–15, 20, 21, 23–26, 30, 36–49, 51, 69, 102, 112, 116, 118, 124, 128, 130, 132, 142, 157, 165–182
transformation, 2, 23, 24, 114, 126, 171
Constitutional Committee (Syria), 138, 145, 148, 149, 154, 157, 176

Contact Group (Mozambique), 98
Context-specific, 1, 15, 38, 40, 63, 103, 178
Convention for a Democratic South Africa (CODESA), 25, 27
Coordination, 42–44, 93, 97, 112n1, 121, 149
COVID-19, 8, 68n13, 118, 130
  SARS-CoV-2, 59, 103

D
de Mistura, Staffan, 145, 146, 148, 149, 151, 154, 157, 173
Demobilization, disarmament, and reincorporation (DDR), 59, 64, 67, 70–73, 75, 82, 83, 98–100, 103
Democracy, vi, 34, 36, 168
  democratic, vi, 34, 36, 63, 69, 95, 128, 132, 168
Determined-designed, 1, 7, 8, 10, 14, 15, 36, 62, 85, 91, 95, 103, 167, 173, 179, 181
Dhlakama, Afonso, 13, 86, 89–93, 95–102, 177
Dialogic, v, 6, 15, 24, 38
Digital transformation, 7
Direct dialogue, 13, 81–103, 148, 172, 173, 175, 178
Duterte, 13, 117–119, 129, 129n8, 130n9

E
Emergence, v, 6, 11, 24, 27, 28, 32, 35, 36, 44, 46, 51, 99, 155, 156, 170, 180, 182
Ethical
  implications, 48, 49, 51
  perspective, 48
  responsibility, 48, 49
European Union (EU), 82n1, 86, 92, 98, 123, 124, 129, 172
Evaluation, 10, 15, 42, 45–47, 49, 50, 170

F
Facilitation
  iterative, 10, 169
  process, 10, 15, 21, 51, 84, 86–91, 96–103, 121, 128, 169–176, 180, 181
Facilitator, 8, 11, 15, 44, 86, 97, 122, 124–128
Feedback, 11, 27, 32–34, 36, 38, 39, 42, 45–47, 51, 169, 176, 178
Framework Agreement on the Bangsamoro (FAB), 119, 123, 126, 129n8
Friends of Peace, 128, 176

G
Geneva Communiqué, 141, 142n4, 143, 145, 148, 157
Guebuza, Armando, 86, 90, 100, 175

H
Harland, David, 2, 165, 166
High Commission for Peace (HCP), 66–68, 177
Human security, 2, 84

I
Indonesia, 120, 121, 121n6, 123
Inequality, 60, 63, 76, 166
Insider Mediation Group (IMG), 128–132
Institutional capacity building (ICB), 13, 57–77

Institutional learning, 103, 158, 176–178
Insurgency
counter, 65, 70, 71
Islamic, 83, 84, 99
International Contact Group (ICG), 98, 121, 123–128, 173
International Monitoring Team (IMT), 121, 123–125
International Red Cross, 5, 72
International Syria Support Group (ISSG), 145, 146, 149
Iran, 143, 145, 147, 156, 157, 174
Iraq, 141, 179
Islamic State of Iraq and Levant (ISIL), 83n2, 117, 145, 146, 148, 155

J
Japan, 82n1, 123, 125, 127
Joint Commission (Mozambique), 91–94, 91n6

L
League of Arab States (LAS), 5, 138–145, 155–157
Lehti, Marko, 2, 5, 6, 19, 21, 22, 24, 38, 40, 153, 166, 170, 171
Liberal, 1, 36, 61, 82, 155, 166
illiberal divide, 6
illiberal "exclusivity," 6
order, 95, 155, 156
peace, 1, 3, 36, 166–168, 178, 179
peacebuilding, 1, 82
Libya, 2, 112, 120, 121n6, 123, 139, 166, 179
Lleras Camargo, Alberto, 61, 62
Local actors, 151n8, 180
local community, 66, 71, 73–76, 83, 102, 124, 154, 180
local conflict, 2
local context, vi, vii, 14, 44, 118, 124, 132, 150, 151, 174, 181
locally grounded, 10, 50, 170
local ownership, vi, 15
local system, 39, 41

M
Mack, Andrew, 22, 71, 157
Malaysia, 121, 123, 125, 128, 173
Management, 2, 4, 7, 19, 23, 24, 42–44, 49, 59, 61, 62, 111, 113, 116, 142, 174
Mandela, Nelson, 5
Manzoni, Mirko, 13, 96–98, 100, 101, 103, 173, 177
Mediation
activity, vi, 5, 6, 11, 67, 85, 140, 144, 150, 153
actor, 6, 14, 21, 84
adaptive, v–vii, 1–15, 19–51, 57–77, 81–103, 111–132, 141, 142, 144, 148, 153, 154, 157, 158, 166–171, 174–179, 181, 182
approach, 4, 9–15, 19, 22, 23, 42, 44, 50, 59, 64, 85, 113, 132, 141, 142, 153, 156, 166–171, 174, 179, 181, 182
blackhole, 98, 102
communitarian, 77
directed, 7, 10, 36, 37, 50, 95, 170, 174–176
domestic, 64–67, 84, 86–91
effectiveness, 2–4, 7, 13, 59, 61, 97, 102, 113, 172, 178
external, 84, 112, 116
formal, 5, 11, 85, 113, 123, 167
framework, vi, 13, 64, 93, 95, 99
high-level international, 84, 85, 91–96, 175
hybrid, 123, 127, 173

informal, 5, 11, 85, 113, 167, 168, 173
insider, 13, 111–132, 173, 176
mainstream, 36, 50, 170
multi-layered, 13, 113, 116, 117, 120–132, 173, 176
outcomes, 6, 95, 113, 114, 117, 149, 155, 157, 178, 179
peace, 3, 6, 8, 9, 14, 19, 21, 24, 51, 170, 171
pragmatic, vi, 3, 85, 102, 103, 137, 147, 149, 173, 174
problem-solving, 23, 41, 177
stage, 13, 40, 63, 65, 71, 75, 84, 85, 87, 90, 91, 94, 96, 98, 101, 144, 172, 176, 177
standard, vi, 6–8, 13–15, 36, 60, 73, 74, 84, 85, 91–96, 101, 113, 141, 143, 155, 167, 173, 175, 179, 181
strategy, 3, 13, 14, 23, 40, 59, 61, 62, 67, 70, 73, 85, 90, 92, 94, 97, 117, 140, 141, 143, 144, 150, 151, 153, 172–174, 177, 179
third-party, 2, 8, 19, 112, 115, 124–128, 132, 173
transformative, 23, 24
Mediator
domestic, 13, 85, 87, 89, 90, 172, 175
insider, 115, 116, 132, 173, 178, 180
national, 13, 87, 89, 90
neutral, 19, 115, 138, 144
Mindanao, 13, 113, 117–120, 117n3, 126–128, 130, 178
Mistura, 145
Monitoring and evaluation, 10, 15, 45–47, 50, 98, 170
Moro Islamic Liberation Front (MILF), 117, 117n3, 119, 119n5, 121–126, 129, 129n8, 130, 130n9
Moro National Liberation Front (MNLF), 117–121, 117n3, 118n4, 123, 124, 129, 131
Moros, 117, 120, 121, 129, 132
Mozambican National Resistance (RENAMO), 13, 81–84, 86, 88–94, 91n6, 96–103, 177
Military Junta, 84, 100, 103
Mozambique, v, vi, 2, 3, 8, 10, 13, 81–103, 165–182
Mozambique Liberation Front (FRELIMO), 81, 88n5, 89–91, 91n6, 93, 94, 100

N
National Agency for Reincorporation (ARN), 71, 75
National Agenda for the Future of Syria (NAFS), 147, 152, 154, 157
National dialogue, 9, 19, 40, 72, 169, 175, 176
National Front (Colombia), 61–64, 68
National ownership, 85, 101, 102, 112n1, 173
Natural disasters, 2, 83, 84, 103
Negotiation
facilitated, 9
formal, 8, 91, 125
Negotiator, 72, 126, 172
Neha Sanghrajka, 96, 101
Non-governmental organizations (NGOs)
international, 5, 15, 84, 124, 126, 153, 154, 157, 173
Non-Linearity
nonlinear system, 31
Non-State Armed Groups (NSAGs), 3, 6, 12, 14

Norms, 28, 32, 36, 128, 131, 132, 167, 168
Norway, 5, 72, 82n1, 98, 99, 123, 172
Norwegian Centre for Conflict Resolution (NOREF), 58, 151, 152
Nyusi, Filipe, 83, 88–92, 94–101, 177

O

Organisation of Islamic Cooperation (OIC), 118–121, 123

P

Peace agreement, vi, vii, 1, 2, 7, 8, 10, 11, 13–15, 19–22, 25, 29, 31, 36, 37, 44, 50, 51, 57, 58, 63, 64, 67, 70, 72, 73, 75n17, 76, 81, 82, 85, 99, 100, 103, 112n1, 118, 118n4, 120, 121, 123, 128, 132, 144, 154, 168, 170–175, 177, 178, 180–182
Peace architecture, 14
Peacebuilding, 1, 4, 14, 57–60, 62n7, 65, 69, 73–75, 77, 81–83, 85–87, 100, 103, 111, 113, 114, 116–118, 121–124, 137, 151, 171, 178
  peacebuilders, 6, 7, 59, 84, 101, 103, 139, 157, 170
Peace gains, 74, 85
Peacekeeping, v, vi, 4, 123, 127, 137
Peace-making
  peacemakers, 4–7, 11, 101, 170
  peacemaking practices, 6, 15, 24
Peace process, vi, 5–8, 12–14, 21, 24, 31, 37, 39, 43, 50, 51, 58, 60, 63, 66, 68, 69, 71, 73, 75, 76, 81–103, 111–132, 140, 142, 143, 145–154, 156, 157, 168, 171–174, 176–178
Pedersen, Geir O., 148, 154, 174
The Philippines, v, vi, 2, 3, 8, 10, 13, 118, 125, 128, 129, 130n9, 131, 165–182
Planning, 9, 10, 14, 22, 41–42, 47, 49–51, 168, 170
Political participation, 63, 66, 67, 72
Popular Liberation Army (EPL), 13, 60, 65, 67, 73, 74
Poverty, 60, 66
Power-sharing, 2, 36, 61, 96, 100, 127, 168
Pragmatic, vi, 3, 85, 102, 103, 137, 147, 173, 174
Problem-solving, 23, 41, 177

Q

Qatar, 5, 142, 145, 156, 157

R

Raffaelli, Mario, 92, 94
Rebel, 3, 60, 61, 63, 65, 74, 97, 113, 115–117, 120, 122, 132, 142, 145, 155
Reconciliation, 37, 62, 87, 97, 100, 101, 103, 131, 178
Resilience, 15, 24, 25, 40, 44, 45, 47, 59, 73, 76, 94, 96, 101–103, 128, 131, 132, 142, 148, 154, 158, 172, 173, 180
  resilient, 10, 24, 25, 32, 34, 40, 45, 50, 58, 116, 170, 177
Revolutionary Armed Forces of Colombia-People's Army (FARC-EP), 13, 57–60, 63–67, 69–76, 75n17, 172, 175
Rosário, Lourenço do, 86, 90
Russia, 139, 141, 143, 145–149, 157

S
Sant'Egidio, 5, 82, 92
Santos, Juan Manuel, 59, 70, 71, 75
Saudi Arabia, 123, 142, 145, 156, 157
Self-organization, 10, 11, 15, 21, 23–25, 27, 30, 32–36, 40, 44, 45, 47, 50, 58, 59, 73, 76, 85, 94, 96, 102, 103, 115, 116, 121, 128, 132, 170, 173, 176, 178
Self-sustainable, 9, 10, 21, 37, 40, 44, 50, 51, 168–170, 174–176, 180–182
  self-sustainability, 10, 11, 20, 25, 50, 170, 180, 181
Sengulane, Dinis, 86
Southern African Development Community (SADC), 5, 86
South Sudan, 2, 44, 166
Special Commission for Rehabilitation (SCR), 61, 62, 62n6, 64
Special Jurisdiction of Peace (JEP), 72, 74
State Security and Intelligence Services (SISE) (Mozambique), 92, 96
Sustainable peace, vi, 2, 10, 50, 87, 112–116, 128, 131, 132, 156, 169
Sustaining peace, vii, 10, 73, 75, 76, 83
Syria, v, vi, 2, 3, 8, 10, 21, 112, 138, 145, 148, 150, 151, 153–156, 165–182
Syrian Opposition Coalition (SOC), 142

T
Team of Military International Observers on the Cessation of Military Hostilities (EMOCHM), 88, 90
Territorial Spaces of Capacitation and Reincorporation (ETCR), 73
Theory of change, 9, 24, 36, 37, 48, 49, 51, 166, 168, 169, 179
Third-Party Monitoring Team (TPMT), 121, 123, 124
Transitional justice, 72, 75, 152
Trust-building, 66, 98, 125, 176
Turkey, 123, 142, 142n4, 145, 147, 148, 151, 153, 156, 157

U
Uncertainty, vi, 3, 8–12, 14, 15, 22, 25, 32, 37, 41, 43, 50, 57–77, 84, 89, 90, 92, 95, 98, 100–102, 113, 128, 132, 144, 146, 157, 165–182
United Kingdom (UK), 98, 123, 127, 139, 142, 157
United Nations (UN), v, vi, 2, 4–6, 20, 39, 49, 51, 82n1, 86, 100, 111, 112, 120, 121, 138–140, 144, 148, 172, 174, 176, 178
  General Assembly (UNGA), 140
  P5 (Five Permanent Members of the UNSC), 5, 140
  Personal Envoy, 103
  Secretary-General (UNSG), 5, 103
  Security Council (UNSC), 6, 138, 180
  Special Envoy, 138–140, 142, 144, 145, 148, 149, 151, 154, 155, 173, 178
  Supervision Mission in Syria (UNSMIS), 141, 142
  UNDP, 116, 129, 150
United Self-Defense Forces of Colombia (AUC), 64, 66, 67, 70, 71, 74, 172

United States (US), 86, 98, 99, 120, 123, 126, 139, 141–143, 145–147, 156, 157, 172
Uribe, Alvaro, 70

V
Values, 1, 23, 34, 45, 47, 74, 128, 131, 132, 156
Violent extremism, 2, 3, 14, 83, 111, 166

W
Whole-of-system, 9, 29, 36, 169
Women, 5, 6, 143, 149, 151, 176, 180

Y
Yemen, 2, 21, 112, 139n2, 166, 179

The manufacturer's authorised representative in the EU is Springer Nature Customer Service Centre GmbH, Europaplatz 3, 69115 Heidelberg, Germany. If you have any concerns regarding our products, please contact ProductSafety@springernature.com

Printed and bound by CPI Group (UK) Ltd, Croydon, CR0 4YY
01/10/2026
02226249-0001